TANGLED

SEVEN
ICONIC MOMENTS IN
WHITE WOMEN'S HAIR
AND WHAT THEY
TELL US ABOUT
POWER, PLEASURE,
AND
COMPLICITY

SARAH MESLE

BEACON PRESS, BOSTON

BEACON PRESS
24 Farnsworth Street
Boston, Massachusetts
www.beacon.org

Beacon Press books
are published under the auspices of
the Unitarian Universalist Association of Congregations.

Printed in the United States of America

29 28 27 26 8 7 6 5 4 3 2 1

This book is printed on acid-free paper that meets the uncoated paper
ANSI/NISO specifications for permanence as revised in 1992.

Text design and composition by Kim Arney

Library of Congress Cataloging-in-Publication Data is available for this title.
Names: Mesle, Sarah author
Title: Tangled : seven iconic moments in white women's hair and
what they tell us about power, pleasure, and complicity / Sarah Mesle.
Description: Boston, Massachusetts : Beacon Press, [2026] | Includes
bibliographical references. | Summary: "Acclaimed cultural critic Sarah Mesle
unpacks the surprising power of white women's hair in shaping American identity,
politics, and pop culture. From rom-coms to TikToks, blowouts to legislation,
Mesle explores how hair-often dismissed as trivial-has been a stealth vehicle for
transmitting whiteness, privilege, and conservative values" —Provided by publisher.
Identifiers: LCCN 2026007726 (print) | LCCN 2026007727 (ebook) |
ISBN 9780807016343 hardcover | ISBN 9780807016350 ebook
Subjects: LCSH: Hair in popular culture—United States | Women, White—
Race identity—United States | Beauty culture—United States | Communication
in hairdressing—United States | Hair—Political aspects—United States |
Television hairdressing—United States
Classification: LCC GT2290 .M47 2026 (print) | LCC GT2290 (ebook)
LC record available at https://lccn.loc.gov/2026007726
LC ebook record available at https://lccn.loc.gov/2026007727

For my grandmothers,
aunts, nieces,
and most especially for my mother:
Dr. Barbara J. Hiles Mesle

CONTENTS

INTRODUCTION

DISCIPLINE AND PONYTAIL

Hair seems to be such a little thing. Yet it is the little things, the small everyday realities of life, that reveal the deepest meanings and values of a culture, give legal theory its grounding, and test its legitimacy.

—PAULETTE M. CALDWELL,
Duke Legal Review, 1991

Lo! Freedom Comes . . . *She moves divinely fair*
Olive and Laurel bind her golden Hair.

—PHILLIS WHEATLEY PETERS,
1784 (original emphasis)

In the spring of 1983, I experienced my first major hair event. Like all American hair events, this event was about race. I didn't recognize it at the time. I was seven years old, a little white girl sitting in a small-town beauty salon, where, extremely against my wishes, I had been taken to have my long hair bobbed. Losing these few inches of straight brown hair felt like a matter of life or death. Now, many years later, I have a better sense of why. My own personal hair feelings that day, like your personal hair feelings, like *everyone*'s personal hair feelings, are knotted into a long racial history. It's those feelings, and that history, this book aims to untangle. What I'm after is a record of recent American whiteness, told through white women's hair.

Does that seem a reach? I'm sure this goal would surprise everyone who was with me that day in the beauty salon. My hometown was so racially homogenous, so deep inside whiteness, that it offered its white residents the privilege of ignoring both our race and our racism. When the stylist looked at me, she saw just another little girl, one whose race I'm sure she didn't notice, cutely angry about an unwanted haircut. The stylist's name was Tara, and she was a little sorry. She herself had prettily permed hair, long and fluffy, her bangs hot-ironed and carefully sprayed. (Do you believe that I remember these details? I remember all these details.) Tara smiled sympathetically as her scissors opened, as I pressed my thighs into the vinyl chair, as my hands white-knuckled around its metal arms, as the long brown threads fell to the floor and the newly short ends brushed against my jaw. To her, this was a normal childhood milestone, not a political conflict.

It didn't feel normal to me. I sobbed ragey tears. In my girlish way, I felt—and, this book would propose, I was not actually wrong to feel—a change with historic stakes. I felt like I was being robbed.

Today, I'd describe it this way: I knew they were cutting my hair. I felt they were severing away a power—a power of respect, a power of beauty, a power that even at seven I had felt myself wield and didn't want to lose. What I didn't know, back then, was to call that strange power whiteness—specifically, white femininity. But that is what it was. My long and pretty white girl hair possessed a symbolic power with a long extractive history and an enduring material force.

What makes hair so meaningful? Hair evokes and exceeds and escapes other bodily phenomena. Hair is your body, but it's pliable body. It's the inside of us outside; it's viscera you can cut and brush and braid and curl and color and straighten and conceal. Emerging from our bodies, our hair seems to reveal our nature, our identity. Readily available to transformation, hair also displays how we *feel* about our nature, what we would like our nature to be.

Hair's symbolic intensity has persisted through time, as so many myths and fairy tales show. In the American context, where race remains a central factor in, to quote theorist Ruth Wilson Gilmore, "group-differentiated vulnerability," hair takes on a particular cultural power.[1] It marks where we belong on a racialized social hierarchy. Unlike many other racial markers, our hair can be changed to show how we feel about our place on that hierarchy. No matter how closely individual bodies align with whiteness as a racial ideal, all of us can display, in how we style our hair, an understanding of what that ideal wants us to be. We can use our hair to show that we recognize it, respect it, desire it—or reject it. We can straighten our hair, or bleach it, or cut it all off. Doing so shapes how we're treated.

When we style our hair in the ways we understand that powerful institutions want us to—whether they are businesses, schools, or cheerleading squads—we regulate our own performance of the social, racial values those institutions find legitimate. Put differently, the inside-and-out quality of our hair makes it one of America's most powerful tools for racial discipline.

Black feminist thinkers and activists have amply shown how Afro-textured hair, a term I take from Jasmine Nichole Cobb, has been a specifically powerful negative reference by which white femininity defines itself.[2] For this reason, this book about white women's hair pays special attention to white anti-Blackness. No matter what Black women do with their hair, and no matter what sphere they enter—romantic, educational, familial, professional—white America will read their hair decisions as a reflection of their attitudes about race (Michelle Obama reflects on this pressure in her book *The Look*).[3] Today, when some official body like the Olympic Committee makes a ruling that discriminates against Afro-textured hair, a forceful protest often rises up to challenge it.[4] These protests are a marker of Black feminist success in public discourse.

But what about *my* hair? What about when I was a little girl in that beauty salon, or my hair now, in a ponytail pulled on my head? In hair, as in most other daily experiences, white culture resists being racially marked. White culture likes to see itself as "normal." White institutions uphold that belief by subtly transmitting to every other group a pressure to comply with racial standards—in language, in fashion, in etiquette—that refuse to recognize themselves as such. White women's hair operates in exactly this way. It represents itself as a norm, a standard, rather than a racial marker tied to status and security. But in the intensity that white women feel about our hair—for instance, crying when getting our hair cut as little girls—we find the lingering evidence of white hair's material, political significance.

White women's hair typically registers as an individual matter. The power it carries seems to be the small-scale authority of personal aesthetics women can wield even when public institutions have excluded them. Because the powers that hair seems to bestow on white women are aesthetic, feminine, and often reinforced through pop culture, they can seem not just private but also trivial. The pleasure, the play, the insecurities that white women feel when we brush or stroke or style our hair are easily sequestered to the realm of fashion and artifice, seemingly outside of the serious places—the courthouse, the capital, the university—where important racial policy is made.

There's a real misogyny at play here. Spending a lot of time or money or emotional energy on our hair (as so many women I know do) can be interpreted, even by other women, as a sign that we're not serious people. But the misogyny white women face serves a complex purpose. Misogyny may keep white women below white men. But the presence of misogyny works like a filter allowing white women to blind ourselves to our own racialized power. Assuming that our hair feelings have only to do with our trivialized femininity, we avoid recognizing how those feelings intersect with our privileged racial position. We use the real misogyny we face as an alibi for the racialized power we enact.

When white women in our daily practices perpetuate the belief that our expressions of femininity—like our intense feelings about our hair—are demonstrations of only our gender and not our race, mainstream culture rewards us with attention, access, affection. It's so easy to turn to those pleasures. Sometimes we even see the complex attainment of those pleasures as pressures, and write ourselves as victims into the stories that lift us up. We feel ourselves move closer and further away from idealized whiteness. We watch Julia Roberts on the movie screen or Gwyneth Paltrow on our phones and are more likely to see how these images make us feel inferior and insecure rather than to see how they validate the worth of a standard that our hair, if always imperfectly, lets us trade upon.

But if hair is a racial sign, it is *always* a racial sign, not just when it signifies Blackness or another racial identity. Black women's hair could signify Black Power only because white women's hair had always, whether overtly or evasively, been signaling white power. Reading deeply in the history of American culture shows that there has never been a moment when women's hair hasn't mattered to the ongoingly contentious question of what whiteness is, and, relatedly, what Americanness itself should look like. Interpreted as merely aesthetic, dismissed as a matter of popular fashion, white women's hair decisions have largely escaped the attention that other vehicles of white power have received. With its racialized power hiding in plain sight, white women's hair has been a versatile technology for securing whiteness's hold on American cultural authority, even as America's political landscape shifts. And this means that those who hope to participate in an honest reckoning with racial power should pay attention when *any* white women's hair occupies the public view.

~

How do you read hair, or understand it? In 1989, Paulette M. Caldwell, the legal theorist quoted above, published an essay called "A Hair Piece: Perspectives on the Intersection of Race and Gender."[5] She wrote the essay at one of America's first critical race theory workshops. I first read it in 2021, when the media was erupting with debate about CRT. Of course, I thought: Women's hair is right here, at the origins of our best (and so, most controversial) language for describing how race works in American legal life. Caldwell's wisdom about hair is exactly what racist white Americans don't want their children to read.

Caldwell's essay focuses on a particular court case, one I'll discuss in chapter 1 of this book. She shows how legal terminology for race often fails to describe how race matters to hair—and thus how it fails to protect Black women from discrimination, hair-related and otherwise. In particular, she criticizes how the court was only willing to protect what it called "immutable" signs of race, like skin color. A hairstyle, it judged, was a merely "mutable" racial expression—changeable, subject to fashion, seemingly, as Caldwell puts it, "such a little thing."

A hairstyle was too trivial for the court to take seriously as a matter of racialized experience, expression, or repression.

In this book, I follow Caldwell's lead in taking hairstyles seriously. Doing so has some risks. Often, the discussion of a hairstyle can be petty, judgmental, misogynistic. Criticizing a woman's hair can be a way to enforce sexist and classist norms as well as racist ones. But acting as though *all* attention to hair is unfair offers a too-easy way out of the reality of hair's power.

Too often, white women use the court's same dismissive logic to avoid taking responsibility for our hair's significance. We pour time, money, and attention into our hair because we correctly sense hair's power. But then we disavow the significance of what we're doing. We act like our own hair efforts are silly, or reactive, or unimportant. Our hair is just pretty, or not yet pretty enough, this narrative encourages us to say. We work so hard. We feel so bad when we have a bad hair day. What we're doing when we spend time in the bathroom or money in the salon isn't something to make a big deal about. Criticizing what a woman does there, in their bathroom or the salon, isn't nice. Can't we leave women alone, white women say. Men wouldn't get criticized this way. In this mode, we are only victims, our hair powers merely palliative. Strapping ourselves into the straitjacket of misogynistic dismissal as though it were a comforting swaddle, we absolve ourselves of any capacity to handle ourselves or our power responsibly. When we place our hair beyond discussion, critique, or interpretation, we participate in our own trivialization.

I think we can do better. So, in this book, I'm trying to discuss white women's hair and its styling in a way that doesn't just judge it as pretty or tacky or stylish. Instead, I want to understand what it's doing, and all that it reveals about our power and our values. Our legal language, Caldwell shows, remains impoverished for this task. So here are the terms I am using:

- Hair is *natural*, a word that's more complicated than it seems. It's true that there are many things about how your hair grows that are beyond your control. But the word *natural* contains many ideological meanings, too—and it's these meanings I'm hoping to capture by using this slippery term. Because hair grows (or doesn't) from your head, it can also seem like an external manifestation of an internal reality: what is commonly called your "nature." Just as many American movies and myths link outer beauty to inner virtue, good hair still seems to reflect some kind of good emotional nature or internal state. (This gives a particular value, for instance, to being "naturally blond" or having "naturally curly hair"—even though both of those phrases can include as many ideas of "nature" as does the label for a "natural" shampoo or hair serum.) *Natural* is the value-laden idea that culture has created to name what emerges from inside us, the parts of ourselves we can only indirectly access or touch.
- But at the same time, hair is *expressive*. Hair can be straightened, permed, colored, bleached, blown out. So, while hair shows your nature, it also shows your emotional relationship to your nature; it shows both your nature and what you desire your nature to be, what you wish your nature was.
- And finally, at the intersection of the two, hair is *temporal*. So is everything, of course. But hair takes time, and it marks time. The question "How fast does your hair grow?" is a question about the nature of your hair that affects everything about how you respond to your hair's

> expressiveness: how long to grow out your relaxer, your perm, your bangs, your braids, your roots, your bad layers. Temporality is how your hair's nature pays for its expressivity. The availability of hair to respond to a moment can make it seem fickle, trivial; that women often do change their hair quickly is often taken as a marker of hair's insignificance. But for the same reasons, the time commitment hair can represent makes it available as a symbol for significant, enduring histories. Hair shows where we are in history, as well as where we are in nature, and how we feel about both.

The word *temporal* helps me mark one of my most important beliefs: No matter what else your hair is—whether it's "natural," permed, dyed, shorn off, or bought at a store—it's always real. You can touch it, and you do. Its materiality offers a path toward a better understanding; how it feels to us (in our hands, and in our, for lack of a better word, hearts) offers evidence about the world.

"A Hair Piece" draws equally on Caldwell's legal training and her embodied expertise, gained while moving through the world as a little Black girl and later as a professional Black woman. Every woman reading this book has gained some kind of similar expertise, even if we're rarely encouraged to move that expertise outside of the private sphere. When I was a little girl, my grandmother, my mother, my aunts, my friends all touched my hair. In their touch, they taught me about beauty, about value, and about love. These things are true. Were they also teaching me lessons about whiteness, lessons they didn't even know they knew?

~

Hair can be many things, and not all its meanings are tied to race, racism, or America's continued history of racial bias. White women's hair, like all hair, can be a powerful conduit for connection, self-making, communal pleasure. These pleasures feel especially valuable because white women, like all women, are often pressured into self-denial.

So, it's often good that when little girls learn how to do each other's hair, they are learning caregiving in the most intimate ways. It's good that thinking about our hair gives us a way to imagine the daily lives of other women in other places and times: other women who wanted their hair to be desirable or wanted it out of their way, wanted it to be touched and cared for by *their* mothers and grandmothers and lovers and friends. My long hair makes me understand my own moment in history, and it helps me think across history. In this way, as well as in the more tactile experiences of touch and tug and twist, my hair gives me daily pleasures. These pleasures, like my hair itself, are real.

But it's also true that since the nation's founding, if not before, white women's hair has been used symbolically to justify white American violence, and also to disguise it. This truth exists alongside the reality of my hair's pleasure: It doesn't mean my pleasure is false or bad. It's only when white women insist that our pleasures are innocent—that because the world denies us some pleasures, all our pleasures are virtuous—that our deployment of them becomes ethically problematic. Too often, white women want our pleasures to hew toward the strict moral standards of virtue and martyrdom by which white femininity has so often been judged. But those standards themselves emerged from, and are entangled with, America's troubling past. We can't free ourselves from those standards if we're also using them to judge ourselves, our pleasures, and each other.

Instead, we have to acknowledge that our pleasures, like our lives, play out in a world styled by both joy and injustice.

My own academic training is in American literary history. So, when I think about the origins of America's obsession with hair, I remember Phillis Wheatley Peters. Wheatley Peters was a prominent early American poet; she was, in fact, the first African American to publish a book of poetry. And she was also, in her youth, enslaved. Seized as a child in West Ghana or Senegal, she was transported via slave ship across the Atlantic. In 1761 a wealthy white woman named Susanna Wheatley purchased her. Stripped of her own home, Wheatley Peters was assigned the labor of making another family's home more comfortable. Among Wheatley Peters's tasks was caring for Susanna and her daughter Mary.

Phillis Wheatley Peters's poetry is now famous for its astonishing capacity to simultaneously flatter and reprimand the white society on which her survival depended. So, I always hear the dark register in Wheatley Peters's poem "Liberty and Peace," which begins by describing the goddess Freedom: "*She moves divinely fair* / Olive and Laurel bind her golden Hair."[6] This poem, the critic Alice Walker would later write, clearly took its golden imagery from "the one thing she saw elevated above all else"—her mistress's hair.[7] In Wheatley Peters's words, we see what her enslavers tried to teach her, along with English and how to clean a house. They tried to teach her the pernicious lesson that American culture, in various ways, still tries to impart: that despite all evidence to the contrary, American freedom looks like being blond.

When I was seven years old in a rural Iowan beauty salon, I was the same age Phillis Wheatley was when, to use her own euphemism, she was "brought" to America. Two centuries later, I absorbed my own version of the lesson Wheatley's poem reflected. *I* had internalized racism. My hair wasn't blond, but it was silky, it was straight, and it had been petted and loved and praised. I had been told that it made me look like a princess. I raged in the beautician's chair because I knew my long hair, if imperfectly, attached me to an American ideal. I fought against the haircut that I believed would sever my connection to it. What I wanted in my little white girl's heart was to move more closely toward that idealization, toward the power I already knew it could command.

I don't think all white girls have the same attraction to their hair's potency that I did. How a white woman or girl understands her hair's power depends significantly on her politics and her personality, and how those lead her to an affirming or oppositional relation to white femininity's conventions. Also, "white" girls have many different kinds of hair. A white girl's sense of her hair's value and force will depend on a kaleidoscope of factors: her hair's color, texture, and heft; on her family's country of origin, her geography, her language use, her religion, her sexuality, and more. But whatever her politics, her background, or her hair, I'm absolutely certain that *every* white woman has navigated the reality of her hair's power. She has navigated it at slumber parties and in high school bathrooms, at job interviews and in bars and at weddings and at brunch.

In the two hundred years since Wheatley's poem was published, America's cultural focus on hair as a reflection of racial status has both evolved in its forms and remained constant in its presence. White women have registered across the centuries our own complex relations to shifting ideals of white womanhood that all of us approach by degree. So, there are many ways this book could be organized, because the history it charts is deep.

This book looks to white women's hair to understand the story of American whiteness between 1979 and 2016—an era marked politically by the presidential campaigns of Ronald Reagan and Donald Trump, two revanchist white men. (Both, not coincidentally, are known for their signature hairstyles.) You can imagine this book as tracing an arc between these events. The election of Reagan struck a blow to feminist and civil rights activism, one from which, with great difficulty, progressive politics worked to recover. Reagan's policies did real harm to racial justice. But it seemed for a while, with the elections of Bill Clinton and then later Barack Obama, America might finally have pulled itself into a new era. Then, just when it felt we had achieved a better consensus about racial parity, and might also elect a woman president, America—steered by an alarming number of white women—veered backward, into a conservativism even more blatant and violently misogynistic than that from which we had escaped.

How did this happen? What about it can hair help us understand? In *Tangled*, I focus on seven moments during this forty-year stretch when a white woman's hair captured the cultural imagination. Because American media celebrates a fairly narrow range of feminine expressions, these white women have many qualities in common (while their hair varies, for instance, all their bodies are thin, and all their sexualities are straight). Some of these women, like Anne Shirley and Rachel Green, are fictional. Others, like Mary Lou Retton and Gwyneth Paltrow, have built their celebrity based on their real lives and real appearances. But all of them have hair that exerted pressure on how "normal" white women's hair was understood. This pressure made them seem—for better and worse—exciting, appealing, and powerful.

I want to ask questions about these white women's hair like the questions our media culture so regularly asks about women of color who enter the public sphere. American culture recognized that Angela Davis, for example, used her hair to signal that she wanted new powers for Black people. *Tangled* asks: What if, in the bob of Mary Lou Retton, the curls of Julia Roberts, or the perfectly straightened hair and perfectly smooth skin of Gwyneth Paltrow, we might see similar attempts to negotiate or advance the powers of whiteness?

The women in this book don't all perform whiteness in the same way, or with the same intention or success. In fact, when we look closely at white women's hair, often we see—as in the moment when Britney Spears shaved away her blond extensions, or Anne Shirley smashed a slate over her schoolmate's head—white women acting out a deep ambivalence about the very same feminized ideals that they otherwise embraced.

What I'll show is that when we tell the story of whiteness through white women's hair, we're able to see a more complex political history than the one presidential politics offers. American electoral politics often boil down to a simple binary—Democrat or Republican—that you can try to track with polls and approval ratings. But American hair politics show us a richer, more complex history. Their traces aren't shown in simple polls.

Instead, this book tracks the political power created in media that, like hair, are often dismissed because of their feminized nature: girlhood novels, tabloids, romcoms, music videos. Looking at white women's hair as it's displayed by these media, we see progressive ideals zig and zag. Often gestures that are understood at the time as "empowering" for "women" ultimately hurt feminist causes by reinforcing the racial hierarchies that divide us. Other times, in the most surprising moments, something radical takes place. This book tracks these undercurrents too, by showing the legacies of women who never became household names but who gave white women ways to envision their femininity that were less attached to the power of whiteness, and of white men particularly—like Tish and Snooky Bellomo, the sisters who founded the Manic Panic hair dye company.

None of the women in this book are melodramatic villains, beyond hope or reclamation. In telling this story, my goal isn't to spread shame. Instead, my goal is to try to see the power of these women's hair more clearly, so that I can try and recognize my own when I see it reflected in the mirror. Because all women, regardless of our intentions, have hair that can teach us how our power works in the world around us. It grows, it twists, it tangles; it's twined through pleasure, through fear, through experiences of beauty, intimacy, and love.

~

When I was seven years old and crying in a beautician's chair, I was feeling something I didn't know how to name: the weight of two centuries of cultural force, two centuries' worth of white culture normalizing its actions and its erasures by its deployment of white beauty. I was also feeling the results of America's ongoing crisis of domestic labor and childcare (a crisis that, as many Black feminists have long pointed out, has roots in slavery, America's own domestic institution.) In the summer of 1983, that crisis played out in my house, in the particular negotiation between my parents that led to my hair being cut. My mother, with two small children, the first woman in my family on either side to complete a four-year college degree, was making the extremely brave choice to finish coursework on a PhD. She and my father agreed that during the week, he would take care of both children so she could pursue the career she loved.

They also agreed that he shouldn't have to manage me and my younger brother and *also* the caretaking challenge of my long hair. The hair would go. I so respect their compromise;

I've made so many compromises around childcare myself. But to this day I have not forgotten my anger at that haircut, and I have never cut my hair short again. Even as I write, my hair grows long down my back—bleached blond now, so reading even whiter.

Despite hair's deep cultural meaning, it's not inevitable that white women's hair should have the effect it does. White hair's power isn't any more natural than race, and it's not something that white women, naturally, have. It's something we do. White women do whiteness to our hair; we do it to ourselves; we do it to other women. We do whiteness as we perm, crimp, condition, extend, shave, twist-up, shake-down, highlight, lowlight, and layer. And also—to riff on the words of a wonderful thinker who, despite being a man, French, and bald, is perhaps our best thinker about power—as we discipline, punish, and ponytail.

The belief of this book is that racial and gender justice depend on reckonings and recognition at scenes large and small: at the level of legislation and protest, and at the beauty salon and slumber party too. To be part of that reckoning, white women need to consider the powers that accrue to their bodies and their pleasures. This book attempts to ask what, if anything, could be found within my white woman hair pleasures, which are considerable, that could help me live with more justice in a world where my hair—the hair that grows from my head—functions with a disciplinary force, ordering the distribution of resources around femininity's white supremacist hierarchies. What have I done—and what could I do differently—with the white power of my hair?

ANGEL

Would you say her hair falls like wings?

Not quite wings, at least not in this picture, the most famous picture. Normally her hair's parted, feathering down softly on each side, as though she's been midair and just gently landed. The show calls her an "angel" because she does good deeds in a mysterious way, because she's beautiful in the way an angel might be, because the person who calls her an angel—Charlie—can tell her what to do without any concern about whether or not she'll do it. Of course she will. She's an angel. Her feathered hair expresses her angelic inner state.

But in the most famous picture, Farrah Fawcett's hair is less feathered, more curled. You remember it: Fawcett posed next to her Mulholland Drive swimming pool in her own swimming suit, a red tank. Her pose turns her pelvis away from the audience even as it reveals to us her slim inner thighs. Her breasts look as soft as her hair, mostly. Her nipple does not look soft! Her nipple is so famously not-soft, so famously visible, that this picture of Farrah Fawcett, which was released in 1976, months before *Charlie's Angels* even premiered, became a media event. The poster, distributed by a marketer outside of Cleveland, sold more than five million copies.[1] It made Fawcett a star.

Not every woman who saw this poster—or every woman who looked at the way straight male America looked at this picture—could attain

Fawcett's curvaceously slim body. Whatever force gave Fawcett the slim thighs and belly, the soft breasts, the tanned skinned and white smile: Those were natural gifts that not everyone had received. But many, many women expressed their desire to be desired like Farrah was desired. They did so by spending their time copying Farrah Fawcett's angelic hair.

The time! I have talked to so many women about the time it took—especially for women whose hair had any texture—to achieve Fawcett's easy-seeming, just-landed-from-heaven look. Women all over America getting up early before school, before work, plugging in the hot rollers. Blowing out their hair, then rolling the curl in, brushing the curl back out just enough so it would fall soft, gentle, feathered, like God seemed to want the best hair to be.

Farrah Fawcett comes before the real timeline of this book begins. But she hovers in its background, so let's pause here to look at her, and her golden hair, her angelic poolside presence.

What if this specific hair look didn't actually come from God—a divine gift to American libidos? What if Fawcett's hair came to us out of a specific moment in American history—as, in fact, it did? What could we see about that historical moment, and its desires, by looking at all the women across America hanging out in their early-morning bathrooms with heavy plastic rollers pinned in their hair?

CHAPTER 1

BO DEREK'S CORNROWS

In the moment that made her famous, Bo Derek, age twenty-three, beachy-blond, soft but slim, runs across golden sand. She wears a golden swimsuit; it shines against her golden skin. She smiles. Her golden hair shines and sways over her slim shoulders. This golden hair is braided into cornrows.

It was 1979. Bo Derek was appearing in the movie *10*. The role she was playing in *10* was the 10, the perfect woman. Even if you haven't seen the movie, you still might know this scene. You can probably picture Derek, running, on the movie's poster, which by itself sold millions of copies.[1] You might have seen the movie's trailer—Bo Derek running as the camera ogles her in sunny soft focus, while her cornrows bounce to the soundtrack of Ravel's "Boléro." She runs straight toward the camera, straight toward the viewer, straight toward *you*, watching. Three years after Fawcett's angel curls became famous, Derek's cornrowed version of sexual desirability arrived. She became America's new gold standard of hotness.

In her excellent book *White Negroes: When Cornrows Were in Vogue . . . and Other Thoughts on Cultural Appropriation* (2019), the critic Lauren Michele Jackson explains how white women often use cornrows to signal their knowledge of Black cultural practices and to enhance their own edginess, their erotic appeal.[2] Although cornrows themselves are not necessarily Black—in *10*, it's implied that Derek gets her braids in Mexico—mainstream American media always braids, as it were, cornrows into Black cultural history. Reading Derek through Jackson, we can recognize what Derek's cornrows promise the viewer—us—watching as Derek runs. Derek's cornrows tell us that she's perfect, but not uptight. She's beautiful, but not removed. She's white, but she's in touch with something a little bit Black. And that makes her hot, but also cool.

Bo Derek's hardly the only white celebrity to appeal to white audiences in this appropriative way: Both before and after her, white women have made the same cornrowed move. But I can't think of another white woman in cornrows who has become the same kind of touchstone. Bo Derek's cornrows show up all over the place. Take Kim Kardashian's Instagram, for example: A few years ago, Kardashian posted a picture of herself mugging at the camera with her hair in cornrows. You can tell Kardashian was thinking of Bo Derek because of how Kardashian captioned the picture: "BO WEST."[3] Or a different example, from a different part of culture: Chimamanda Ngozi Adichie's best-selling 2013 novel *Americanah*, which takes place almost entirely in a Trenton, New Jersey, braiding salon filled with African and West Indian immigrants. Midway through the novel a young white woman enters the salon. "The woman sat down and said she wanted cornrows. 'Kind of like Bo Derek in the movie. Do you know the movie *10*?"[4] It seems like no matter where culture goes—to Instagram, to fiction, and even, as we'll see, to court—Derek eventually follows. It's weird. Derek's always running in slow motion. But somehow America can't get away.

What can a hairstyle hold? Picture Derek's cornrows—all those delicate braids. In orderly rows, they trace lines across her scalp, moving at an angle away from a neat center part at her forehead. At the crown, they begin to dangle, loose. Her blond ends slip neatly into white beads. A few feathers appear. The cornrows are an artwork, crafted with precision. They bear an enormous investment of someone's skill and time. If we unbraided them, what would we see? What histories are tied into Derek's cornrows that give them such a grip?

That's the question this chapter tries to unravel. Derek's braids look orderly. But trying to comb them out, I found strands from different decades, different movies . . . a whole history of twentieth-century race and hair. And most especially, I kept finding connections between Derek's cornrowed run on the beach and another event happening at exactly the same cultural moment: Ronald Reagan's first successful run for the presidency.

Derek and Reagan may seem like an odd pair. Reagan had been a movie star, but by the time he ran for president he was decidedly uncool. Reagan was folksy and old-fashioned. He offered a parental rebuke to the counterculture's indulgences in sex, drugs, and rock 'n' roll. Derek, in *10*, *was* an indulgence, a golden embodiment of pleasure. Her hair—those cornrows—might seem to have signaled an appreciation for the very cultural freedoms that Reaganism wanted to leave behind. But white America wanted both. *10* became a surprise hit, and Reagan won a landslide election.

Here's what I want to know: What did Derek's cornrows allow voters to carry with them, as they made their revanchist turn? A hairstyle may seem trivial compared to a world-defining presidency. But Bo Derek's cornrows have a surprising amount to teach us about how white America got to the place—after Kennedy, after LBJ, after the cultural rebellion of the '60s and '70s—where Ronald Reagan, the '50s star, could become, in his own way, hot.

~

In my imagination, the story of Bo Derek's braids starts here: with a little girl, brushing up against the velvet of a heavy curtain, peering out from a backstage darkness onto a brightly lit stage. The girl presses against her mother, standing backstage with her. It is 1967, so the girl is eleven; her mother has brought her here, to this Las Vegas backstage, where the mother has a job. The mother does hair and makeup for Ann-Margret, who is performing all month at the Hilton.[5] But apparently the little girl is not watching only Ann-Margret. She sees someone else.

This little girl, the hairstylist's daughter, is named Mary Cathleen Collins. Just a few years later, she'll change her name to Bo Derek. And many years after that, the trace of this experience will show up in Bo Derek's Twitter. In the explosion of online irritation that erupted after Kardashian posted her "Bo West" photo, Bo Derek will defend them both. The hairstyle isn't a problem, Derek insists; it's a tribute! Derek, in this tweet, says her style was an homage to "Ann-Margret's backup singer from her Vegas Nightclub Show."[6]

The tweet is real, but we have to imagine the details that gave rise to it. Despite all my trying, I have not yet found any images from Ann-Margret's Vegas show that include any backup singers at all, so it's possible that this backup singer is a lie or a fabricated memory. But let's imagine that she's real. That in 1967, young, blond Mary Cathleen Collins saw a woman with cornrows, a woman who appealed to Mary Cathleen in a way she would remember in 1979, when she wanted to become famous, when she wanted to become a 10.

~

In 1967, the year Ann-Margret performed in Vegas, Mary Cathleen Collins and her mother weren't the only people whipped up about hair. *Hair*, the musical, had premiered on Broadway just the year before. *Hair* was called *Hair* because hair had become a visible symbol of the counterculture that was attempting to shift the balance of American power, both politically and aesthetically.

But it would be a mistake to make *Hair*, or the counterculture it represents, into an easy emblem of how America was feeling in 1967. We love to remember the free-wheeling sixties, people going to San Francisco and hippies with flowers in their hair. But the same year that *Hair* premiered on Broadway, California voters elected Ronald Reagan their governor. Reagan had promised a return to law and order, committing to, for instance, "cleaning up that mess in Berkeley."[7] He meant the protests, but he didn't *not* mean the messy long hair.

And Ronald Reagan himself was enough of a hair icon to know something about hair's power. Reagan, as a handsome young white man in the '30s, went to Hollywood, making his first movie in 1937.[8] In the posters, you can see Reagan's dark hair, carefully combed back. Pomade gives it a little shape and curl. Can you picture the hair? If you've ever seen Ronald Reagan, you've seen this hair. He never changed it. A whole forum on Quora devotes itself to the question of what strategies Reagan did or did not use (hair dye? Brylcreem?) to keep his thick, dark coif so steady over his long career.[9]

In the '40s, Reagan joined the army. But he didn't see any combat. Instead, he spent his active duty serving in a role I was shocked to learn existed: the "1st Motion Picture Unit," which made the army's training movies.[10] His unit produced more than four hundred movies. I've only watched a few. But in the ones I've seen, Reagan's hair looks just like Reagan's hair always does, pairing neatly with his uniform. His handsome image helped blur the line between heroic soldier and Hollywood leading man. His job was to make soldiers feel like stars.

And when Reagan came back to Hollywood, he found it eager to celebrate veterans like himself. He made movies set in so many time periods—World War II, the Civil War, the Old West—but somehow, he always had the same hair. This unchanging image conveyed an enduring sense of American heroism. Because Reagan had literally been an official image of the WWII soldier, he could look like he was fighting for freedom no matter what he was doing, or no matter when we were imagining him doing it. Fighting the Germans? That's American freedom. Fighting "Indians"? That's freedom too. In 1951, he actually played a captain in the *Confederate Army*.[11] He was literally fighting against the American Union, but he still had American hair on his Brylcreemed head.

Through the media images of Ronald Reagan and actors like him, the actual veterans of WWII came to symbolize all American experience. Such images placed a white, masculine hero at the symbolic front of a rising American story: the myth of the "greatest generation."

It's worth mentioning that one of these other actors in Hollywood with Reagan—a man whose career followed a less successful version of the exact same trajectory—was Bo Derek's husband, John.

Around the time *Hair* opened on Broadway, Reagan had a recurring role on the TV western *Death Valley Days*. Same hair. Reagan's roles and his celebrity changed as he shifted from Hollywood to politics, but his dark tidy hair was enduring (it kept enduring until he died).

Hair's hair and its politics expressed a specific and new thing, something that could only happen in 1967. Reagan's hair, on the other hand, did the opposite. It expressed an intense aversion to any cultural change. In fact, Reagan's hair, with its long unchanging life on movie screens and television, helped create a particular fantasy in late-twentieth-century America. Reagan's hair made the values he represented look "timeless." His hair served up a comforting vision: *His* values, America's values, would always endure—no matter what the hippies, in Berkeley or on Broadway, were doing with their long, messy, radical hair.

~

When I think about the '60s counterculture—the many Americans who resisted the narrative of postwar white male ascendency—I think about all the work it took to create the world in which I live. I think about activists who helped bring about the Civil Rights Act of 1964, Title IX, Title VII. I remember how women won the rights to no-fault divorce, to get credit cards, to get birth control, to get abortions.

None of the legal or legislative accomplishments of the '60s and '70s, that I know of, involve rights pertaining to hair. (California's CROWN Act [Creating a Respectful and Open World for Natural Hair] would not be passed until 2019.) But it makes sense that hair became so important to '60s political movements. Hair matters to every political movement. This is because hair's pliability gives it a special social, even ideological, power. For most of human history, hair has been the part of our human nature, our embodiment, that was most available to our manipulation. As I've said: When we do our hair, we express how we desire our nature to be.

How we desire our nature to be: What kind of desire am I talking about here? Political desire: the desire to belong, to be recognized as part of the body politic that a given government pledges to protect? Aesthetic desire: the desire to have symbolic status within that body politic? Erotic desire: the desire to be desired, to be pleasured, to have pleasure? Yes. All these. Hair matters so intensely, I think, because of how it tangles all these desires together; because when we do our hair, we can't tell which desire we are doing.

~

Hair, also, in US contexts, exists as the second most important visual marker of race, after skin. Which means that race is one of the things your hair allows you to "do."

~

Whiteness, like race more generally, works much like a currency: It's a set of physical and social properties that have become valuable for exchange.[12] It's a source of credit and prestige. Like other currencies, whiteness becomes powerful when it's backed by real resources. Its value grows when more people want the resources it represents.

Some people's physical features look like a fat wallet full of whiteness. I would put myself in this privileged category, along with Bo Derek and Ronald Reagan. Almost everywhere I go, I can trade on this currency. The world works for me like a series of metaphorical racial currency exchange kiosks, with clerks who hardly scrutinize my features. My whiteness means that I can go to a job interview, a police station, or a nurse's office, and my currency looks so legitimate the people there hardly realize they are putting it to the test. They help me exchange my whiteness for other resources: money, protection, respect. For other people, with different features, such systems work differently. Even for me, in some places, I experience some kinds of scrutiny—sometimes someone peers at me intently, skeptically, as though I were a ten-dollar bill held up to the light. In these moments, I can experience an anxious worry, an ugly desire for a way to make my whiteness, my understanding of whiteness, clearer.

It's in that exact desire that hair becomes especially valuable to all of us negotiating with whiteness's power. Only some people have bodily features like me and Bo Derek that are automatically read as white. But all or most of us have hair, a pliable version of ourselves. More than many other bodily features, our hair can easily be stylized to indicate our aspirations toward whiteness. With our hair, we can show that we value, that we *recognize as valuable*, the currency of whiteness. In this way, our hair becomes, as the legal scholar Paulette M. Caldwell explains, a "proxy for legitimacy."[13] Styling our hair toward whiteness's currency, we increase our access to that currency. We show how we want to be read.

And I mean "we" intentionally: me, and the world I help make. I am white; I also dye my hair blond. Every time I do so, I do more than thicken my own whiteness wallet. I'm also investing in blondness, in whiteness, as a currency. I throw my desire behind its meaning, not only for myself but for everyone else who sees me. Because not many people do see me, the effect may be pretty minimal. I'm a small bank. But it's not zero.

When Bo Derek braided her hair, she juxtaposed a body that American media read as white with a hairstyle it interpreted as Black. What did she hope to gain? I'd argue that she wasn't divesting from whiteness. Instead, she was changing the way whiteness could be recognized. She was expanding the territory whiteness could claim. It was still the old currency—but

Derek put a significant new style there in the center of its ten-dollar bill.

~

What is it about cornrows that allows the white women who wear them to seem, as Lauren Michele Jackson explains and Bo Derek shows, edgier, sexier, hotter? It has to do with the specific form American racism has taken—a form that associates Blackness with sex. Since the nineteenth century, the scholar Patricia Hill Collins argues, Americans have been trained—by media, by (racist) theories of medicine, and even by the law—to associate Blackness with heightened sexual appetites. This means that Black people encounter what Collins calls "a highly visible *sexualized racism*."[14] Whiteness, she's saying, looks so normal that its currencies work almost invisibly. Blackness, on the other hand, becomes "hypervisible"—*and* a symbol of sexual deviancy.[15]

Collins doesn't talk about hair, but her discussion of hypervisibilty helps us get at why hair matters to race. The same white institutions that associated Blackness with animal appetites tended to read Afro-textured hair as less normal, even less human, more like an animal's "wool," and one of many symbols of Black sexual difference. When white women like Derek adopt a style like cornrows, developed for textured hair, they're taking a style that white America interprets as a symbol of sexual, racial difference, and braiding it onto their own heads.

Collins's work also explains some pressures that Black women face about their own hair decisions—and how new hair technologies could change how those pressures felt. In the early twentieth century, chemicals that could dramatically curl your hair, or color it, or straighten it, suddenly became much safer. You could (I have) put a permanent in your hair that will last as long as the hair does. When it comes to hair, even a permanent really isn't; new hair will always grow. But even though none of these hair changes would last forever, all of them expressed a long-term commitment. That made them ideologically powerful.

Historian Shirley Anne Tate vividly describes what could be at stake in the decision many early-twentieth century Black women made to straighten their hair. Because Afro-textured hair had been read as "wild and primitive," straightening your hair offered a way to reject those racist interpretations.[16] It's like the opposite of a white woman getting cornrows. Black women could straighten their hair to show, externally, something that should always have been obvious: that they were equal to white women and deserved to be afforded the same respect and same security.

But Black equality was not something most white America wanted to see. So instead of seeing how straightened hair expressed a desire for equal treatment, white America chose to see straightened hair as a desire for white femininity itself—an investment in whiteness as a currency. Soon, straightened hair became a standard against which white America judged Black women. It became a way to measure, and discipline, how Black women felt about whiteness. In Black women who weren't willing to make the longest temporal commitment to looking white, white America saw more than a styling decision: It perceived racial insubordination.

Simply growing the hair on your head became an "assertion of the self," as Paulette M. Caldwell would put it, "in direct conflict with the assumptions that underlie the existing social order."[17] So it's no surprise that when some civil rights activists *did* want to challenge those assumptions, hair became a tool they could use, a way to resist the currency of whiteness. In the face of white racism, textured hair could look radical. Like pride. Like power.

In the 1960s, when Reagan was appearing in westerns and preparing his run for governor, the actress Cicely Tyson was using her hair to send a message that pushed back against Reagan's show of enduring, heroic whiteness. She became the first woman to wear her hair in cornrows on American national television. For Tyson, braiding her hair was a tribute to the specific women she represented in characters on TV—mothers, caregivers, powerful Black women. It was also a broader act of redefining what braided Black hair meant.

Braids, in a special way, show care that takes time. You can't see braids without seeing how long it took to braid them—and how long it took to *learn* to braid them. In her autobiography, Tyson vividly describes her braids as a tribute to the wisdom of Black women: "Our foremothers created the world's most ornate, intricate and diverse hairstyles, squeezing their youngs between their thighs, swapping laughter with every braid and twist." Hair "represented intimacy," she writes.[18] Tyson refused the idea that Black hair was a metric of sexualized racial difference. Her hair wasn't about Black availability. It was about Black love, and the enduring commitment Black women make to caring for each other.

~

When Bo Derek was a little white girl from California backstage at an Ann-Margret show, she probably did not think about the choices that Ann-Margret's backup singer or Cicely Tyson made when they decided to wear their hair in cornrows. But maybe she did. It's hard to say.

Bo Derek is a white woman—like several in this book—whose actual intelligence (whatever it is; we really can't know) remains hidden by a public performance that can only be described as some kind of strange evil genius. Derek's public performance emphasizes Derek's fundamental passivity. Tracking down her motives—about her hair or anything else—becomes nearly impossible because she continually disavows that she had any.

In 2020, Reelz—a streaming television station with a tabloid feel, which is the kind of under-the-radar place where news of Derek remains in steady circulation—devoted a whole episode of its *In Their Own Words* series to Derek. Derek took the opportunity to repeatedly assert her essential blankness. "I have no real sense of achievement," Derek reflects; "I don't care if anyone remembers me." "I don't think I've changed or evolved at all." "Despite my indifference, opportunities kept presenting themselves."[19]

In Derek's version of herself, she can't be the source of any wrongdoing, because she hardly did anything at all. She defers all agency away from herself—and onto white men. It's a white man—her husband John—whom Derek most often credits as the source of her cornrows. In this version of the story, Derek didn't get the idea of braids from a backup singer. They were her "husband's idea." But John Derek, although a director, was not directing the movie *10*. The final authority rested with *10*'s director, Blake Edwards, another white man. "So," Bo goes on, "I had it done and went into Blake's office and he wasn't too sure. He wasn't on board right away."[20]

In 1979, Derek was twenty-two years old; she had been partnered with John (fifty-seven) for six years. When John and Bo Derek talked about "having it done," did they talk about race? Was the picture she had in mind, or John had in mind, Cicely Tyson? Bo and John had been living through the hair history I've just described. Even if they'd never thought about race carefully, it's hard to imagine that the Dereks talked about cornrows without using the word *Black*. But maybe they didn't. Maybe they used some euphemism, some other word.

~

"I had it done," Derek says about her cornrows. It's not exactly a passive sentence. But it doesn't tell us the key thing: who braided them. It also doesn't tell us how Derek described to the stylist what she wanted the stylist to do. Writing this chapter, that's what I wanted to know, more than anything else. I spent months trying to track down this information. Derek's stylist, unlike her costar's, isn't listed in the movie credits.

The woman who braided Derek's hair is named Eunice Ann Collins—I think. I found this name in a 2019 *GQ* essay called "The Meaning of Cornrows" that offers a link to an inactive twitter account.[21] But once I had Collins's name, I found it a few other places, most notably a 2018 thread on Lipstick Alley (an online chat forum originally created for African American women).[22] According to this source, Collins saw Derek in a restaurant with braids she had tried to do herself and stepped in to offer her services. Apparently, the Dereks hired Collins to come to the set in Mexico so she could redo the braids as needed.

Braids take time. Imagine Derek with Collins during the long hours while Collins traced the end of her comb over Derek's scalp, sectioning the hair carefully, working to maintain the right tension, slipping the beads over each braid. Did they make small talk? Discuss how, strangely, they had the same last name? Chat about Derek's hair, John, the movie, which kinds of beads to choose? Did Derek roll her shoulders, stretch, get stiff? Is Derek the kind of person who complains when her hair is pulled? Did Collins apologize, reassure, boss around?

The difference between appropriation and paying tribute, Lauren Michele Jackson explains to us, lies in how a moment of cultural exchange activates or relies upon differentials of power. When someone with more power takes up the aesthetic practices of someone with less power, what typically results is an intensification, rather than an amelioration, of the power differential.[23] When Bo Derek pulls toward herself an aesthetic resource—the beauty, the knowledge, the symbol of Black intimacy that braids imply—without moving other kinds of resources in the other direction, the imbalance on the ledger intensifies. It's not a tribute if the person or people whose style you are replicating become harder to see, become less secure, in the aftermath of your action.

Eunice Ann Collins, it seems, was paid $1,200. But I cannot find a single source published over the last forty years in which Bo Derek mentions her name.

~

10 is a very strange movie. It can feel like a trivial one. Although it was well-reviewed and a surprise box-office success, I don't think the movie would matter now if Bo Derek, in cornrows, hadn't run—like a train or a bullet, cinema-of-attraction style—straight out of the film and into the cultural imagination.

The movie's basically a sex romp, a two-hour, two-minute-long delivery service for slapstick comedy and boobs. But the movie critic Gene Siskel, in conversation with Robert Ebert (two thumbs up!) insisted the movie was also about "serious stuff." It was, specifically, about learning how to be adult in a world where sex had changed.[24]

10 tells the story of a man, George (played by Dudley Moore) who's a famous, Academy Award–winning songwriter, and whose forty-second birthday throws him into a midlife crisis.

George's problems include wanting to stay young rather than grow old and (his word) "disgusting," wanting more young people to prefer his romantic orchestral songs to vulgar rock ones, and being bored with his age-appropriate and extremely talented girlfriend, Sam. Sam is played by none other than Julie Andrews. (I didn't remember this; no one I've ever talked to remembers this. That real-genius Andrews is eclipsed in memory by Derek is just more evidence of Derek's cornrowed appeal.) Sam, too, has a problem: She wants to "make love" (her words), and she's frustrated by George's lack of desire for her.

Frustration also saturates George, who feels sure nothing can stop his descent into what he semi-ridiculously calls "invalidity." But driving one day through Beverly Hills, he catches sight of a woman so beautiful that her appearance feels, maddeningly, intoxicatingly, like the solution to all his problems. The beautiful woman is played by Bo Derek. Her name in the movie is Jenny, although George doesn't learn that until later. He only knows that she's "the most beautiful creature" he's ever seen. Despite the fact that a woman's wedding seems like a poor opportunity for a meet-cute, George pursues Jenny aggressively, even following her to the beachy resort where she's gone on her honeymoon. Ridiculous circumstances involving a shark and a bad sunburn (literally, this is the plot) finally bring George and his perfect woman together. But when the opportunity to "do it" (her words) finally presents itself, George finds himself . . . turned off. He doesn't like that she gets high. He's irritated when her hair, with its beads and feathers, falls into his mouth. When she puts on her favorite erotic music, "Boléro," the record skips. The stuck record works like a metaphor for what happens next: Jenny's husband calls. Jenny's not worried about the infidelity, and neither is her husband. But George is appalled to discover that he's not "special." Disgusted, George returns to his age-appropriate fiancé, Sam; the movie ends by affirming the familiar Hollywood lesson that when it comes to erotic fulfillment, there's no place like home.

Julie Andrews charms her way through the movie, at every moment grown-up, talented, and smart. Her hair is short and carefully coifed. It looks, I cannot help thinking, much like Nancy Reagan's.

This summary leaves out a key part of *10*: its intense scopophilia. *10's* characters—most of them—want to have sex, but they also want to have the right kind of sex, and to have their sex lives be perceived by other people as desirable. By "other people" the movie means other white men: It literally gives George and an unnamed male neighbor telescopes they use to spy on each other. This neighbor hosts sex parties attended by multiple gorgeous and typically naked women, and he often purposefully stages these parties on his patio for George (and the film's lucky viewers) to watch.

And George does watch those parties, though he's not sure what he thinks of them. He mutters "un-fucking-believable!" with something like disgust. But he doesn't peel his eye away from the telescope. What does he see? The flamboyant clothing of the neighbor and his guests seems to mark him and his sex parties as a glammed-up free-love counterculture. In this way, the sex parties become one of the strategies *10* uses—along with mentions of OPEC, gay rights, and birth control—to make its comedy not just about one man's sexual crisis, but rather about sex in 1979, in general. About, as Siskel said, "serious stuff."

George isn't sure he wants the sex parties. But he also does not want to make love to steady, reliable Sam. He is stuck: He wants erotic delights but not to be vulgar. He wants a sexual partner who will be as enviable and admirable as the naked women at his neighbor's parties, but who will be available to him alone.

It's risky to boil a whole period of history down to a simple analogy, but here I'm going to propose one: The conflict that George faces in this dumb movie mirrors, sort of perfectly, the conflict that white male America faced on the verge of the Reagan revolution. Like George, white male America wanted to manage its attraction to the counterculture's sexual revolution while retaining the privilege—and sense of domestic certainty and comfort—that the counterculture, at least in part, existed to criticize.

~

Here's something about which I feel quite confident: that at the time John Derek had his "idea" about Bo Derek's cornrows, both of the Dereks would have had Farrah Fawcett's image in mind.

The photographer who took Farrah Fawcett's swimsuit picture, Bruce McBroom, credits the success of the photo to Fawcett's "fresh face," her "girl-next-door" quality. It's an account that makes admiring her feel normal, as American as apple pie. But communication studies scholar Chadwick Roberts sees something more historically specific. According to Roberts, Fawcett's nipply, long-haired image told viewers that she had absorbed only the most crowd-pleasing lessons of feminism and the sexual revolution, removing from those lessons any criticism of the status quo. Here she was, now, in her swimsuit with her free breasts and long hair—but not *Hair* hair. She looks willing to offer herself up to the desires of any appreciative viewer, fully available for pleasure without any critique of that viewer's power. Roberts suggests that "her whole persona grows out of a need to be somewhat liberated without being dangerously exposed."[25] Fawcett had taken white erotic norms and done with them what she did with her curls; she made them *looser*.

One piece of evidence for how intensely Fawcett's image "meant" sexuality that was hot and liberated, but de-politicized: Almost all the naked sex-party women in *10* have exactly Fawcett's long, loosely curled hair.

When Bo and John Derek talked about Bo's hair for *10*, they surely were aware that Derek and Fawcett had similar slim bodies, golden skin, and golden hair. Derek, I am sure, was just as aware as every other white woman of her hair's comparative power; she knew that her hair didn't grow with the same thick abundance as Fawcett's. She needed some other way to compete. Somehow, between them, the Dereks decided on cornrows. Maybe it really was John Derek's idea. Maybe it really was Bo Derek's memory of a Vegas backup singer. Maybe they thought the waystation of a Mexico beach, where white women often really did have their hair braided, would wash enough Blackness out of Derek's braids to make them look as apolitical as Fawcett's curls.

Cicely Tyson and others had fought to make cornrows and other braids a sign of Black care, Black intimacy, Black power. These activists had defined what Black braided hair meant. They'd rejected the racist interpretation of unstraightened Black hair as an external symbol of an internal primitive state. They'd made Black braids into a sign of Black women's love for each other.

I won't say that Derek undid all Tyson's work. She's not more important than an entire Black feminist tradition. But nevertheless, by putting cornrows into the lineage of white pinup sex stars, by using a Black hair style to one-up Fawcett's angelic hot-girl hair, the Dereks made a decision that still reverberates today. Derek's braids, like Tyson's, might signal that she has spent time being cared for by Black women, close to them. Yet, with her exposed body, she presents that Black intimacy back to white viewers as a signal of exactly what Tyson didn't want it to be: sexual availability.

Put differently, Derek's hair sent to white audiences the racist message that sexual looseness was what Black braids meant.

~

It's hard to overemphasize the effect of Bo Derek's in *10* on the media world of 1979. She was on the cover of *Playboy*, on Australian *Playboy*, on Italian *Esquire*, on *Playboy* again. She was on the cover of *US Weekly*, on *People*, on special issues of *Movie Release* magazine that promised instructions on how to "do your hair like Bo." I have watched human interest stories from multiple "local news" outlets that featured reporters visiting braiding salons to show (white) women lining up to get a "Bo," interviewing women getting their hair braided and the women braiding it.[26]

All of this was not an accident. It was not a "natural" response to Derek's appearance or to the movie. Instead, it happened because Derek's image appeared at a key moment, right after Farrah Fawcett's, when mass-marketed celebrity images gained a new cultural power—right when pinup posters became what Tressie McMillan Cottom might describe as an "institution" that could "legitimize the 'right' ideas" about beauty and desire.[27] Selling pinup images had previously been an informal sales network; after seeing what happened with Fawcett's image, other advertisers turned selling licensed posters into a $100 million a year industry.[28] The Dereks wanted to be part of it. They hired a photographer to photograph Derek in her swimsuit, recreating the scene from the movie. Along with a poster distributor, they chose three of these images and mass-produced them so they would be ready to sell at the time of the movie's release. By four months after the release of *10*, a *New York Times* article would quote a marketer as saying: "Farrah Fawcett is dead, at least as far as her poster goes." Now, "Bo Derek is all the rage."

In the posters for *10* you are most likely to see, Derek's full form—swimsuit, smile, cornrows—appears under the number 10, with Dudley Moore's face beaming down over her, his face grafted into the number. Every poster with Derek's picture and *10* on it reasserts to us the lesson that to be overwhelmed with attraction to this particular woman, looking this particular way, is only to be experiencing a normal human response. What are you going to do? She's *perfect*. She's a 10. She doesn't feel like a marketing campaign. She feels like a natural value: like pure gold.

~

What does it matter that these posters were everywhere? Are we silly to complain about them, notice them? What does hair in a dumb movie matter, anyway?

Well, here is one answer. One person who apparently believed in the transcendent power of Derek's image—and Derek's hair—was a man named Abraham D. Sofaer. In 1979, the year that *10* was released, Sofaer was appointed judge for the United States District Court for the Southern District of New York. Sofaer was appointed by Jimmy Carter, a Democrat, on the recommendation of Senator Daniel Moynihan, also a Democrat, and a name that will immediately grab your attention if you have any interest in twentieth-century American racial history.

Moynihan, before he was a senator, had written a report for the Johnson administration called *The Negro Family: The Case for National Action*. It's a document better known as the

"Moynihan Report," and it helped direct how US policy treated Black families. The problem with Black American families, according to white man Daniel Moynihan, was that they were "pathological" in their matriarchal orientation. Black families failed because they were too focused on the agency, will, and resources of Black women.

It may seem like a long way to travel to get from a famous political document like the Moynihan Report to an artifact of popular culture like *10* or Bo Derek's braids. But that connection played out in 1981 when Judge Sofaer, recommended by Moynihan, ruled in a suit brought by a Black woman named Renee Rogers, who wanted to wear her hair braided at work. Rogers worked as a stewardess for American Airlines. American Airlines said that Rogers's braids were unprofessional and that she could not wear her hair that way at work. Rogers sued on the basis of racial discrimination. (This case became the basis of one of the first published works of critical race theory, when Paulette M. Caldwell wrote about it in the *Duke Law Review.*) Determining what kind of hair was work appropriate for Rogers, Sofaer referred to the most famous cornrow wearer of his moment: Bo Derek.

Rogers, in her suit, claimed that braided hair should be protected as an expression of her race under the Thirteenth Amendment. In the case she and her lawyer made, she positioned herself within a legacy of Black public figures—some of the women I have mentioned here. Rogers and her attorney argued that cornrows are "historically, a fashion and style adopted by Black American women, reflective of the cultural, historical essence of the Black women in American society."[29]

The defense, and then Judge Sofaer in his ruling, disagreed.

I don't know if Judge Sofaer ever saw the movie *10*. But he knew enough about Derek's surging popularity—the presence of her cornrowed image everywhere—to affirm the American Airlines argument that Rogers's braids could not be expressing her Blackness. Her braids, Sofaer ruled, had nothing to do with the texture of her hair, or a legacy of Black culture, or the example of Cicely Tyson. Instead, Sofaer refers to cornrows as a style "popularized" by "Bo Derek." His ruling literally mentions Derek by name.

I have spent a lot of time imagining what it was like for Renee Rogers to walk into a courtroom and argue about her hair in front of Judge Sofaer. Did Rogers wear her hair braided to court? How else did she dress? How did she feel as a Black woman with her hair on trial, sitting in a row with three white attorneys?

This information isn't written into court records. As with the name of Eunice Ann Collins, it's hard to know how to find it. To try, I tracked down headshots for all the attorneys in the room. All three of them—Rogers's attorney James L. Meyerson, and American Airlines' attorneys Charles B. Updike and Nancy A. Connery—have virtually the same, short, salt-and-pepper hair. I don't know about the other people in the courtroom, whether the bailiff or the court recorder, had ever spent time in a braiding salon or negotiated with their textured hair. I also can't know if Judge Sofaer—who I learned had been born in Bombay, in a Jewish family originally from Baghdad—identifies as white. (I do know, per his webpage at the Hoover Institute think tank where he is a fellow, that he is a fan of jazz.)[30]

But it's clear what Judge Sofaer was thinking, or at least assuming, when he sat in his bench looking down at a Black flight attendant in a row of white lawyers. What he saw, looking at her, feels to me as scopophilic as the movie *10*, or as Derek as a young girl backstage at the Vegas nightclub. He sees a Black woman with braided hair. He imagines this Black woman watching Bo Derek run down a beach, all eyes on her. He pictures Rogers flipping through a magazine, any of the many magazines published after *10*'s release, explaining how to get "Derek's Style." Maybe he envisions Rogers at a newsstand, seeing Derek on the cover of *Playboy*, on Australian *Playboy*, on Italian *Esquire*, on *Playboy* again.

When Judge Sofaer sees Rogers's braids, he cannot see the Black women who braided them, the Black women who cared for her, the Black women who put themselves on the line so that cornrows could mean Black strength. He cannot see the tradition of these Black women because Bo Derek has colonized his entire field of vision.

So what Judge Sofaer sees when he looks at Renee Rogers's braids is like a fun-house movie version of racial appropriation. All Judge Sofaer could see in Rogers's braids—what he saw, even though *it was not even there*—was an expression of Rogers's desire to look *like a desirable white woman*. So all he could imagine was that Rogers wanted the men who stared at Bo Derek to look at her in the same way.

~

In the fall of 1980, Bo Derek made her second appearance on the cover of *Playboy* magazine. This time, her hair is not in braids. But her eyes gaze out at us between two names: her own and Ronald Reagan's. They were the two headlines of this magazine, focused on, as it then claimed, "Pleasure for Men."

Derek gained celebrity because of her cornrows, an expression of Blackness she could take off and put on at her convenience. The flexibility of her hair, and the nature of her celebrity, makes the Black culture her cornrows represented seem silly, trivial, merely—to use Judge Sofaer's word—popular. Derek herself, appearing in tabloids and soft-core porn, seems hardly to register in significant history. But perhaps, under Reagan, this was the safe place for sex to be: minor, fun but not threatening, easy to enjoy and not think about. This wasn't at all what the counterculture had proposed that sex, or hair, might be: a location full of political or emotional transformation.

~

In November of 2022—as civil rights were again under attack, as conservative white America pressed back against the civil rights gains made in the wake of George Floyd's murder—Bo Derek ran down a beach and into my hand. She was framed there by the blue metal of my iPhone, in a video sent to me by my friend Dan.

Dan was at a Los Angeles Chargers football game, and Bo Derek—still gorgeously luminous—was in attendance too, to celebrate her birthday. In honor of the occasion, the stadium Jumbotron projected the video of Derek's famous beachy run for all the fans in the stadium to see. In the video Dan sent me, you can see both the Jumbotron with the movie clip, and sports fans cheering for it. The video was a strange replication of the movie's own fascination with watching, with knowing our desire is affirmed, correct, and seen.

It was also a moment staged for friendly good cheer in the midst of a heated football game. The moment told everyone at the stadium what the movie and its posters had been telling viewers for forty years: Here is something we can agree on, should delight in, all desire. Forget about your disagreements. Forget about politics. Forget about the NFL, about what it did to Colin Kaepernick. Forget about race. Remember that Bo Derek, braided, is still hot.

When you look at Derek's smile in the video, her apparent delight in her beachy experience, her seeming pleasure at coming right toward you, you do not see an image that American culture encourages us to see as ominous. She looks like the opposite of conflict, like acquiescence, like the word *yes*. What about her could threaten? But put into context, the image becomes a perfect example of how the idealization of white womanhood continues to function in American cultural life. It breezes along, looking beautiful and joyful and free, accreting to itself all possible markers of attractiveness—and thus wreaking havoc for everyone who must inhabit a world where this idea of perfection, of being a 10, is written into court documents that determine how the real women who represent the word *American* should look.

MANIC PANIC

Picture the punks. Picture their hair. The spikes, the bleached ends, the sharp bristly ridges and the bare-shaved skulls. To picture punk hair is to see punk anger. Even to viewers unaware of that anger's source—people who didn't know how punk emerged out of Margaret Thatcher's cruel austerity, London's racist police violence, and the crackdown on English labor unions—punk anger was apparent.

And whatever else it was, punk anger was exciting. Here were people who gave no fucks. In every fashion choice they made, they enacted their disdain for convention. They wrote their rage into their skin with safety pins and tattoos; they cut it into their clothes. Feeling rejected by their world, they rejected it right back. They refused its terms. Their hairstyles were a part of that refusal. Their wild hair was a way they showed they were free.

Right around the time *10* appeared in theaters, a new business opened up at 33 St. Mark's Place in New York: Manic Panic. It was the first punk-style boutique in the US, run by two sisters, Tish and Snooky Bellomo. St. Mark's, like much of Greenwich Village, was then nearly abandoned; their rent was $250 a month. Tish and Snooky sold shoes and clothes they thrifted while shopping with their friend Debbie Harry. And they sold hair dye that they brought back in suitcases from England. When their distributor became unreliable, they found a way to produce and market their own.[1] Punk in general often had an aggressive, masculine tone. But in the US, two women drove its signature hair dye, its most famous tool for hair's decoration.

They did it in their own way. Trish and Snooky describe the style they promoted as "glam into punk." They prided themselves on their fabulousness, their friendliness, and on making hair dye that was vegan and cruelty-free. When I was a little girl, I never heard of them. But even I, in rural Iowa, could see their influence. I saw it, for instance, in the hair of one of my favorite singers: Cyndi Lauper, the Bellomo sisters' friend.

I first saw Cyndi Lauper in my friend Kate's living room—Kate had just gotten Lauper's album *She's So Unusual*. The tone of the music was friendly, even pop, but Lauper's style reflected her New York punk scene. Kate and I stared and stared at the cover. It was like the opposite of Derek's pinup poster. Nothing here is soft. No one smiles our way. The image captures a woman in the midst of a whirling dance: Her legs rotate inward, knock-kneed; her torso twists; one hand fists around a bunch of flowers that are not offered to us. Her red skirts swirl up, and so does her red-orange hair.

Red-orange like a candy, like a warning sign, like a box of crayons sharpened into spikes, both bright and begrimed. Part shorn, part short, partly still long enough to toss. This hair shows want and intention, but it disregards ideas like "pretty" or "hot." Across her body, words scrawl out the album's title, the aesthetic ambition for which this woman reaches and by which she'd like to be judged: "She's so unusual."

I cannot confirm that Lauper's hair was dyed with Manic Panic in this specific photograph. But I can confirm that manic panic—a name for a moment, an energy and ethos—is what this picture shows. Lauper got her first hair dye from Manic Panic, the Bellomo's website tells us; and in interview after interview, still, Lauper recommends their dye.[2]

Cyndi Lauper's record made her a breakout star. Many people saw this picture: Billboard Records ranked it the seventh-best album cover of all time.[3] And part of what all of us saw, what my friend and I saw, a thousand miles away from St. Mark's Place, was a world of imagery made by women. We felt the creative power of the Bellomo sisters. Years later, when I learned that Annie Leibovitz had taken this photograph, I could understand what I was seeing in it: two women, women who celebrated all sorts of not-straight pleasure and desire, rethinking together what a woman's image might mean.

My sophomore year in college, still in Iowa, I went to a basement vintage thrift store that carried Manic Panic dye. I bought a red that was more burgundy than burning, but still just a shade different from Cyndi's. And even though I was still far away from New York, and from punk, I felt a kind of solidarity with a long line of unusual women as I leaned over my kitchen sink so my friend—laughing and bossy and loving—could streak the red dye throughout my waist-length hair.

CHAPTER 2

MARY LOU RETTON'S BOB

In 1984, Mary Lou Retton also became a 10, after she executed—not once but twice!—a perfect vault at the Olympics. In the busy months immediately following, she endorsed a medley of carefully chosen products, each selected to support her developing brand as America's sweetheart. One of these, in keeping with her iconic hair, was a hair-care line. Another was America's campaigning president Ronald Reagan.

Significantly, Mary Lou Retton managed to be an American sweetheart, an emblem of patriotism, an ideal of girlishness, and a hair icon, all while having short, closely cut, hair. I'm calling it a bob, but it's actually shorter than a bob. I tracked down a hair stylist who had worked in a Vidal Sassoon hair salon in the '80s and asked what the right term for the cut would be, and he told me he'd call Retton's hair a "basic layer cut." Unlike Bo Derek, whose intricately cornrowed hair implied tremendous amounts of leisure time spent parting and combing and braiding, Retton's close crop strongly implied she just did not have *time* for that kind of hair-centric frivolity.

That's not the only difference between Retton and Derek, of course. Derek's hair became famous for how it grafted a Black style into her white woman's sex-symbol appeal. Retton's short hair, on the other hand, expressed a specific version of no-nonsense femininity almost entirely internal to whiteness. Many women, across race, obviously have feelings about their hairs' length. But only white women can cut off, and thus symbolically reject, the particular, feminine power of long, flowing white woman's hair.

Mary Lou Retton was not the first short-haired American sweetheart, and she was hardly the first white girl to attach herself to a powerful adult white male figure. But the coalition of Retton and Reagan helps us see a function that short white women's hair performed during the so-called Reagan "revolution."

In the early '80s, many white women cut their hair short: Versions of Retton's tidy, basic bob appeared everywhere, on movie stars, in shampoo ads, on real princesses like Diana, and even, unwillingly, on my own head. But Retton, unlike Derek with her cornrows, did not start a trend. My parents didn't take me to get a bob *because* of Mary Lou Retton. By the time Retton executed her perfect vault, I'd been living with my short hair for almost a year. Rather, bobs were somehow in the early-'80s air that both Retton and my parents breathed.

I knew why my hair was cut short: because my parents were too busy with their small incomes and demanding jobs to take care of it. Short hair became a matter of practical necessity. But why, I wondered, did so many emblematic girls with so many options *also* have such short hair? Were their parents busy, too? I stared at images of their short hair—on the TV, in the grocery store magazine aisle, at the movies—and felt an uneasy gap between my own understanding of the currencies of girlhood and the smiling images I saw on my screens. What was short hair giving these girls and women? What was *its* value? What had these short-haired people gained that made up for the long hair they had lost?

Could the punks explain it? When punk women shaved and spiked their hair, they seemed to free themselves from the expectation of spending their time beautifying themselves for anyone else's viewing pleasure. Shorn punk skulls perform a specific form of radicalism that seems very different from Retton's tidy trim. But I think Retton too wanted to signal a cultural break. Like the punks, she was interested in freedom and strength. Before her, gymnasts were known for a "traditional model," which one biographer described as "ponytailed and spindly thin."[1] Like the punks', Retton's image rejected a feminine norm. Her hair carried the sense of a powerful, world-changing energy. But on Retton's all-American head, that revolutionary energy was repackaged and redirected for mainstream, conservative purposes.

In this way, Mary Lou Retton's short hair expresses something bigger than her own busyness, her personal unwillingness to spend time caring for her hair. Her hair tells us something about all of USA Gymnastics—and through gymnastics, about American patriotism in the Reagan era. Retton embraced Reagan, literally, in photographs that were widely distributed during the 1984 presidential campaign. Partly as a result, Reagan could turn Retton (and USA Gymnastics) into emblems of his version of America, to help bolster political support for his economic and political policies. My claim, which may be surprising, is that Mary Lou Retton's short hair made her particularly valuable to Reagan's project. Retton's short hair became a metaphor for Reagan's austere politics. Translated into a little girl's no-nonsense haircut, reactionary conservative policies—including a broadscale retraction of public welfare and social safety nets—could look revolutionary, and even sweet.

~

Mary Lou Retton fell in love with gymnastics as a child, watching Nadia Comăneci win her 1976 Montreal gold medal. In memoirs, Retton describes lying on her living room floor in front of the television as Comăneci spun on the uneven bars, the first gymnast ever to earn a perfect 10. Retton was eight years old.[2] Later, when I was eight years old, I crowded into my parent's hotel room bed—we were on vacation, and I remember perfectly the small TV and the sound of the window air conditioner—to watch Retton earn her 10 in the 1984 Olympics.

Later still, in another gymnastics memoir of sorts, the lawyer Rachael Denhollander would describe her own childlike fascination with watching Olympic gymnastics, in her case the 1996 "Magnificent 7" gold-medal-winning team. "These little girls with perfect bodies," Denhollander would write, "had done what no other US women's gymnastics team had ever done. They'd paid a high price, including the injury of a teammate, and still they had persisted. It was incredible."[3]

Denhollander titled her 2022 book about her experience with USA Gymnastics *What Is a Girl Worth?* That is my question, too. What is the special worth of "little girls with perfect bodies"? What did I see, what did Denhollander see, what did Retton see, in women's gymnastics, that we admired so intensely? It was sports, but it was more than sports. It was an epic battle. It was a contest with national stakes. And somehow, it was a patriotic battle that young girls seemed uniquely able to win.

Gymnastics became patriotic on purpose. It happened in the 1950s when, despite the long tradition of the sport, its status at the Olympics was on the wane. The USSR realized that Western athletic programs weren't committed to the sport and saw an opening for success. Nations across the Soviet Bloc invested in the sport. They imagined Olympic gymnastics competitions as venues to display the triumphant outcomes of the communist way of life. They succeeded. The Soviet Bloc won a jaw-dropping 94.8 percent of Cold War gymnastics medals. That figure includes the 1984 Olympics.[4]

Gymnastics isn't the only sport in which competitions feel like referendums on entire ways of life. But because of how gymnastics is tied to childhood training, and because of how it put girls' bodies on display—and because of how gymnastics rewards bodies that are small and look young, even when the athlete is grown—it has the rare capacity (ice skating is maybe the only other sport that comes close) to bind the narrative of sports to the story of the American Sweetheart. When a young American girl competed in gymnastics against a girl from the Soviet Bloc, the competition was different than when, say, a group of burly college-age boys padded up and went after a hockey puck.

Gymnasts, no less than hockey players, are highly skilled athletes, and their success depends on their determination, their discipline, their strength. But in gymnasts, all these qualities appear in a vulnerable guise, dressed in sparkles and decorated with careful hands and smiles. When a gymnast competes in the Olympic Games, the victory she might win, or might lose, is not only a symbol of American strength. She's there to demonstrate the worth of all the qualities we associate with girlhood: innocence, virtue, goodness itself. Americanness itself. And so, in my childhood, and into my adulthood, Olympic women's gymnastics competitions became scenes in which the contests between global superpowers—the United States and the USSR, democracy and everything else—felt like they could be decided by the twist of a girl's body, a step or misstep of a girl's foot.

In the '60s and '70s, when American girls were regularly trounced in gymnastics competitions, it caused America a particular kind of worry. Were we raising our girls right? Was *America* all right?

It's hard to distill the illogics vibrating through Cold War fears. One of the tropes about the USSR was that it demanded a cold, effective, hyper-discipline, the opposite of our unruly individualism. This concern shapes a whole range of Cold War competition movies: *Miracle on Ice*, *Pawn Sacrifice*, *Rocky IV*, even the dance movie *White Nights*. Soviets, in the broad American imagination, sent their children off to be schooled in rote repetition. They were tied to tradition and thus un-free, but in an excellent way. They hated our freedoms and wanted to punish us for having them; they worked tirelessly for our defeat. Soviet scientists engineered victories with special training regimens that verged on cheating, and certainly *would* cheat if they could, because they had no ethics or morals, and the athletes cared only for national success. Even in my liberal family, we believed that Soviet daily life was so impoverished that a whole family's future might depend on a young girl making that future slightly more endurable by making herself valuable to the state. I'm not saying that any of this is true; I'm saying that somehow I believed it. The Russians wanted to beat us at everything, and to that end they would beat their very flexible girls into gymnastic icons, and the girls would go willingly, not because they loved gymnastics (no one in Russia loved doing anything) or communism (which was unlovable) but rather because their world made them scrap for bits, and they would do anything they could to keep their family safe from the secret police, and possibly secure a big enough apartment, or a nicer one. It was a disturbing and undesirable system, but it seemed to be working. Americans wondered: How could we have Soviet success while also distancing ourselves from its values?

In the 1980s (and into the '90s), the answer to that highly irrational question was seemingly resolved with a quick fix solution: We could do it with Bela Karolyi.

An icon of Eastern Bloc athletics, the famous coach of Nadia Comăneci, Karolyi grew frustrated with government meddling in his methods and defected to the US. Then he moved to Texas. He liked to hunt. He became a perfect crossover figure: He had the discipline of the East and loved the freedom of the West. For more than thirty years, Bela and his wife, Marta, held powerful control over USA Gymnastics. We Americans—by which I mean me in the 1980s, too—believed he could help us win. With Bella, our girls, our gymnasts, our virtues, would become the best.

VAULT I: MARY LOU RETTON IN LOS ANGELES

A vault takes only a few seconds. Judges, when judging, view vaults on screens that allow them to parse intricate details that the naked eye, in the instant, can hardly see—the point of the toes, the alignment of the thighs, the solidity of the landing. Only in slow motion can watchers perceive all the strength and talent and tenacity that those few flying seconds condense. Years of discipline and endurance compress into quads and wrists and core muscles, so that for those few seconds the gymnast can fly free.

The "Vault Without Fault," Mary Lou Retton's vault, the vault that won her an Olympic gold medal, the one that made her a champion, a sweetheart, a star, went like this:

From the edge of the mat, Retton raised her arms. The crowd in Los Angeles quieted. They knew, Retton knew, that her score had fallen behind that of her main competitor, the Romanian Ecaterina Szabo; Retton had only this last chance to take the lead. Retton, at the edge of the mat, did not look like Szabo; she did not look like Nadia Comăneci; she did not look like a gymnast was "supposed" to look. Her coach called her "Booboolina" which, she would later write, "means fat."[5] The press compared her thighs to spark plugs, her body to a "toy truck."[6] She was fast. She began to run.

She did not run like Derek on the beach—relaxed, lithe, unrushed, her body barely covered by stretched-thin gold. Retton ran toward gold, a victory not a luxury, and she wore the colors of the country's flag. She pounded. She exploded. She needed every bit of the force in her powerful thighs to push her toward the vault, so that when she leapt, reaching for its leather skin, she would rebound off its hard surface, flying high into the air: high enough to stretch all out in the air, twisting once, twisting twice, piking. She snapped her body into a fold, pulling her legs in hard to her chest so they landed evenly on the ground. It is the Tsukahara vault, and in 1984 Mary Lou Retton was the only woman who attempted it at the Olympics.

When her feet stuck a perfect landing, everyone could see her arms pump into the air. Everyone could see her short hair settle around her head. Everyone could see that she knew she had it: the 10, the victory, America's first Gymnastics Olympic Gold. "You couldn't see it," she would later say. "But I was smiling on the way down."

~

Four months after her famous vault, Mary Lou Retton officially became America's sweetheart. It's not a standardized process; no one votes. But in 1984 no one spoke more officially for America than the journalist Walter Cronkite, and so it mattered when Cronkite introduced her that way: "Mary Lou Retton, America's sweetheart." It was at the Kennedy Center Honors. The Reagans were there watching. Mary Lou Retton was not there to receive an honor, and she was not honoring any of the honorees. The *New York Times* article reporting on the event described her as there "to lighten things up, evidently."[7] In a red, white, and blue leotard, she completed tumbling passes across the stage, in front of all the guests in their formal attire. It's a little hard to picture because it's a little strange that it happened. But it's one point of evidence for how, in that post-Olympic moment, Retton had become an emblem for all American triumph, every kind of success.

"America's sweetheart" is a curious category. All the Dallas Cowboys Cheerleaders lay claim to the title, according to their coaches and handlers. Early movie stars like Mary Pickford and Shirley Temple are often considered sweethearts. Both of those sweethearts were also hair icons, indicating the long relation between hair and sweetheart-ability. (The DCCs also have a signature [mandated] long, flowing style.)[8]

In the stories and fantasies in which they feature, sweethearts often want love. They want *to* love. Their victories, like their personalities, are virtuous: Consider Pollyanna (a fictional sweetheart played originally by a real sweetheart, Hayley Mills), who, per the trailer of the eponymous 1960 Disney movie, "taught a whole town how to laugh, how to love, and how to live." The success of a sweetheart seems to make a collective project a simple goal, no more complicated than the bland affirmation you'd find on a tea towel. Live, laugh, love! Retton's universally praised cheerful bubbliness made her perfect for the role.

"America's sweetheart," as a phrase, emerged with the movies. Studios created particular kinds of stars, with particular kinds of star images, who could draw audiences toward particular narrative desires. Despite the historical specificity of the term, the concept it names has become so powerful that it can absorb figures and characters from earlier eras, slotting them into particular roles in the American story of progress and patriotism. It's a concept that uses the values we associate with little girls—innocence, sweetness, virtue, beauty—to make us believe in happy endings, to make us feel that when we acknowledge the status of the sweetheart, her happy ending belongs to, and can happen to, us.

A gymnast sweetheart, with her body tightly encased in a flag and a gold medal around her neck, could vault, as it were, the sweetheart feelings to new heights. To love her was to love America. To see her smile back was to feel American, in a wonderful way. It was to believe not only in the truth of girlhood as a good; it was to see the romance, the evidence, the magic, of the American dream.

~

In her 2022 memoir, Rachael Denhollander describes going to her gym, which was in a mall. "[W]orkers at Claire's Boutique were peddling scented lotions and sparkly hair clips," she writes, while next door, "flipping through the air," were gymnasts with "bleeding hands and utilitarian ponytails."[9]

For Denhollander and others, the ponytail is the signature hairstyle of the gymnast. Nadia Comăneci wore one, with a white ribbon, when she won her gold medal in Montreal. Cathy Rigby, whose success at the 1968 Olympics helped popularize the sport in the United States, typically wore two, also be-ribboned, just like the Russian genius Olga Korbut. I personally feel that if you're wearing two, it's *pigtails*, not a *ponytail*, but I have learned that this is a regional difference. Regardless of the number and of which farmyard animal's name they bear, pigtails and ponytails are a distinctly modern hairstyle—dependent on the 1957 invention of an industrial product that would become the ponytail holder—of a consistently girlish kind. Early packaging for ponytail holders regularly featured sketch drawings of little white girls with hair pulled up from their smiling faces.

Here's something I wonder: Did Mary Lou Retton ever ask another girl for a ponytail holder? Did anyone ever ask for one, from her? Without a ponytail, how did she make her way into the small circuits of exchanged care out of which so many girlhood relations are made?

A ponytail might not seem significantly different than short hair or a bob. Given that in many stories, girls' hair is pulled into a ponytail precisely to be cut off, a ponytail might actually seem halfway down the road to short hair. There's a reason why Denhollander, above, called them "utilitarian." They're how you do your hair when you're not "doing" your hair. Girls with long, smooth-textured hair wear ponytails because they're simple to put in and keep in, and also simple to put *back* in when they come out. It's possible to make a ponytail complicated—I have seen one million Instagram tutorials explaining ponytail improvement strategies, designed to cater to the Ariana Grande fans among us—but even so, ponytails have a "get up and go" quality that distinguishes them from many other hairstyles like braids, blowouts, and hot-roller curls.

So, it might seem strange to linger over the difference between Retton's bob and the ponytails of many gymnasts as an important signifier of Retton's femininity. It's true: A ponytail isn't as different from a bob as a bob is from, say, Sleeping Beauty's flowing locks or—to take a different but related example—a Dallas Cowboys Cheerleader's required long curls.

But looked at differently, there's a world of difference between these two styles. You pull your hair up into a ponytail, rather than cut it off, because you still want and value the possibility of wearing your hair down some other time. The wearer of the ponytail may be utilitarian at that moment, but she's also visibly holding on to more extravagant aesthetic possibilities available to her in other contexts. A ponytail, more than a close-cut do, displays the gymnast's belief that beauty, and appeal, and gender, are sometimes worth caring for. Long hair can mean a lot of things to girls and women, including a whole world of care, attention, and appreciation. A ponytailed gymnast is showing she can be focused, and strong, and girlish too.

For me as a girl, watching the Olympics on my TV, I felt intuitively that the aesthetic value of the ponytail ran parallel to the patriotic, moral-feeling value of the gymnast as I understood her; it was the perfect hairstyle for a disciplined but still feminine girl, the kind of girl the media trained me to admire—the kind of girl that I absolutely wanted to be. Watching Retton's short hair scrambled those desires.

My young girl's intuition that *hair mattered* had latched on to something important, even if I didn't fully understand it at the time. Retton, her hair showed us, was casting one kind of girlishness aside. Was it a frivolous femininity, something we'd be better without? How could *frivolous* femininity be separated from other kinds? Retton mattered so much to 1984 American that looking at her short hair gave me the sense that what girls were worth, and what made girls worthy, was changing too.

~

I wasn't the only one. Vidal Sassoon, the famous haircare company seemed to feel the same change. At the 1984 Olympic Trials, months before the Olympics themselves, the fast-growing company set out to associate their brand with Retton's. They sent an official hairstylist to the trials to give Retton a "complimentary haircut" as soon as she'd officially been given a spot on the Olympic team.

The haircut took place in the arena, still full of fans, but tucked into a lower corridor so that the young girls watching—the press coverage tells us that it's young girls who were watching—had to fight for the chance to see the haircutting action.[10] They all wanted to see what Sassoon's stylist would do.

I'm curious too. It's honestly a little hard to say specifically what happened. Retton's hair had always been short, since she was a little girl; after the haircut, it was still short. Grainy TV footage from ABC's *Wide World of Sports* broadcast makes the hair details hard to see, for all my rewinding (maybe I need one of the judges' special screens). In footage from before the haircut, Retton's hair looks structured, short and straight back from the ear. From what I can tell, the Vidal Sassoon stylist layered the back and sides. Comparing the hair footage from the Olympic Trials and the Olympics themselves, it looks like at the Olympics Retton's hair, though still short, has a looser shape. Retton's new hair, like Retton, moves.

A girl's haircut is the kind of hair event Vidal Sassoon was good at staging. In 1968, when Vidal Sassoon himself flew from London to Los Angeles to cut Mia Farrow's hair on the soundstage of *Rosemary's Baby*, more than four hundred journalists were in attendance. By the time of the Olympic Trials, Vidal Sassoon, the company not the person, had already been named the "Official Hair Stylist" of the 1984 Olympic Village—they set up two salons there, where any athlete could get their hair cut. Sassoon's haircuts had always been famous for their movement. Now, the company literally promoted a "science" of athletic haircutting: They called it "pilo-dynamics." I'm not making this up. They claimed to develop sport-by-sport strategies for enhancing an athlete's appearance at the photo finish. A gymnast, the *Philadelphia Daily News* reported, is given a "graduated cut" that is "layered for extra body and bounce."[11] Retton's haircut was their trial style.

Vidal Sassoon's marketing describes their Olympic haircuts as a move into a new, marketing-friendly modernity. At least one journalist covering Retton, though, recognized that her Olympic haircut was full of old-fashioned intensity and a deep cultural narrative about what a girl's haircut means. "Big brown eyes strained heavenwards," the reporter from the *Philadelphia Inquirer* writes, "pleading for mercy from the swiftly hacking hands of the merciless hairdresser." "Oh, please, don't bald me," Retton is reported to have said. It's a sentimental moment—and a real feeling, I'm sure, even for a girl who had short hair even as a child, but who still worried about it being *too* short, or somehow not right. In a haircut, something might be gained, but in every haircut, something—some identity, some appearance—is always given up.

It's worth remembering that for all the moral qualities the sweetheart displays, sweetheart is also a marketing category. Sweethearts themselves hadn't traditionally talked about money—they talked about virtue, and community—but that was a norm the '80s abandoned. Retton, in one of the many articles discussing her post-Olympics branding success, cheerfully recounted that she'd discovered "a little businesswoman inside me!"[12] It's a tribute to Mary Lou Retton's genius force of personality that she could leverage an affective identity based on girlish optimism into a commodity, a brand—and she has published articles about how to strategically brand yourself—without losing the sense of innocence or charm that were long considered antithetical to commercial desires. If they are not now, that's because we're living in a moral world that Retton, willingly if without full consciousness, helped make.

Retton's conquest of the American marketing scene was described, by the American press, as another kind of victory, parallel to her gymnastics success. The *New York Times* touted gold medal champions as a "gold mine for marketers." While Retton kept most of her earnings secret, journalists and other sports marketers widely reported that she had earned by far the most post-Olympic endorsement money (surpassing comfortably, if just for the moment, the second most successful athlete, Michael Jordan). She signed contracts with General Mills, McDonalds, Energizer, and Vidal Sassoon. She "fits the image of our teenage market," Vidal Sassoon's spokesperson said. "She's very clean, very wholesome, very All-American." These qualities were something she could sell.

In the world of endorsements and sponsorships—in the world of marketable girlhood—a girl's worth was subject to a financial calculus. Vidal Sasson explained Retton's value by describing her as "wholesome." But there's something unwholesome lurking behind this thinking. In this mentality, it seemed that a girl became worth a brand's care when she was a success, and if there was something from her to be gained. If there was no profit to be found in her, if there was no victory to be claimed through her, was a girl worth anything at all?

After Retton's haircut, the fans who had been held back by security guards were released, and a crowd of little girls "swoops forward," the same journalist tells us, to retrieve the locks of hair from the floor: mementos, from a sweetheart, a star. It's a perfect Retton moment. A haircut proposed by a brand, for a marketing opportunity, for financial profit, enhancing the company's own value by drawing on girls' heartfelt love for Retton, captured in the enduring symbol of her hair.

VAULT 2: DIANNE DURHAM, FT. LAUDERDALE

Or maybe the story of Retton's heroic vault into history begins even before her haircut: with another vault, one that never became famous, and for that very reason, is just as important for Retton's story.

Retton was a favorite going into the Olympic trials, but she was not the only one. In spring of 1984, and for several years previously, America's best gymnast had been Dianne Durham. It is worth saying that Durham also had short hair, about the length of Retton's. And it's also worth saying that Durham, unusually for a gymnast, then and even now in the age of Simone Biles, was Black. How much this matters to her story is the subject of some debate.

Durham was taller than Retton, and like her, very strong. She was an accomplished vaulter. Like many athletes, Durham was also in a constant state of recovery from injury. When she pulled herself back to earth from the sky at her Olympic trials vault, she landed hard on one ankle, spraining it. Recounting the moment later, her coach said that he was relieved it was just a sprain. She only had one event left, the uneven bars. "It's the bars, you won't be on your ankle," her coach told her. She could go on; he was sure she could go on. A gymnastics official tried to comfort her, but her coach was having none of it. He recounted the moment later: "Dianne," I barked, "get over to the god damned bars."[13] That was how he proudly described his treatment of a re-injured sixteen-year-old.

In footage from the Olympic trials, Durham sits on the sidelines, surrounded by worriers working at her ankle. She looks tired and hurt, slouched. She faced a dilemma. She could, while injured, compete for her Olympic spot. Or she could withdraw from the competition, trusting that her high rank would earn her a spot even if she didn't perform in this last event.

Caregivers around her—although not her barking coach—apparently assured her that she could still make the team. If I felt like she looked, and if someone told me that I could still make the Olympic team without landing yet another event on a damaged ankle, I would listen. I would be grateful. I don't know if Durham was grateful, but she followed the caregivers' advice and withdrew from competition.

Her coach was appalled. He couldn't believe she didn't push through; he felt other coaches pushed her out. And—he was not totally wrong. Despite the reassurances she'd been given, and despite her status as, with Retton, America's most accomplished gymnast, Durham was not given one of the spots on the Olympic team.

The moment on the sidelines with a vault-injured ankle was the end of Durham's competitive career. Literally at the very same time that Retton was getting her hair cut, Durham was reckoning with the status she had lost.

I don't know what Bela Karolyi, Durham's and Retton's coach, did in the aftermath of the decision. I don't know if he helped Durham pack, or if he watched his new star Retton receive her new Olympic-ready look.

~

Bela Karolyi is one of the white men most associated with Mary Lou Retton. Another, as I hinted, was Ronald Reagan. What did Reagan mean in 1984? He was the ogre of my childhood, which makes my childhood very different from many American childhoods, I assume. A lot of people voted for Reagan in 1984, and their kids must have known about it, heard about it, thought it was a good idea. I don't know what their parents told them about the whole "he cut school budgets so much they had to count ketchup as a vegetable!" situation, which my parents and their friends described to each other over and over, in shock and horror. My parents were liberal and anti-war, and they had felt some sense of betrayal by their country for much of their lives. Reagan's clear cruelty, its broad embrace, felt to them like a continuation of Vietnam: a murderous horror glossed over in chirpy optimistic tones.

Mary Lou Retton, in 1984, claimed to want to "stay away" from politics. But judging from the many pictures of the occasion, she didn't seem to mind when politics came to her—when, at the end of the Olympic Games, Ronald and Nancy Reagan came to Los Angeles to meet the US Olympic Team.

Retton stands front and center as the team awaits the presidential couple. She's the athlete who has been chosen to hand Ronald his honorary team jacket. After he puts it on, she reaches her arms up toward him for a hug. They both seem delighted, smiling and laughing.[14] In the widely circulated photographs—they were sold as postcards—they stand with their arms around each other's backs. In some of them she beams up at him, with the same wide smile that Little Orphan Annie, another short-haired sweetheart, not coincidentally, beamed up at Daddy Warbucks. During his remarks, Reagan praises the team for showing that Americans were "generous." "There's a new patriotism spreading across our country," he claims, and he praises the athletes for creating an America to believe in. He tells them to win one "for the Gipper." He's the Gipper. It's been his nickname since he played the once-famous football player in a movie. America, Reagan: In Reagan's speech they are the same, and so to win for Reagan is to win for America too.

It's not a campaign speech technically. But it takes place less than three months before the 1984 election, and the electoral implication is clear. It seems that Retton didn't mind, because she appeared at a Republican fundraising dinner shortly after. Reagan's cheerful tones must have seemed perfectly in tune with her own smiling marketing persona. ("I'm a pretty happy person," she would declare in a *Washington Post* article titled "Cashing In on That Winning Smile.")[15]

In his cheerful affect, Reagan took a very different pose than his cross-Atlantic counterpart and frequent collaborator, Margaret Thatcher, who came into office just a year before him. Whereas Reagan embraced the feel-good "Gipper" nickname, Thatcher was known for her coldness, for being the "Iron Lady." The Thatcher comparison helps throw Reagan's political pose into sharper relief. Thatcher and Reagan shared their hardline political positions on defense, on empire, on privatization, on unions, on the counterculture (both maintained a deadly inaction during the growing AIDS epidemic), but only Thatcher made being hardline, or "resolute," to use her term, into a personality or a rallying cry. Reagan, on the other hand, made it a point to appear infinitely friendly and personable, smiling in the face of his brutal policies.

And his policies were brutal, especially for the American poor. Reagan wanted more military spending, an arms buildup that would signal American strength to the Soviet Union, and a "strong" America primed for an economic, moral fight. Reagan tasked his economic policy advisor, David Stockman, with presenting a "Program for Economic Recovery" that would balance the budget while increasing the defense budget and also—this part was not directly addressed in campaign speeches—protecting the wealth and resources of Reagan's political allies.

So Stockman never proposed, for instance, balancing the budget by eliminating subsidies for republican Jesse Helms's tobacco farmer constituents (I mention Helms because in my childhood, he was an ogre too). Instead, Stockman cut programs for those without powerful political advocates—those who didn't already have connections, power, or success. According to the most recent Reagan biography, as a result of the 1981 budget cuts, "as many as five hundred thousand families lost their eligibility for the main welfare program, Aid to Families with Dependent Children, and another three hundred thousand families had their benefits reduced; a million people lost Food Stamps; and only 45 percent of the jobless in 1982 received unemployment benefits, compared to 76 percent during the recession of 1975."[16] Reagan's first term was marked by economic upheaval, a surge in homelessness as funding for public housing and mental health care retracted, and dramatic suffering among the Black families who were the most common recipients of the particular kinds of aid that Reagan's budget cut.

My parents were so anti-Reagan that as an adult, I wondered if their stories were exaggeration, a projection of their values, a falsely framed good-versus-evil story that just reversed the characters in the stories that Reagan himself liked to tell. Did his administration *really* count ketchup as a vegetable? That seems to me insane. But, my dear readers: That is not an exaggeration. It is true. In 1982, the Department of Agriculture met Stockman's budget demands by overhauling the school lunch system. Both ketchup *and* relish (!!) suddenly became "vegetables." Servings of milk shrunk from six ounces to four.[17] Kids eating school lunches received fewer calories, and less nutrition in those calories. Can you *get* more melodramatically villainous than stealing milk from kids?

Yet Reagan sold the story of himself as the hero, not the villain. Sure, he was taking lunch from kids. But he was doing it for their protection—to protect them from welfare cheats and moral weakness and Russians. Reagan swept to a landslide 1984 victory by convincing white American voters that he was helping to protect their economic interests. Even as Reagan's economic policies hurt the American poor and middle class—and set in motion the path to the extreme and dangerous economic stratification we're experiencing today—he convinced white voters that he was protecting them from the real threats to their economic security: the cheating, lazy, and racially coded poor. Not to mention the Russians, who would easily prey on the weak.

I remember the morning Reagan was elected, but most of my life has been spent in his world. That means I hardly remember a time when the phrase *welfare state*, like *welfare queen*, wasn't a political third rail, something to be rigorously worked against; when even many liberals were scared that their economic liberality would be perceived as anti-America, anti–hard work, anti-well-being. I have to make myself recognize how strange this state of affairs really is. How could it possibly become taboo for a government to prioritize the welfare of its citizens? How could protecting each other, looking out for each other, come to seem like injuring our national well-being?

Yet that is the line Reagan sold us, and that "we" white Americans collectively bought. Reagan won his very first campaign, back in 1966, by rallying white Californians around the fear of "a segment of society capable of caring for itself but which prefers making welfare a way of life, freeloading at the expense of more conscientious citizens."[18] He rejected even Nixon's proposal for universal income for parents by claiming that it would "weaken" the nation's "moral fiber," that it would "drain the productive wellspring of America."[19] He would, as his famous ad would promise, make it "morning again in America" by teaching us all that the way to protect our moral fiber, our integrity, our future, our way of life was by rejecting any mandate to extend care to each other. He was retracting care from us, but for our own good.

Retton and Reagan are not the same. But one reason, I think, why they made such a perfect smiling pair—why the image of them struck such a perfect cord—is because her soaring gymnast's body seemed the perfect illustration of the worldview that Reagan constantly advanced. When Mary Lou Retton, then fifteen, left her family, like Dianne Durham had left her family, to go train in Bela Karolyi's Texas gym, she did it because, as she said a year later in the book that she and Karolyi cowrote, "I wanted someone to push me, even yell at me." She felt she couldn't move to the next level without stiffer competition, without that stiffer training that everyone knew had produced Nadia. Retton went even though she'd heard "terrible rumors," that Bela was "this monster, he starves you, he makes you into a robot."[20] But she wanted to improve.

I cannot really convey how disturbing it is, with the benefit of hindsight, to read Retton and Karolyi's book. This is not to say that they don't have a rapport, visible in ample video footage, or that brutal was all he was. But the cheerfully told stories of rigor and discipline and withdrawal—of being yelled at while injured, while bleeding, while one pound overweight—are very hard to take. "Some girls," Retton tells us, don't get through what she calls a "hard time."[21] But some do. "I had to," Retton says, "and I did." She wanted to win one for America, for the Gipper.

That she did win made the logic she represented seem true. In Retton, Reagan found the perfect metaphorical evidence for the America in which he wanted us all to believe: an America in which the way to succeed, the way to soar, the way to reach freedom, was to make sure that no one would take care of you, be kind to you, at all.

VAULT 3: SIMONE BILES, TOKYO

In 2021, Simone Biles was the best vaulter the world had ever known. She was the reigning world champion, the reigning gold medalist. A young Black woman, she was the face of America's gymnastics team when America first voted for Trump, and while USA Gymnastics was roiled by its own calamities. These are not the only burdens she has carried. In the documentary *Simone Rising*, Biles and her mother describe at length the ongoing criticism Biles has faced for her appearance, for her hair especially. To be beautiful, Biles explains, was to have long, straight hair.[22] Since she didn't have the right hair, she could never be beautiful. Criticizing her hair is one way the media has expressed general ambivalence about whether this young Black woman's success makes her a sweetheart too.

At the Tokyo Olympics, Biles planned to do an Amanar vault: two and a half full twists.

Yet in the first night of the all-around competition, somewhere in the air above the vault, Biles lost track of ground and sky. She did not feel free; she felt lost. At the same mid-flight instant that Retton told us she was bursting into a smile, Biles was throwing out her arms to slow her spin. It looked like she was reaching for something steady to hold her. She landed low, lunged forward. She left the mat and the competition and the Olympics. She headed straight into a maelstrom of media heat. Why didn't she press through?

Didn't she love America? Wasn't she tough? Why didn't she care more about winning America, winning USA Gymnastics, a victory?

Gymnasts around her explained that Biles was experiencing "the twisties," a well-known psychosomatic manifestation of anxiety that interferes with a gymnast's proprioception, or body awareness in space. It's a real and terrifying experience with dangerous consequences. To push through the twisties, in the way much of American media wanted Biles to do—and in, we should note, the way Karolyi wanted Dianne Durham to push through her damaged ankle—is to risk a catastrophic injury.

I'm not a gymnast and I've never had the twisties. I don't know what experiencing them during her best event meant to Biles. But I do know that when I was watching Biles in 2021,after Trump 1, after the pandemic, after watching three generations of American gymnasts on the vault, Biles psychic experience of terror, her radical sense of lost confidence, her physically felt confusion about where she might find solid, steady ground, made absolute emotional sense to me.

~

The week in 1981 that his tax cuts were approved by congress, Ronald Reagan wrote in his diary that he was "d—n lonesome."[23] He wasn't feeling alienated from his country or party; he missed his wife. Nancy was away in London. She was attending a major short hair event: the wedding of Princess Diana and Prince Charles.

In 1981, I was a five-year-old white girl, which means I was already well into my lifelong investigation into princess hair. I had avidly consumed all the major texts: *Sleeping Beauty*, which had been rereleased by Disney in 1979, and *Cinderella*, which was rereleased in 1981, the same year Diana got married. Foxy *Robin Hood* (with its carriage and King Richard wedding) would be rereleased in 1982. A princess, these movies taught me, was like a sweetheart, but on a timeless, universal scale, and with a castle instead of a picket fence. Any little 1980s girl in the world of Disney's orbit could learn the lesson that the princess and the sweetheart were two parallel roles, two roles in which a girl's happy ending could matter to a whole country's cause.

I remember Princess Diana's face and dress framed by the box of my TV screen—watching it on the news, on commercials, on PBS. Princess Diana got married in the most princessy dress I could have imagined. Anyone who has read L. M. Montgomery's *Anne* books knows exactly how I continue to feel about Diana's puffed sleeves. There was Diana in a carriage, Diana walking down the aisle, posing with her pages, waving from her balcony. Receiving the ring that was its own special kind of crown. I was thrilled. The church, the blushing smile, the applauding witnesses—they were storybook, they were fairy-tale. What these adjectives mean is that, like *Cinderella* or *Sleeping Beauty*, they created the feeling of being timeless. They felt connected to some enduring, feminine truth. What I believed, and what all the fairy-tale trappings of Diana's wedding seemed to affirm, was that to be a princess was to be eternal—to be in the smiling, starring, role forever. This is a lie, but it is a very powerful one.

In all the fairy tales I had seen, long hair mattered to being the princess. Even Fox Maid Marian's wimple is a long-hair cipher. But in Princess Diana's wedding, in the middle of the silk taffeta and lace, between Diana's blushing face and her billowing dress and interrupting the confluence between them, was . . . her hair, that feathered bob. Her hair made no crown at all. Princess Diana's short hair punctured the illusion of the eternal princess, even as she seemed committed to holding on to that illusion in every other respect.

Mary Lou Retton was not a princess. She came from a mining town in West Virginia. But I would posit that for all the differences between them, we can learn a lot by comparing Diana Spencer to Mary Lou Retton. Like Thatcher and Reagan, they were cross-Atlantic counterparts. These two much-admired women both became emblems of their era, emblems of the best of their country, in a way that only young women and girls can be. The Princess and the Gymnast Sweetheart—these are two roles in which it was acceptable for young, white women to receive attention and admiration for their status and their power, two roles in which your girlishness can enhance your role in your world, rather than diminish it.

Compare these feminine spectacles of my childhood: Diana, gliding down the aisle, her hair in a feathered bob. And Retton, sprinting toward a vault, her hair a clipped mop around her head. Diana's body was encased in flowing, obscuring white fabric; Retton's lithe form was left mostly exposed except by the small piece of fabric printed in the red, white and blue of the American flag. But both young women's bodies were hyper-disciplined to prepare for the elaborate performance at hand. In one complicated feat, each woman would win a victory that would bring her into the arms of a powerful man and an adoring, celebrating nation.

What were each of them doing with their surprising short hair? I had read many stories about girls who cut their hair to do good, or to get free. Perhaps that was what Diana or Mary Lou wanted. Maybe they wanted to be modern—to cast some old mold aside. They wanted to be strong, not frivolous. But what version of "freedom" was this, that was dressed in the same old fantasy, and moving into what felt to me like the same old story?

What would modern hair mean if the girlish woman wearing it wrapped her arms around Charles, around Reagan, around emblems of a return to the past?

~

Short hair, like Diana's and Retton's, participates in a very specific and well-established symbolic white tradition. It began in the 1920s, when white women began bobbing their hair in droves. The trend generated a significant amount of media narration, with headlines that indicate the deep symbolic power that white women's hair possessed. If white women, en masse, were changing their hair, then something significant in their world had changed. What was it? Was that change for good, or for ill?

What this trend meant to the many individual women who navigated it, it's hard to know. Surely many of them were thrilled, many regretful, many ambivalent; some were surely motivated by pleasure and others by pressure. Histories of the moment chart intensely divided feelings. Headlines from the era announce that young women had literally killed themselves out of overwhelming regret about their new bobs; other headlines report that young women had killed themselves because their fathers wouldn't allow them to get bobs. In both kinds of headlines, short hair was life or death. Or maybe, because short hair was a *new* way of life, it also always meant the death of the old one.

Revealingly, the bobbed and cropped hair that became trendsetting in the '20s returned in the '60s, another moment of self-perceived gender modernization: Picture Twiggy's short hair, or Nancy Kwan's famed five-point-bob, which was also cut by Vidal Sassoon. In both the '20s and the '60s, the consensus interpretation of a woman cutting her hair was of a dramatic break with conservative ideas of femininity. Many condemned and others applauded this outcome, but few disputed that cutting your hair was a way to free yourself from tradition. The language of liberation infuses interviews and testimonials, scholarship and blogs, in the 1920s, in the 1960s, and today as well. Vidal Sassoon would praise his signature bobs for how they would "eliminate the superfluous."[24] The woman who received his haircuts, would be "liberated" from weekly salon visits and elaborate styling, needing only a monthly trim.[25]

Another hairdresser who helped make the bob famous—by cutting the hair of the French actress Eve Lavalliere in 1911—recalled his motivations in a way that seems to have perfectly captured the consensus about the cultural rupture: "A bell rang inside my head," he wrote. "The time had come for women to have their hair cut short. This new automobile in which women sat open to the winds, these new women with careers, this busy life. And these changing clothes, which demanded small, neat heads, not enormous masses of hair."[26]

In this account, white women (he doesn't mention that they are white) need to fit in new machines, in new fashions, in new jobs or the newly held possibility of having jobs; together these new situations comprise new lives, and the new lives are busy ones.

There's a tension here that grips me. The lives that short hair represented—and also enabled, and also required—are almost universally described as *liberating*. And yet, while short hair seemed to signal access to opportunities, those opportunities have not only less security ("open to the winds") but also less space ("small, neat heads") and less time ("this busy life"). What kind of freedom requires such constriction?

My Grammy, born in 1926 (two years younger than Vidal Sassoon), was the youngest of six children. She grew up in a series of hardscrabble midwestern situations at exactly the time the bob was catching on. Her whole life, she recounted with delight her childhood memories of *her* mother, my great-grandmother Odessa, washing and brushing her hair. That sounds wonderful to me too. But when I think about Odessa, washing the thick hair of six children without reliable warm running water or shampoo or conditioner, I understand why Odessa bobbed her own hair. The bob freed her from work, work that was real. It gave her time to run her various side businesses, keeping her children fed through the Depression.

But what short hair did not offer her, this working-class rural woman, was the mobility of motorcars and careers that Antoine, the French hairdresser, imagined. Bobbed hair was not a way out of the constriction of feminized labor. Chopping your hair can certainly feel like freedom or escape, and its symbolism can be deeply powerful—but not necessarily. For my great-grandmother, bobbing her hair was mostly about a reduction of labor. She cut her hair because she did not have time to take care of it, because she was too busy taking care of everyone else. Like my parents who cut my hair in the '80s because they couldn't afford childcare, she "chose" the "freedom" of short hair because other changes that might have made life better were too expensive.

The bobs of the '20s and the '60s might have signaled some kind of gender revolution. The '80s, whatever they were, were not a gender revolution era, as Phyllis Schlafly would be happy to tell you. The Bellomo sisters and their punk friends were laying the foundation of something new in a burned-out strip of the East Village, but they were not the prevailing national sentiment. The '80s were an era of a conservative economic reaction. They were an era when collectivist policies that feminists had worked for in the '70s began to be rolled back, when protections for families eroded. In practical ways that mattered, women—particularly working-class women—became less free to make real choices about their lives.

Yet short hair, and bobbed hair, became the emblematic hair of the early '80s. Diana's short hair, Mary Lou's short hair, my short hair, borrowed a liberatory meaning from feminism and transferred it onto the economic realities of 1980s life. Celebrities made their short hair look glamorous, like a deliberate decision to focus on the success they cared about rather than frivolities they didn't.

I've talked to a lot of women who cut their hair short in the '80s, and many of them definitely describe the relief and pleasure of the experience. They were glad to abandon a long hair ideal, with all the drying and brushing and curling it often required. Short hair meant a lot of things, not just the "dress for success" image Retton and Diana Spencer tried to marry it to. It could be punk or new wave or queer. It could be breaking up with the demanding and apparently vapid and anti-feminist loucheness of Farrah Fawcett and others—Christie Brinkley, Cheryl Tiegs. It could feel feminist and proud.

But a lot of women in the '80s—the women in the '80s whose kids lost school lunch, who lost unemployment benefits, for example—probably experienced their short hair freedom more like my great-grandmother, scraping by, and less like Mary Lou Retton with her million-dollar hair-care endorsements. What they *weren't* experiencing—and arguably what even Mary Lou Retton wasn't experiencing—was the freedom to decide what you do care about, or what kind of care counts as valuable, to you.

~

There's something dangerous about being a sweetheart. Because they are sweet, sweethearts have value, and what we value, we often feel compelled to sacrifice. And sacrifice often becomes the sweetheart's narrative fate. Pollyanna fell out a window. Shirley Temple and Mary Pickford played orphans and abandoned children: abused, drugged, lost. Shirley Temple (a real American Sweetheart) played Little Eva (perhaps the most iconic fictional sweetheart), the consumptive moral center of Harriet Beecher Stowe's *Uncle Tom's Cabin*, whose virtuous death—the story goes—helped move America away from slavery.

Little Eva's death, played over and over on America's stages and screens, became famous because before she dies, she cuts off—to give as mementos of her sacrificial love—every lock of her hair.

Mary Lou Retton never played Little Eva. She did, however, play Tiny Tim, Little Eva's cross-Atlantic nineteenth-century sacrificial counterpart, and the rare boy sweetheart figure. (As Reagan is to Thatcher, and Mary Lou is to Diana, Little Eva is to Tiny Tim.) Tiny Tim is a character in Dickens's *Christmas Carol,* and Retton plays him in *Scrooged,* the very '80s Dickens retelling starring Bill Murray as Ebenezer.

Scrooged is a strange movie; I remember watching it in theaters. To be really accurate to its complicated plot, which involves a lot of '80s-specific imagery like TV sitcom dads, overwhelmed homeless shelters, and Black secretaries without adequate health care enduring the whims of their pernicious white male bosses, in *Scrooged* Mary Lou Retton plays herself *playing* Tiny Tim in a made-for-TV Christmas special. This means that everyone in *Scrooged* both gets to see Mary Lou Retton as Tiny Tim *and* gets to comment on how weird it is to cast Retton as Tiny Tim. She literally does a huge tumbling pass, in a leotard and old-timey jacket, and perfectly sticks the landing as a prelude to saying Tim's famous line: "God bless us, every one."

What we can take from Retton's casting is that even in the '80s everyone thought it was kind of comedic and absurd that Retton was doing her gymnastics everywhere—at the Kennedy Center, in nineteenth-century London—and also that in the '80s, everyone acknowledged that she was literally everywhere. However strange it might be now, or at the time, that an explosive world-class athlete was 1980s America's analog to consumptive hero/ines like Little Eva and Tiny Tim, it's a truth that *Scrooged*, shruggingly, accepts.

Retton doesn't cut her hair, though—it was already short, which is maybe why she could play a boy. She'd already given that part of her girlhood up. And this interests me. Many sweethearts cut their hair as a gesture of sacrifice, whether they were sacrificing themselves or because someone else was sacrificing them. Joan of Arc's hair is shorn before she is burned at the stake. Fantine sells her hair to a "hair crone" in *Les Misérables* in a desperate attempt to care for her child. Once, on an airplane, I wept so intensely over Jo cutting her hair in *Little Women* that a stewardess asked me if I was okay. "Jo just cut her hair!" I said, and the stewardess gasped and clutched her chest, her eyes filling too. "Her one beauty!" we both said, together.

Mary Lou Retton always had short hair, and she is a model of vigor rather than frailty. But it's worth remembering the tie between short hair and a sacrificial sweetheart. For all her vigor, for all her difference from Tim and Eva, it's worth considering what Retton had sacrificed—and what her success taught America about what we should be willing to sacrifice too.

VAULT 4: KERRI STRUG, ATLANTA

1996 was no longer the Reagan era. It was no longer the Cold War. Things were different. Clinton was in office. We had started to think about tomorrow again. Yesterday was gone.

But some things remained the same—among them, the leadership of USA Gymnastics. Coaching the '96 women's team was Marta Karloyi, Bela's wife. Bela was still on the floor. The team's athletes sported a medley of ponytails, except for two, whose short, practical curls always reminded me of the woman who was both their and my childhood gymnastics role mode: Mary Lou.

One of these short-haired athletes was named Kerri Strug. She had Retton's hair, and Durham's hair, and like Retton and Durham, was a Karolyi-coached vault specialist. Mary Lou Retton was the standard that Strug had been pursuing her whole life. Maybe you remember what happened to Strug in that pursuit—or, put differently, what she did.

Maybe you remember the moment: how, for the first time, the US women's gymnastics team had been primed to defeat Russia and Romania in the Olympic team competition—the first time when all three teams were in competition, and when all the teams had a chance. It was no longer the Cold War, but it didn't matter—the old political antagonism and nationalistic fervor still fueled the athletic rivalry. All America still felt on the line. And we had been winning, it had felt like a lock, and then it all began to fall apart. Because of a series of tiny wrong steps by Strug's teammates, the team medal depended on her last event: the vault. The event that had made Mary Lou Retton a sweetheart. The event that had swept Dianne Durham out of memory.

Strug's first vault did not go well. She flew into the air, and, like Durham, she landed hard; wrong.

She was in pain. She was clearly in pain; even I could see it, even though I was a thousand miles away from the Atlanta Olympics, watching through my TV screen in Iowa. Even though the vault happened in a flash, I could see the result the same way I had seen Retton's triumphant arms thrown into the air. Strug's rough landing had torn the fibers holding together the strong muscles in her foot, her calf. What remained could hardly hold or steady her.

I can picture, right now, Strug limping away from the vault and toward the large man, Bela, who loomed over her. I can see her close-cropped curls, and her hopeful eyes and her pain, her pain, her pain. "You can do it!" Karolyi yelled at her, red in the face, urging her on. It was a kind of cheerleading.

So Kerri Strug, ankle roiling, limped with compact determination to the mat, raised her arms on uneven feet, took a deep breath, and stared down the long stretch of padded mat stretching between her and a leather-covered vault. If she could do this, if she could run, jump, throw, twist, and land, through her injury, the US Olympic team would be assured its gold, no matter what the Russians did. All she had to do to be America's golden girl was turn this one last trick. Staring, Kerri lifted her foot.

When it was over, when she had done it, Strug collapsed, weeping, joy and pain wrestling in her form. The Karolyis were elated, America was elated, Rachael Denhollander watching, was elated, and I, too, watching, I was elated. I had never seen anything so beautiful. I wept. It was not the '80s and everything was different; it felt like a new, better version of the past. A new American sweetheart would smile with a new, cheerful president, one who did feel, to me, kind. I didn't think about all the things that hadn't changed: the same exhorting coach, the same presidential posturing, even the same presidential policies. I didn't think, a month later, when this Democratic president signed into law his welfare reform law, about how it borrowed directly from Reagan's economic strategy. I'm not sure I even really worried anymore about Strug's short hair, like I did about Retton's.

Watch the video of Strug's vault now, even if you remember it. Find it on YouTube. Watch Strug's vaulting beauty; watch her collapse. Watch Bela Karolyi gather up her agonized form and hand her directly into the arms of her doctor, the team doctor: Larry Nassar.

~

Rachael Denhollander, the lawyer and advocate who wrote *What Is a Girl Worth?*, did not become famous for her on-mat gymnastics accomplishments. She doesn't have a gold medal, like Retton or Strug. But Strug and Denhollander did have something in common, besides a love for the sport and a deep intense drive: Both women were treated for gymnastics injuries by Larry Nassar, US Olympics staff doctor. And Rachael Denhollander was the woman, many years later, who filed the criminal case that ended in Nassar's 2017 conviction for sexually abusing the athletes entrusted to his care.

Denhollander, as her book makes clear, wanted to be a gymnast because it was a sport that would celebrate her girlish drive, where the particular girlish strength of "perfect" girls' bodies could be put in the service of a great cause. The same tenacity that, many years later, drove Denhollander to expose and press charges against Nassar was what compelled her into his orbit in the first place and made it hard to free herself from his gravity. Larry Nassar, who treated Denhollander for escalating pain in her wrists, feet, and back, was the unusual sports' doctor who attentively looked girl athletes in the eyes and witnessed their suffering. He saw that she was persisting, and he praised her for it. And he tried—and for a very long time succeeded—to blur the lines around her willingness to persist, telling her that his abuse was pain relief, and banking on her capacity to endure whatever further harm he caused. Strategic and predatory, he seems genuinely to have not anticipated that girlish persistence could be turned against him.

More than 250 women, the women drawn into gymnastics in the generations following Retton's success, joined in Denhollander's suit. One of them was Simone Biles.

One of the most wrenching experiences of that trial era—the one that Biles had lived through in the years preceding her "twisties" during the Tokyo vault—was reading about the athletes' slow and painful realization that the medical "care" they had received, the "care" from a doctor that the powerful coaches in their lives endorsed, wasn't care but abuse *described as* care. They had been gaslit into believing that abuse was the treatment they needed.

You will not enjoy it, but I do recommend reading Denhollander's astonishingly brave and precise accounts of what, physically, Nassar did to her body: how he moved his hands, how he positioned the medical robe and his body and *her* body and a towel, so that even when Denhollander's mother was there in the exam room watching, her mother couldn't really *see*. It happened quickly, and repeatedly, like a vault, but with no judge trained to look for infractions. Where was the moment when care turned into abuse—when someone promising to help you succeed instead sacrificed you to their own cause, their own desires? These are precisely the questions that three generations of athletes, of aspiring American sweethearts, had been carefully trained to sweep aside, lest they be swept aside too.

Kerri Strug was not one of the women who added her name to the suit. She has not accused Nassar. She does mention Larry Nassar repeatedly in her post-Olympic memoir, heartbreakingly titled *Landing on My Feet* (1997). In one instance, she recounts a night in the midst of a gymnastics competition, when yet another injury has left her ability to compete uncertain. Nassar comes to her hotel room for massage treatment at 1:00 a.m.[27] In another instance, injured again, she tells him, "Try anything."[28] She tells her readers how desperately grateful she is for his willingness to help her, for his care.

~

Short hair has no inherent politics. It's not necessarily conservative or rebellious; by itself, it's neither ethical nor cruel. Short hair's meaning comes from its context rather than from some built-in quality. Long hair, too, is neither necessarily feminist nor anti-feminist. Neither spending time on your hair nor refusing to spend time on your hair are necessarily decisions that help make a feminist, collectivist world.

Nevertheless, I have always hated short hair, with an animosity that feels ethical, that feels political. In my early '80s childhood, long hair—in picture books, in old family photos, in journalism—seemed to condense both the attractions of fairy-tale femininity with the radical world-making possibility of feminism. To have long hair, to braid a friend or a loved one's hair, to sit closely together in the act of pleasurable beautification, seemed a return to nature and an escape from the world's unjust demands. It seemed like the kind of interaction that could lead to making a better kind of world.

This was a fantasy, obviously, which isn't to say that it's all bad or has no power. I think our fantasies matter to us, as we commit our energy, here in reality, to the daily labor of making the world. When I say it's a fantasy, I mean that it's not history, not a real account of what the counterculture was like, and also that it's always mixed up with complicated desires (like my desire for a radically equitable world in which I would somehow remain a princess), and those can be hard to recognize and confess.

In particular, my fantasy of long-haired feminism reveals the blinkers of my whiteness. I never considered what that fantasy meant to women of other races, with other kinds of hair.

But maybe because I felt the power of my own long-haired fantasy so intensely, I was primed to recognize that the short hair of the '80s was full of fantasy too. You might put what I was sensing this way: If, in the '20s and '60s, cutting long hair was a symbol of freedom from patriarchal expectations, in the '80s, for many women, cutting long hair became a symbol of freedom from collectivist caregiving politics. These white women of the '80s made a version of success, something we'd now call "white feminism," by giving up long-haired, hippie-dippie consciousness raising and turning toward career success. Don't waste your time criticizing the man; become more like the man. In fact, be more *liked by* the man. Tidy, short hair took a gesture of feminist freedom and used it to make women look free only when they had cut away their attachment to collectivist feminism itself.

Fantasies are, by definition, not bound to reason. So, in the same way that long hair could straddle, for me, traditional and radical worlds, short hair, on Retton's head, could simultaneously mean womanly, corporate "dress for success" *and* girlish sentimental sacrifice. That these two modes were opposites didn't undermine the fantasy; they intensified it. They seemed to show that you could succeed by being sacrificed; that your own sacrifice was identical to and necessary for your success.

You needed to always be working toward freedom. If you didn't have it, if you didn't get it, it was probably because you weren't working hard enough and didn't deserve it.

I loved Mary Lou, and Simone, and Kerri, and all of them, all the gymnasts, Nadia and Olga and Ekaterina, too, because they made the girlishness of my world feel bigger, more important, richer with possibility. This is a great gift that they gave me.

And it doesn't take away from that gift to acknowledge all the complexity of what happened: of what Retton's iconic short hair, especially, in all its iterations, came to mean. To me, there is no image that more perfectly distills the misdirections of the Reagan era—the purposeful and successful and sustained effort to describe austerity as abundance, and brutality as care—than a short-haired Retton in her flag leotard, turned into a generation's most powerful image of what an American girl could be worth.

Reagan's era hammered home the fantasy that the real freedom was freedom from receiving care, and freedom from the responsibility to take care. Short-haired gymnasts on the medal podium were the perfect metaphors for that fantasy, its best icons. Retton seemed to be a kind of observable proof, tying that fantasy to reality. And in what happened to the gymnasts around her, we see a condensed, visceral parallel to what happened to women and families across America in the era when she was our star. We see the great architecture of suffering and sacrifice that could be rationalized by a single, smiling sweetheart's success.

MIXTAPE

"Do you want this, Sarah?" My dad handed me a mixtape. "Jean made it for me." Jean was his student assistant, and I knew her a little: dark, thick hair, strong bangs slicing a line across her forehead. Jean liked my dad, and she took it as part of her job to keep him updated on youth culture. Jean had grown up far away, in a city with clubs and underground radio. But in my tiny Iowa town where Jean had come to college, youth culture was hard to find. Official infrastructures limited cultural transmission. The man who ran the local cable company was religious, and he blocked any broadcast of MTV. Pop music beamed in, irregularly, from an FM radio station in the state capital, seventy miles away. So Jean took matters into her own hands, as kids often did back then. She made my dad a tape.

My dad liked Jean too, but he had his own clear taste in music: jazz, classical, folk. Those were the sounds of my childhood. A tentative good sport, he'd slid the mixtape in the car's deck while he and my mom drove home from teaching. The music seemed unusual, but okay at first—just a voice whispering, "Wake up!" Several strange voices joined the whispered message over a melodic piano line. But then, a minute in: chaos. A tinny rush of synthetic garble, a monster's growl, a woman's fiercely chanted lyrics about roses! and bleeding! I can almost see my parents' heads jerk. Nope! They popped out the tape. Whatever "cool" this music offered wasn't for them. I don't know if they even looked at the name carefully printed on the tape's liner. Kate Bush, "Waking the Witch."

I was eleven. When my dad handed me that clear plastic box, still a little wide for my girlish palm to hold, he didn't understand he was giving me a precious object. It wasn't a big deal to him. He didn't know any of the names, and neither did I. In my basement bedroom, I stared through the plastic at the white cardboard sleeve with its narrow lines. In careful letters, written in a pink fine-line pen, I read: Kate Bush. Siouxsie and the Banshees. Suzanne Vega. Sinead O'Connor. A few songs from each. There were no pictures.

I clicked the cover open, slid the tape into my boom box. What I heard in the garble, in the chanting and caterwauling that had made my parents toss the tape away, was the sound of a different way for white women to be.

How did my hair look that day? Probably a ponytail or a braid. Maybe my hair was down. I didn't have many other hair examples. It was the '80s. My family, a few of their friends, were outliers in a town and a country where Reagan's aesthetic orthodoxy ruled. I didn't want to be a part of it, but I also didn't really know another way to look. There wasn't a clear contemporary feminist movement I could see pictured in the newspaper. My only image of protest hair was the long '70s hair on my parents' folksy records: Joan Baez, Carly Simon, Carole King. I owned both *Like a Virgin* and *She's So Unusual* on LP, and I loved these pop glimmers of a joyful faraway scene: Cyndi's shaved red, Madonna's bleached tousle. They looked like they were having fun, which I liked. I wanted to have fun; I knew the power and appeal of girls whose looks conveyed a sense of their happiness. But happy was only part of how I felt. "Having fun" wasn't always how I wanted to look.

Coming out of my boom box, from my new mixtape, I was hearing the sound of the rest of my feelings, the ones pop music so often filtered out. There was something new and dangerous to be angry about, this music said. I agreed. I imagined the women who went with these names, these rumbling, whispering, strange sounds. My mind rippled. What did you look like, what might your hair look like, if you were singing like this?

And of course, all these women did have strange, brave hair. I didn't know yet what it looked like. I didn't know yet that Jean's bangs looked a little like Suzanne Vega's. I'd never seen anyone in person with the ratted wild shag of Kate or Siouxsie. I didn't know yet about Sinead's bald head.

But I could hear the sound of women who cared more about being wild than being pretty or polished. Coming through the music, on this channel that had opened accidentally in my small-town room, these women were sending me a message about how angry white women's art, their aesthetics, could be. And they carried, too, a message about what hair could be, even though, on my mixtape's cover, I couldn't see their hair at all.

CHAPTER 3

ANNE SHIRLEY'S CARROTS

"How *dare you!*" Anne Shirley seethes. Anne stands in her one-room country schoolhouse wearing a gingham dress. She grips in her girlish hands the pale wooden frame of her writing slate—or rather, what remains of it. The rest of her slate has flown in pieces around the school room. Anne Shirley has smashed her slate over Gilbert Blythe's head.

Anne Shirley is the heroine of L. M. Montgomery's 1908 novel, *Anne of Green Gables*. Gilbert Blythe is her enemy. He has taunted her beyond what any eleven-year-old girl should have to endure. He has pulled her long braid—but that's not all he has done. Gilbert has lifted Anne's braid, holding its red length up for the students around them to ridicule, and hissed the mocking word: *carrots!*

Anne of Green Gables is one of the most enduringly popular Anglo-American girlhood novels. Never out of print, continually adapted to stage and screen, in the 1980s *Anne* was enjoying a surge in popularity unprecedented even in its own successful history. Across every retelling, every book cover, Anne's red hair remains central to the story's drama. The famous "slate-over-the-head episode," as Margaret Atwood once described it, anchors every adaptation.[1] In it, Anne Shirley displays the full-throttle girlish passion so many of us love her for. She has acted out. But for us readers, for viewers, she has acted rightly.

When Anne brings down her slate, full force, on Gilbert Blythe's head, the students in the schoolhouse gasp. Her teacher punishes her. Even she feels a little shocked. But she is not sorry. Righteous anger fuels her. "How dare you call me carrots!" And truly, how dare he? Even if he didn't really mean it or understand the full scope of what he had done. What worse insult could you hurl at a sensitive, story-loving girl than to say: You have the *wrong hair*.

~

America loves the past. For all our sense of ourselves as forward looking, uniquely modern, and ahead of all the rest, we remain nostalgic for our origins. Our "city on a hill" sense of our own exceptionalism emerges from "our" national story, one about our foundations in freedom, godliness, liberty and justice for all. We fought a war of revolution. We bravely set out into the wilderness. We fought for freedom again and again.

Our history, it's implied, inaugurates the best version of our future. We narrate the transition between our American past and our coming American destiny all the time. We tell the story over and over *as* a story. We want to get back to greatness, again. "In no other country on earth," said a campaigning Barack Obama, "is my story even possible."

In my girlhood, I learned to love the past in a very particular way: by devouring classic novels of white, anglophone girlhood. I liked novels about the past, and I especially liked novels and stories *from* the past. I liked how these stories connected my American girlhood to a long history of American girls. The books made my life feel important. Books like *Anne* took part in an overarching cultural project by which, as Toni Morrison would later write about her own novel *The Bluest Eye*, a whole idea of a culture "could take root inside the most delicate member of society: a child; the most vulnerable member: a female."[2] These novels told me that, much like the past, I was lovable. In fact, one lesson of these novels seemed to be that American girls were loveable in much the same way that America's past was—as an ideal. (The problem is that, as the books themselves sometimes seemed to know, ideals are always different from reality.)

Sometimes the historic girl novels I loved traveled outside of the US itself. They took place in British great houses, or other reaches of the British empire, like India. *Anne of Green Gables*, famously, is Canadian, and it may seem strange to include it in a catalog of novels specifically for American girls. But *Anne*, in fact, was published in Boston—its setting is Canadian, but its publication and marketing history are entirely American. No Canadian press published the book until the 1980s. The global scope of this novelistic narrative reach only made my sense of my American girlhood more powerful. The books' capacious geography felt like a girlish form of manifest destiny. And indeed, girls' fiction was literally a part of the US imperial project. (In the aftermath of WWII, US State Department libraries in Japan distributed translated girls' fiction like *Anne* as a part of a cultural reeducation project.)[3] America was the best version of a vast and astonishing project, these books conveyed. American girls, these stories made it seem, were the best of all possible girls.

Here's the problem with America's past: Despite how much Americans seem to love it, when you look at it squarely, it's a mess. Anytime you try to pluck out a heroic act of liberty and justice to admire, you're likely to find a hydra-headed tangle of cruelty, displacement, selfishness, violence. Much like whiteness itself, America can only admire its virtues by strategically omitting most of its own history. It's thorny and uncomfortable, and it's been a problem for white Americans since our founding moment.

For nearly that whole time, popular fictions have been trying to make American history more palatable. Girlhood fictions, for reasons I'll explain, perform that flavor-enhancing role in particularly powerful ways. Because girls are believed to be delicate and vulnerable, virtuous and admirable "sweethearts" even when also strong willed and unruly, stories about girls can, by a kind of narrative moral alchemy, make the places they are from seem as though they have those qualities too. Just like a winning gymnast could amplify a nation's victories, an impassioned girl character could also smooth over a nation's violence. Synecdochically connecting girls to country could make a country's mistakes seem like admirable unruliness too.

American girls—at least, *some* American girls—can find a tremendous kind of power by reflecting back to America a flattering version of itself. But as Mary Lou Retton shows, that power comes at a cost. This flattering version is not true; it's not real. And to become its emblem, you have to try and make yourself into a less true, less complicated, less honest version of yourself. This, too, feels thorny, uncomfortable, bad. Girls often want power, the power granted to them by the myths of America's happy story. Also, they resent that power's demands. They are conflicted. I was conflicted.

And my theory is: This inner conflict finds a symbol in the many girlish fictional heroines who have—who hate having, yet whom we love for having—the wrong hair.

~

"If I was very beautiful and had nut-brown hair," asks Anne, "would you want me?" These are some of Anne's early words in *Anne of Green Gables*. She has just learned that the people she believed had adopted her—a lonely, aging brother and sister—do not want her after all. Anne's arrival at Green Gables is a mistake. Maybe the problem is her lack of beauty. Maybe the problem is her hair.

The aging brother and sister, Matthew and Marilla Cuthbert, quickly dismiss Anne's sense that the problem involves hair or beauty. They wanted a boy. They need help on the farm. Marilla, especially, feels determined to send Anne back. "I don't want an orphan girl," she tells Matthew, "and if I did, she isn't the style I'd pick out." Marilla does not specify what "style" she would like. Anne, loquacious and emotional, seems not to be it.

Anne's surprise arrival at Green Gables happens in the novel's second chapter. You might expect that the question of whether Anne might stay at Green Gables would create an organizing tension for the novel's plot, give its story a shape. But in fact, the Cuthberts adopt Anne in fairly short order. The remaining story has very little "plot," if you compare it to other orphan novels like *Harry Potter* or *The Wizard of Oz*. There's no villain or dramatic conflict driving a conflict forward. There's just—"just"—the picaresque pleasures of reading about Anne's adventures as she adapts to her new home. Another way to put this is that the pleasure of *Anne*—and L. M. Montgomery's true literary genius, across her oeuvre—comes from finding significant and dramatic the subtle machinations of acceptance and judgment that make up most girls' lives, every day.

Adapting to her new home, for Anne, is hard. Is it hard because of her hair? Despite the Cuthberts' eye-rolling, the book itself seems uncertain. "People who haven't red hair don't know what trouble is," Anne explains. Anne is sweet-spirited and loving and tries to be good, but she's also hot-tempered and drama prone. It's not just the slate. She "flies" in a rage at a neighbor who calls her ugly and redheaded. She accidentally gets her best friend drunk. She buys hair dye from a peddler that turns her hair green (she was aiming for black but got the symbolic color of her envy instead). She also saves a dying child from the croup, falls off a roof, and almost drowns in a pond.

No one in her small town has ever met anyone like her. The question of the novel is: How will living in her new home change her? What will it take for someone as impetuous as Anne to fit in? "Her temper matches her hair I guess," says the insulted neighbor. The red of her hair is the visible sign of her fiery, unregulated nature. If her hair can't change, can she?

~

My personal first encounter with *Anne of Green Gables* came in 1983. I had gotten a hardcover copy of the book for Christmas. I have a visceral memory of my Aunt Nancy reading the first pages to me. We were sitting in my parents' bed, on the white-and-green-leafed sheets my mother I'm sure had picked out. The book was large, with a picture of redheaded Anne holding her flower-bedecked hat onto her head and gazing into the distance. Aunt Nancy's voice was quiet and even as she read the opening pages about the Green Gables creek and the watchful eye of Mrs. Rachel Lynde. My mother and my aunt were with me as I turned toward the past that, through stories, we felt we all shared.

But my particular hardcover edition, I did not then know, wasn't one that any other woman in my family could have held. In 1983, the *Anne of Green Gables* copyright had just entered the public domain. Publishers around the world jumped at the chance to reap the benefits of the novel's long-standing popularity. Editions exploded. Between 1908 and 1983, the original publisher reissued the novel 30 times; between 1983 and 2009, 781 new editions would appear. One of these was my own beloved hardcover, one of the most precious objects I ever owned.

Anne was everywhere, and she wasn't alone. My edition of *Anne of Green Gables* was part of a renewed and intense 1980s uptick in stories about historic anglophone girls. All of L.M. Montgomery's novels were reissued: the *Emily of New Moon* series, the *Story Girl*, *Jane of Lantern Hill.* As publication of girlhood books surged, the books' stories moved into other media. In the late 1970s and 1980s, mass-media productions of girlhood novels were everywhere. Laura Ingalls Wilder's *Little House* books were on TV from 1974 to 1983. Francis Hodgson Burnett's *The Secret Garden* was made into a movie twice (1987, 1993) and also a Broadway musical (1991; my Grammy bought me the CD). In 1990, Disney and the Canadian Broadcasting Company collaborated on a *Story Girl* television show. In 1986, a woman named Pleasant Rowland (her name is really Pleasant Rowland) began her extremely successful efforts to mass-produce the historical novel experience, starting her line of American Girl dolls and their companion books after, as she puts it, "an inspirational trip to Colonial Williamsburg."[4] The 1994 movie of Louisa May Alcott's *Little Women* starred ur–'90s girl emblem Winona Ryder, showing that even the edgy among us harbored an inner love for the pinafore.

I read all these stories, and I watched all these shows. I like to think I would have loved these novels—and I do love them, more than almost any other books I have ever read—even if they had never been adapted for screen. But it's undeniable that the media spectacle intensified their attraction. Every girl I knew, not only the bookish ones, understood themselves through these stories. Most white women my age will still sort ourselves into types around our favorites. Some (me) love Anne best, some Emily, some Laura, some Jo. Regardless, we were all old-fashioned girls.

But even for girls with other favorites, *Anne of Green Gables* became a 1980s event. In 1985, the director Kevin Sullivan produced, with primary funding from the Canadian Broadcasting Company and support from PBS, a record-shattering *Anne* miniseries. Its enormous success and rave reviews meant that, as a 2013 *Vulture* article would claim, "for girls growing up in the '80s, *Anne of Green Gables* was seminal TV viewing."[5]

It's true. *Anne* was for girls. But importantly, it wasn't *just* for girls. It was also for everyone who cared about girls or wanted to think about them. Critics hoping to draw large audiences to the *Anne* television spectacle emphasized its universality. It's "[o]ne of those rare television efforts," said the *Chicago Tribune*, that "serves up, for the youngsters, both rebelliousness and silliness, and—for the adults—bite, wit, irony and just plain joy."[6] Jay Rayvid, director of PBS, made an even more expansive claim in the *Montreal Gazette*: "What Kevin has managed is what Lucy Maud Montgomery did with the novel." "He has created a universal story based in Canada, in an era that holds a great deal of nostalgia for all the western world."

Rayvid's words capture the slippery history I described above: *Anne* is about a girl in Canada, he concedes, but it is really about all girls, and in fact, all of us—all American PBS watchers, and everyone, everywhere. I'm not surprised that Rayvid, facing the threat of tremendous budget cuts to PBS under Reagan's austerity budget, advocated for his programming under exactly these terms: the "universal" appeal of Anne's "era." America loves the past! In the 1980s, it loved this sunny Reaganite nostalgia—much like, now, it loves an angrier

MAGA version. To a budget-cutting president, Rayvid offered a story that was simultaneously about "all the western world" and, specifically, a young, white girl.

I, too, find it extremely pleasurable to consider Anne's turn-of-the-century era in the way Rayvid described it: as a time full of "just plain joy." It's pleasurable for me even though I know that claim isn't true.

And I don't mean a little bit not true: It's not true *at all.* The 1890s, Anne's moment, saw, for example, the instantiation of US legal segregation (in the *Plessy v. Ferguson* decision) and the extension of the Chinese Exclusion Act. It was an era of surging extralegal violence against immigrants and racial minorities, amply documented by Ida B. Wells, among others. But PBS didn't argue for its worth by broadcasting any of Wells's accounts of *Southern Horrors*—lynchings, mob rule. Instead, it focused on *Anne*, a novel about a well-meaning orphan. Doing so, PBS could make telling a sanitized history feel pleasurable and virtuous. How could it be wrong to tell a story of an orphan girl's struggle to find love? Isn't a child's struggle to feel accepted a genuinely universal one, even as it's also protected and niche?

This sanitized history had the added benefit of appealing to many viewers who felt, as critics have throughout American history, that the 1980s present was degraded compared to the idealized past. Take for instance one punchy critic in a Long Island newspaper, who claimed that "the story of brave little Anne Shirley" is "a splendid antidote" to "the songs of Madonna and films about getting high in high school."[7]

The songs of Madonna! Here this critic snaps our focus away from *Anne's* "timeless" appeal to its specific appeal in the 1980s—a moment when government resources were on the line, and a debate was raging about women and what role they might play. The famous television version of *Anne of Green Gables* was being produced just as Madonna was on her enormously successful concert tour promoting *Like a Virgin*. Americans in the 1980s loved both these unruly women. What can we say about their overlap? Is there any connection to make between Anne, smashing her slate, and Madonna, "touched for the very first time"?[8]

One interpretation might be that Anne and Madonna are opposites. It's not hard to see *Anne* as a part of a conservative backlash to, or rebuttal of, other '80s media. Set against cultural products like Madonna's albums, art that was economically and sexually frank and that openly emerged from New York's diverse downtown scenes, *Anne* offered a literally whitewashed (there is, in the books, whitewashing) version of a sweet, clean, anglophone historic ideal.

It's true that Anne was often positioned in just this way: the innocent opposite of more contemporary, complex, urban stories. Sullivan's *Anne* first aired on PBS the very same night, for instance, that the erotic multicultural dance fable *Flashdance* was first shown on network TV. *Anne* won the 1986 Emmy for children's programming over another show about an orphan girl with iconic hair: (the more Madonna aligned?) Punky Brewster.

But for all the conservative positioning of Anne as a rebuttal to more urban, racially diverse, multicultural programming—and for all the real danger in Sullivan's historic erasures—Anne had more significance than this neat divide between contemporary culture and conservative history. Conservative pundits may have wanted Anne to be a model orphan, but that desire just threw her unruliness into sharper relief.

For me, the gap between Anne and Madonna (or Punky) was not so extreme as it may seem from the outside. I loved all three. All of them, in different ways, expressed something confusing that I myself felt: a desire to be admired and desired, alongside a sense that the admiration on offer was rigid, judgmental, and unfair. Anne's old-fashionedness may have made her seem, to the casual viewer, more conservative than Punky. But Punky, for all her pigtailed, torn-jeans contemporaneity, never did anything so passionate as to smash a slate. She never showed the friction that came from being the emblem of a falsely "joyful" history. Punky endured difficulties, but she was never anything but adorable. Nobody who mattered ever told her she had the wrong hair.

~

What does it mean to have the wrong hair? There are so many ways for hair to fail. Your hair might be thin, or oily, or the wrong texture. Its color might be drab (as in a fantasy novel I once read, in which the male lead describes an undesired woman's hair dismissively as "simply brownish"[9]). It could be striking, but in an unpleasant way.

The girls in the novels I'm describing had wrong hair in all of these ways. Carrot-headed Anne Shirley pined for her friend Diana's "raven tresses." Brown-haired Laura Ingalls Wilder resented her sister's blond curls. In *The Secret Garden,* Mary Lenox's thin yellow hair "straggled" around her thin, yellow, choleric face. Jo March has a thick "chestnut mane" but finally, and with great intensity, she cuts and sells the hair that her family considers her "one beauty," leaving her like a "shorn sheep."

None of these girls have hair that's as irredeemably wrong as they suppose. In all these stories, the right kind of person might admire red hair, or brown. But these happy outcomes don't undermine the truth that Anne and Laura correctly discern: Hair is hierarchical. Some hair has higher social status, and some hair—their hair—does not. Laura is not making it up when, as a young girl, her family first goes to town and the shopkeeper there praises her sister Mary's blond hair, rather than her own hair that looks, she tells us, like "dirt."[10] "'That's a pretty little girl you've got there,'" the shopkeeper says about Mary; he "admires" Mary's golden curls, "but he did not say anything about Laura, or about her curls. They were ugly and brown."[11] Anne isn't pretending when Gilbert calls her carrots, or when Mrs. Rachel Lynde does, or when the narration itself notices that, when Anne's temper bursts out at Mrs. Rachel Lynde, "her hair had never looked redder than at that moment." To whom had it "never looked redder"? Mrs. Lynde? The narrator? Us? What kind of truth is a hair goodness judgment?

Hair, right and wrong, matters to all these girlhood books, but arguably it matters the most to *Anne* because red hair is the wrong-est hair. That's not a claim that I actually believe, of course. I love red hair. But it's an idea that has a lot of power, both within the novel and for us as readers. Across white European history, no hair color has been as consistently "wrong" as red. "Carrots" might be an aesthetic judgment, but there's a greater significance, an interpretation of nature, that lurks behind red hair's undesirability.

Across centuries, negative aesthetic responses to red hair have been explained by the idea that red hair is alternately, or sometimes simultaneously: a symbol; a (protogenetic) ethnic marker; or somehow a literal extension of a personality, of a person's inner state. The empire-building Romans encountered red hair in both the Celts and the Vikings (red hair is a Celtic-Germanic genetic trait) and considered it barbarous on both counts. Sometimes the Greek god Pan is described as redheaded; in the book of Revelations, Satan is described as a "scarlet beast." Cain, Lillith, Mary Magdalene, and Judas often appear in paintings as redheads, despite the lack of biblical evidence (perhaps through association with Cain, *Beowulf*'s

Grendel too is sometimes depicted redheaded.)[12] Red hair means violence, licentiousness, misrule, mischief. "Red hair is a minority feature," writes the historian Ruth Mellinkoff, describing (implicitly) white visual culture, "and this fact is sufficient to explain why it is used in the visual arts as a negative attribute and why it is still widely treated with suspicion."[13]

Across literature, art, and theology, "all the western world," to borrow Rayvid's hand-wavey phrase, has ascribed a kind of moral, temperamental intensity both to red hair and to the people who have it. Charting the forms of that intensity helps remind us of two related hair truths. First, in the intense response to hair's redness, we can see something that is true for all hair, if in more muted forms: More often than many of us would like to admit, we respond to hair as an extension, a manifestation, of its owner's inner life, personality, even ethics and moral worth. That is part of why hair so readily lends itself as a symbol to negotiations about race. And second, it shows us that the particular kind of racism that plays out in hair's symbology is more complex than a simple, neat, divide between black and white. Laura Ingalls, Mary Ingalls, and Anne Shirley all have hair racially marked as white—but they don't have white hair status in the same way, or to the same degree. Whiteness is a spectrum, an ideal, that gains its power by measuring each individual's always imperfect attempts to achieve it.

Tressie McMillan Cottom, for instance, has described the powerful feeling of being a Black girl seeing redheaded characters in 1980s media. In watching, for instance, Molly Ringwald in a John Hughes movie, Cottom could see a model of an outsider finding her way in.[14] Red hair feels intense to white culture because red hair, like (as we will see) curly hair, exists at the tail ends, as it were, of whiteness—the place where boundaries can be felt and must be carefully patrolled. In talk about red hair, we see the force of hair's meaning for whiteness, and for women, writ large.

Yet precisely because of the negative intensity surrounding it, red hair becomes ripe for, as one book calls it, "vindication." If a majority viewed red hair "with suspicion," that made red hair valuable for a minoritarian embrace. Only something truly hated and scorned can feel meaningful to intensely defend. No one ever wrote, for instance, a vindication of brown hair—you don't need to vindicate anything that has already achieved something like blandness. (This is one reason why brown-haired me loves red hair and feels jealous that the red hair in my family line seems to have gone only to my cousin.) We may not know "why," if there is a discrete why, Queen Elizabeth wore a red wig, but we do know that she, too, lived in a world where red hair was often viewed with suspicion. She took its outsider status and made it a source of difference and strength. In so doing, she made it possible to interpret red hair's power as more than disruptive; or, maybe, she took red hair's power to disrupt and used it to her own strategic ends.

Mary Magdalene, Grendel, and Queen Elizabeth may hardly seem relevant source texts for Anne Shirley. They seem both out of scale (in that these figures are world historic, while Anne is a fictional little girl in a gingham dress) and out of time, in that by the time 1980s television critics were responding to Kevin Sullivan's *Anne* production, most of "the western world" believed itself to have left superstitions about appearance and typology behind. By the time I was a little girl reading *Anne*, it would have seemed shockingly outdated to openly interpret red hair as a symbol of evil. Doing so would have been as weirdly superstitious as, for instance, considering left-handedness a sign of the devil. But the long cultural history that associates red hair with wickedness and with grandiose figures—with their unruly passions, their tempers, and their potential power—trickles down into Anne Shirley's world, and into ours.

Looking at the critical reception of the CBC *Anne* shows us how even 1980s Americans associated red hair with a set of values. These critics would probably not have considered themselves superstitious. They would not likely have considered their response to red hair as part of their racializing moral vision. But review after review implies that red hair signals a kind of personhood. As such, they show the persistence of otherwise-disavowed belief systems about hair, nature, and interiority. The *New York Times* review notes Anne's "freckles, carrot-red hair and obvious determination."[15] The *Minneapolis Star Tribune* describes Anne as "strong-willed, red-headed"; *Newsday* similarly chooses "plucky, red-headed."[16] The *Orlando Sentinel* makes the point at length: "Not only does Anne have an imaginative mind, but she can no more refrain from speaking it than change the color of her pigtailed hair—a carrot orange."[17] Red hair is intractable, innate; it is nature. And so is the outspoken temperament of which red hair is the outward sign. Even if these critics don't think they are talking "about race," their language shows them making racializing moves.

There's an interesting tension here. Almost everyone in Anne's story notices her hair as some kind of problem to be endured, managed, or solved. But for all the critics I've cited, red hair amplifies their praise. Anne's red hair and unruly temperament are why, the reviews imply, we might find pleasure in Anne's story. What's going on with this tension? Why could the wrong hair make a story feel so right? What does hair have to do with stories anyway?

~

It's true that Laura's hair is brown; that Anne's is red. Is it also true that Laura's hair is "ugly," like the narrator tells us? What's the difference, in these scenes, between an observational fact and a cultural value?

For young girls navigating worlds where they have very little power apart from the attention they receive, the difference between a "fact" and a "value" might not matter at all. When girls have the wrong hair—no matter how biased or unjust that judgment of "wrongness" might be—they get the wrong attention, or no attention. The quality of attention girls receive has its own, very real, effects. You might be lifted up, praised. You might be made safe, kept secure. Other, much worse, things might happen to you. As in the realness of real girls' lived outcomes, facts and values blur together in these novelistic accounts of girlish hair. Girlish hair, in other words, carries the same blurry mix of reality and fantasy as does American nostalgia writ large.

Anne, Laura, Mary, and Jo are fictional girls of the nineteenth century. All these fictional girls express their awareness of a key lesson of the nineteenth-century culture that surrounded them: that in order to have the right story, you have to have the right hair. They also knew exactly what "the right story" would mean.

They knew because these fictional girls were, just like me, always reading. The historic girlhood novels that I read in the 1980s were all intensely metafictional. In these novels—*Anne of Green Gables*, *Little Women*, *Little House on the Prairie*, *The Secret Garden*—women read about other women. This fact is part of the novels' realism, which is to say, their close attention to what women and girls' lives are really like. The characters in these books, like their real-world counterparts, had ready access to the world's first mass-media culture, which produced newspapers, magazines, and books made by early mass-printing technology and distributed them via the newly available railroads. As Angela Davis would argue in *Women, Race, and Class*, the "ideology of femininity . . . was popularized and disseminated through the new ladies' magazines and romantic novels."[18] Many of the first best-selling novels—today *Uncle Tom's Cabin* remains the most famous—were written by women, and they targeted women as readers. Even Laura, living deep in Wisconsin's woods, sees her mother and aunts reading *Godey's Lady's Book*, the enormously popular women's magazine that was a direct antecedent for contemporary women's media like *Good Housekeeping* and *InStyle*.

Nineteenth-century media for women, like much media for women today, often told stories about falling in love: They take part of something we call the "marriage plot," wherein finding the happy ending and the happy-ever-after romance are made into the same thing. This is an old story, familiar from Shakespeare and before, but in the nineteenth century it came to take a new shape. Literary historians call this shape "sentimental." Sentimentalized stories take a classic narrative of good versus evil and route it through a new, middle-class, domestic scene. In its anglophone version, the romantic heroine, about to fall in love, is always a virtuous force for good. She herself might endure tribulations from the world, but this particular kind of heroine rarely faces internal struggles. She's good, through and through. And because she's good, she can bring about the sentimental novel's real change: She can inspire a manly hero to be his best self. Once in love with her, he will protect the vulnerable. He will resist temptation. He will push back against the dastardly villain. This sentimental heroine is marked by her essential qualities of self-abnegation and self-sacrifice. She's at the center of these stories not because of anything particular she does, but because of the attention she unselfconsciously demands. Despite herself, her existence commands behavior of the men around her.

And also: The sentimental heroine is beautiful. In her most iconic form, she may not always be aware of her physical perfection—in fact, her ignorance of her physical perfection is one sign of her moral perfection—but she always *is* physically perfect. She always has a lovely figure, well-formed, soft in the right ways. And she always has wonderful hair.

Her hair may be blond or brown or (less often) lustrously dark, but it's always thick, lovely, simply and non-anxiously well maintained. The heroine of a sentimental novel may well endure some humiliation at the hands of other women for styling her hair in an outmoded fashion or for covering it with (horrors) the wrong kind of bonnet.[19] But her hair itself transcends frivolous fashion—which, anyway, an ideal woman shouldn't care too much about—thus transmitting her natural beauty. The heroine's natural goodness, represented partly by her naturally beautiful hair, is part of what makes her happy ending feel natural, which is to say believable, to readers.

Here is a short list of the widely popular nineteenth-century novels that I have read that enact, directly, this highly ideological good hair–to–happy ending pipeline: *The Lofty and The Lowly*. *The Wide, Wide, World*. *The Planter's Northern Bride*. *Northwood*. There are so many more.

These are the kinds of novels that Anne, Laura, Jo, and Mary might have read. They were the stories that taught girls about what growing up would mean, what girlhood should be preparing them for. When these characters rage against their own hair, they are expressing their correct knowledge that their hair keeps them out of the central roles in the stories around them. The stories in the novels bleed into the stories of their own lives. Stories come through these layers, double enforced, down to girl readers like me.

~

For much of the twentieth century, the "women's fiction," as one critic calls it, that defined the nineteenth-century literary marketplace and that Anne and Laura and Jo read was ignored by historians and literary critics. It was cast aside as aesthetically and culturally insignificant. Instead, literary historians lifted up stories by men: *Moby-Dick*, *Huckleberry Finn*, *The Red Badge of Courage*. Even *The Scarlet Letter*, about a woman's experience of motherhood, homes in on a man's perspective on women. Critics for a long time believed that only these masculine novels captured something essentially American.

But in the 1970s and '80s—the same time that I was reading novels about young nineteenth-century girls reading nineteenth-century novels and magazines about young women—academic feminists were engaged in a massive effort of historical recovery. What if, as the great critic Nina Baym wrote, American literature wasn't just "melodramas of beset manhood"? What if American literature had more to do with women's lives? Novels that had been forgotten were tracked down and put back into print. Feminists archived these stories, tracking their patterns and pondering their significance. Baym herself published a major catalog: *Women's Fiction: A Guide to Novels by and About Women, 1820–1870*. If you think I am exaggerating the importance of hair in these novels, you may be interested to learn that in her recounting of women's fiction, Baym carefully indexes each heroine's hair color alongside the plot in which she appears.

Note, here, a fascinating practical parallel between 1980s feminist scholarly culture and popular marketing culture: As academics were recovering nineteenth-century women's novels as part of a feminist project, popular presses were busily reissuing nineteenth-century girlhood novels as part of an often conservative-leaning nostalgia project. Despite the political friction between these two efforts, they strangely reinforced each other. Feminist recovery could connect itself to the widespread affection for history; popular reissues could act as though their nostalgia was part of empowering women and girls. As in the appeal of *Anne*, it's hard to trace easy political alliances.

Note also that while nineteenth-century *women's* fiction had fallen by the wayside, historic *girls'* fiction had persisted. I have taught many classes on the history of American literature. Very few students have ever read Melville or Hawthorne for pleasure, and fewer still have read or even heard of *The Wide, Wide World* or *Northwood*. But like me, so many of the girls have read *Little Women* and *Little House* and *Anne*, often held on their mother's and aunts' and grandmothers' laps.

This may seem surprising—but in fact, it's not entirely. Historian Robin Bernstein, among others, has shown how the "materials and practices" around childhood—rearing children, representing children, and also the games and play of children themselves—"have unique abilities to recapitulate adult culture while seeming to deflect it."[20] Jokes, fashions, stories, games, and other cultural practices that are out of fashion or even unspeakable within adult culture often have their own life in childhood's scenes, where, no matter how potentially "problematic" or even offensive, they absorb the gloss of innocence from the children who perform them. No one goes to minstrel shows anymore. But everyone buying an ice cream cone for a child hears the old minstrel hits like "Turkey in the Straw."

So too, I think, with girl novels. Just like the TV critics of *Anne* comfortably transmitted, seemingly unaware, the same very old associations of red hair and temperament that trouble Anne in the book, my mother and aunts and grandmother were transmitting to me—and I have transmitted to all the friends' daughters to whom I've given *Anne of Green Gables*—all the stories of sentimental womanhood that Anne (and Laura, and Jo) read. So, in one sense, it didn't really matter to literary history that no adults in the twentieth century had read nineteenth-century adult women's fiction, because all the *girls* in the twentieth century had been reading about nineteenth-century girls reading that fiction. Girls always got the women's fiction anyway even before feminist critics recovered it. And not only did we get the fictions, we also got—in the form of the girls' novels intense and angry emotions—what might be called a feminist critique of women's fiction's ideological demands. No matter the date of our birth or the differences in our belonging, we were inoculated into the nineteenth century's complicated lessons—including its lessons about how hair was a symbol of who we were, what might be asked of us, and what kind of woman we might want, or not, to become.

~

Consider the "Carrots!" slate-smashing event more fully. No matter the production, no matter the retelling, the slate scene appears. On YouTube, you can find a fan-made video called "Carrots! A Compilation" that registers all the different levels of smashing Anne achieves.[21] (In a 1934 black-and-white production, Gilbert ends up with the slate's frame hung around his neck.)

In the Kevin Sullivan production, Anne Shirley, orphan, recently adopted, has just appeared for her first day of school in Avonlea, her new town. She's eager to fit in. She enthuses, wide-eyed, to her teacher Mr. Phillips, that she aims to be a "model pupil." When the students around her try to tempt her into bad behavior, she initially resists. She keeps calm in the face of spitballs, gossip, even a croaking frog shoved alarmingly into her face. She and her friend Diana whisper about a classroom romance, how their teacher seems to be "dead gone" on the lovely Prissy Andrews, an advanced student, who blushes at his attention. Here, even in Anne's little classroom, is a model of the perfect heroine: strawberry-blond, modest, receptive. She is the story book heroine, the good young woman, with good hair.

Anne, instead, is none of those things.

When Gilbert Blythe pulls Anne's hair and calls her carrots, her response is immediate and furious. "You mean, hateful boy!" The slate goes flying. "How dare you!" Mr. Phillips, distracted from his instruction of the admirable Prissy, feels similarly furious. He drags Anne to the front of the classroom. On the chalkboard above her head, he writes: "Ann Shirley has a very bad temper." The classroom gasps. Gilbert feels terrible. Anne must write this diagnosis of her identity one hundred times.

I'm inclined to read Mr. Philips's punishment, and in fact the whole scene, as a very complicated metaphor. Anne, the character, wants nothing more than to be an ideal girl, the romantic heroine of a story. When Gilbert calls her carrots, Anne takes her slate and smashes it. She destroys the place where she writes; she has bad-tempered herself out of her own storytelling. When Mr. Phillips tells her to write, "Ann Shirley has a very bad temper" one hundred times, he's not only humiliating her by spelling her name wrong. He's sticking her narrative in a rut, like a needle skipping in a record. She's stuck repeating a description of why she can't, in a conventional story, move forward. (In the novel, Anne doesn't get to write at all. Even worse, she has to stand, facing the classroom, under

Mr. Philips's own written phrase.) Ann Shirley has a very bad temper! No girl with a very bad temper can grow up to be the heroine of a sentimental story. No girl with a very bad temper can inspire a man to his best action.

Mr. Phillips does not write, "Ann Shirley has very bad hair," but the scene connects those two qualities: To have red hair is to have or be provoked into having a temper, and to have a temper is to be someone who only has that temper, over and over forever, and no other story at all.

What was I learning, when I read this scene, when I read it over and over, when I watched it over and over in productions? Why has *this* scene, the one about hair and story, been so central to the story that I myself loved?

There are a lot of reasons, I think, and they don't all fit together. One, simply, is that Montgomery was showing us that there are many kinds of stories. The novel reassures us that there are lots of ways to be the right kind of girl. Anne, and Mr. Phillips, may think that Anne's story has been shut down by her red hair and temper, but the reader of *Anne* sees Gilbert's regret. We see that there are many ways to appeal to someone who might become the right kind of man. There's a kind of comfort here, in the idea that the marriage plot might have room for even those among us who aren't exactly the right kind of girl.

But at the same time—by which I mean, literally at the same time I'm reading and rereading, or right now, when I'm writing about what I've read and reread—the pleasure of the marriage plot's potential feels better to me, as a reader, when I'm also experiencing Anne's rage. "The iron has entered my soul," Anne tells Diana: She won't ever forgive or change or go forward. No reader believes it; we all rightly anticipate how Anne and Gilbert's romance will unspool over many more novels. But I keep liking the slate-over-the-head episode precisely *because* it holds Anne back from the role of inspirational heroine. We have that future, and we have our resistance to it too.

~

Who gets access to what kind of past? What kind of story? What kind of future?

Any nineteenth-century woman who read a nineteenth-century woman's sentimental novel was feeling her way through a complex cultural belief. The belief was that women were very, very, important, but only in a very particular way. Women—at least some women, women you might try to be more like—were almost otherworldly, angelic. America needed them. America needed them for an important job: to inspire men to do more and better things. Women's happy stories were predicated on men's valorous actions.

True, there were other kinds of stories. Many books have moments of irony and ambivalence and uncertainty; many tell different stories entirely. Some books—like the first known novel written by an African American woman, Hannah Crafts's *The Bondwoman's Narrative*—layer competing versions of the sentimental story on top of each other. But I don't personally think the great variety of narratives changes the fact that even in the past, women were under tremendous pressure to live up to an always-nostalgic image of what women should be. (That some women were precluded from this role entirely, or developed what belle hooks might call an "oppositional" relationship to it, doesn't mean they weren't aware of the pressure.)[22] In every era, women were pressured to be the tool that would make America—through its men—great.

Girl readers always knew this. Even as culture was changing around us, we felt—we read, I read, Laura Ingalls Wilder read, Hannah Crafts read—the transmission of an enduringly narrow vision of our own worth. We felt how, in order to have a good story, to do a good job of carrying forward what was best about the past, we would need to be a good kind of person. We wanted to do it, and also, we didn't. We wanted the good hair. We liked to read about other girls who didn't have it. We—and I mean me, but not only me, if not you—wanted to have it both ways.

One reason we always wanted to have it both ways is because we always have known that good hair is both real and a fantasy. It's true that some girls have "better" hair than others. But does anyone ever really have hair that's good enough? It's an impossible standard. No one has hair good enough to make all of America's past look great.

The narrator of Toni Morrison's *The Bluest Eye* (1970) knows something about hair, and story, and attention and rage. This narrator is Claudia, a young Black girl. *The Bluest Eye* is Morrison's story for adults about the stories told to girls. It's about what those stories do to girls, and what those girls are asked to do, sometimes forced to do, by the world around them—a world that always seems to want girls to reflect back a version of that world that doesn't really exist.

Claudia is very young when she is given a doll that she knows she's expected to love. This doll has white skin, blue eyes, and yellow hair. "I knew that the doll represented," she tells the reader, "what they thought of as my fondest wish." "They" here is her parents, who give her the doll—and it's also everyone around her. No one can imagine she wouldn't love this doll.

Claudia does not love the doll. She hates it. She wants to pull it apart, slowly. "I had only one desire," she tells us. "To dismember it. To see of what it was made, to discover the dearness, to find the beauty, the desirability."

Claudia knows that the yellow-haired doll is an ideal. Her world judges the blond doll to be far superior to the other doll she has, a Raggedly Ann doll, a type of doll that appeared (coincidentally or not) right around the same time that *Anne of Green Gables* was set. Raggedy Ann, Claudia tells us, has "orange worms hair." Orange worms: This is how Claudia describes Raggedy Ann's red yarn hair. Red hair, Morrison shows us, is part of how even this little Black girl learns about the hierarchies of whiteness, of red and yellow hair, of blue eyes, of bluer and bluest eyes, of racial markers. There is no Black doll for Claudia; she learns about Black hair's unworthiness through Raggedy Ann's orange worms. Comparing her dolls, seeing her world's evaluations of them, makes her hate them both. Together, what they teach her is that she can never be good enough. Who could ever actually have the blondest hair, or the bluest eye?

Reading *Anne* lets some girls, especially white girls, read about the kind of rage that Claudia displays as she dismembers her yellow-haired dolls. Acting decorously, sitting quietly with our books, we read about rage even as we look to the people watching us like perfectly calm girls. Here we are, sitting quietly in our aunts' laps. We read about smashing and yelling and acting out. We read these stories over and over. We're never done not quite yet fitting in.

~

Very near the end of *Anne of Green Gables*, Anne reflects on the five years she has spent at her new home. She's trying to describe how things have changed. Unsurprisingly, her language turns to hair. "People are nice enough," she says, "to tell me my hair is auburn now."

All girls, I think, no matter how good their hair, feel that the world wants them to have better hair. White girls like me are not wrong that we, too, feel hair pressure—the pressure of whiteness telling us we can never be good enough. We're right to want to resist the sentimental stories that tell us of our inadequacy, school us in desiring to overcome that inadequacy, in our nature and in our hair. We're right to see these stories as a kind of oppression.

But what ragey white girls often miss is how the very stories that oppress us also lift us up. When we stage ourselves as the victims of the story of our burdening, it's easy to miss how that story, even when it damages us personally, was still made by and for white women. It elevates us up as a group, even as it tells each of us of our individual unworthiness.

Anne's red hair had seemed intractable. But her novel's ending shows everyone—me reading, Claudia reading—the fundamental category gap between red hair that is wrong, but still redeemable, and hair that is fundamentally excluded. Anne's judgy world, like our judgy world, extends a graciousness to some girls that it doesn't to others. It is willing, if Anne acts properly enough, to read her hair a different way. She can become auburn, not red: she can, through behavior, escape a racializing marker. Claudia knows she cannot. The real lesson, then, of the pleasure so many of us take in Anne and other wrong-haired nineteenth-century girls, is not to quietly indulge our rage, our ambivalence, while otherwise accommodating the world's demands. Anne may have disciplined herself into auburn. But the rest of us can do something else. It's possible to reject the empty promises that some stories give. To turn toward stories, like Morrison's, that take a more honest past into a different, better, future. This may mean holding on to the rage: finding all the slates to smash, and smashing them. The smashing, in fact, might be the happy ending.

FARM BALLERINAS

In the Instagram post I'm thinking of, Hannah Neeleman has parted her long blond hair down the middle and pulled it into a simple ponytail. It looks clean and glossy and unfussy. She looks like she's not very worried about styling her hair; she also lets us see that she has beautiful hair. Like a gymnast's ponytail, Neeleman's simple hairstyle toes the balance point where feminine and utilitarian meet.

Significantly, though, Neeleman's extreme sport isn't a vault—it's domesticity. And for her events, Neeleman gathers her ponytail neatly at the base of her neck, rather than high on her head. In this particular post, it drapes down her back, over the clean white fabric of a folksy wrap dress, flattering but modest. In other posts, the exact folksy dress changes, but the low ponytail often remains. As you watch her engage in some of her social media activities—baking bread with one of her eight children, eating from-scratch pasta, wandering through her barn—you can watch her low ponytail swing over her back, slip over her shoulder.

I notice this decision about her ponytail. In subtle ways, it signals Neeleman's values. Securing a ponytail high on the head for any length of time requires a ponytail holder, made of rubber or (now) elastic. You need that tenacious pull to resist the weight of your hair. Low ponytails, gathered rather than lifted, can stay in longer even if they're only fastened with a ribbon or strip of leather cord.

Neeleman's low ponytail might in fact be held by a black elastic band, like the one in my hair right now. Elastic hair ties are everyday, mass-produced, industrial objects. I bought mine at the Walgreens around the corner from my apartment. Neeleman, too, might have gone out to Walgreens. But we don't know. Her low ponytail gives her plausible deniability. It projects the sense that ponytail holders are yet another modern convenience—like store-bought bread, public education, and gender equity—that Neeleman has performatively rejected in order to build her digital empire.

This folksy low-ponied post appeared quite recently—in 2025—on Hannah Neeleman's social media account, @ballerinafarm. So far in this book, I've been giving you a chronological history of white women's hair, starting in the 1980s. Jumping forward to Neeleman—a media figure from the 2020s—may seem confusing. After all, Neeleman's post appears neither in the 1980s, when *Anne of Green Gables* came out on PBS, nor does it really represent the 1890s, when L. M. Montgomery's novel was set. Why mix her up with *Anne of Green Gables*, or the '80s, at all?

I'm telling you about Hannah Neeleman here, out of chronological order, because the whole point of Ballerina Farm, a huge part of its media success, comes from how it jumbles our sense of time. Ballerina Farm falls into the category of "tradwife" influencer accounts; it's one of the most successful. Like almost all tradwife accounts, Neeleman's features video footage of herself, a contemporary woman, doing old-timey things, and wearing old-timey hair, often braided or in buns, or in Neeleman's low ponytail. As of this writing, 10.4 million people follow Neeleman on Instagram.[1] You can log onto the Ballerina Farm website right now to buy "mountain raised meat," "organic farm flour," aprons, salt, and candles. Tradwife influencers purport to show the appeal of an old-timey life, one that would make women and their families consistently happy, joyous, and fulfilled.

For instance, in the low-ponytailed post I'm thinking of, Neeleman describes her marriage by saying, "Daniel and I always laugh." *Always.* It's a tossed-off remark, about hamburgers—the post is called "We love a good hamburger." They "always laugh" because "when we're really hungry, we always talk about hamburgers." So funny! The point isn't that they're literally always laughing. In this Instagram reel, for instance, when Hannah Neeleman talks about laughing and hamburgers, no one laughs. But her phrase "always laugh" still catches my attention. It's both an idiom and a flex. It reveals what the Neelemans really sell, along with the aprons and the meat. Their real product is emotion. You buy their meat or aprons because you're pursuing how the Neelemans feel. This beautiful farm couple with their beautiful eight kids: They're always laughing, or, if not actually laughing, then visibly full of contentment, well-being, deep joy.

To state the obvious, "always" is not a real time in which real things can happen. "Always," like "traditional," is a fantasy. Just like in 1985 the director of PBS could only describe the story of Anne as "universal" by ignoring actual history, you can only indulge the fantasy that something "always" happens by ignoring a lot of what actually happens.

And that's exactly the move made by tradwife social media accounts like Ballerina Farm. Crucially, Neeleman draws neither her hairstyle nor her lifestyle from a specific tradition. Like all tradwives, she blurs a range of old-timey imagery to create a general feeling of not-now-ness. Because the past depicted isn't a real time, it can stand in for an eternal and expansive time: for something like "always." A time when women were happy at home, a past before women moved to the city or cut their hair, when women's families felt contented because of those women's commitment to doing things by hand, from scratch. This is how things always were, the accounts tell us, and how they can always be again, if only you, or me, adopt this traditional life (and hair) style.

Neeleman's "We love a good hamburger" post perfectly captures the dehistoricized tradwife sense of tradition. In it, Needleman makes her family hamburgers. She does it all from scratch. The video edits together scenes of her making burgers with her lovely children: She makes the buns, she makes the ketchup, she makes "a simple pickle." She makes mustard and mayo ("so simple, actually."). At the end of the video, Daniel and Hannah Neeleman (still low ponytailed) both take appreciative head-nodding bites of their burgers. Look: Tradition! It tastes so good.

But, to again point out the obvious, burgers "from scratch" aren't part of any real tradition. I'm sure Neeleman's "from scratch" burgers are delicious. But they hardly refer back to a practice that was ever, as one commenter described it, "the NORM." Burgers became globally popular in the twentieth century specifically because they were so easy to mass-produce. The sight of a low-ponytailed Neeleman eating a burger strangely combines imagery from the nineteenth-century past with the 1950s, blurring together our sense of very different eras that share an association with gender conservativism. It's not actually history. Instead, like the phrase "always laughing," it's a flex, one that only becomes desirable (or, really, feasible) in an incredibly well-resourced contemporary household. Maybe someday someone will make a "from scratch" iPhone that will work really well, but that won't be a historical item either.

While making the buns, the ketchup, the mustard, the mayo, Neeleman's lovely white wrap dress never gets dirty. Her ponytail swings, a little bit loose. Unlike many other Mormon influencers, Neeleman spends no daily time putting in elaborate "Utah curls." The simple hairstyle expresses her sense of the past as a simple time. And it lends an essential verisimilitude to her posts overall, which contributes to her uniqueness, and to her success. To curl her hair and then make from-scratch hamburger buns over a hot oven? That would clearly be impossible. But because Neeleman's hair looks natural, simple as a pickle, easy and often unstyled, it transmits the sense that everything else she does is simple, easy, and natural too. Despite her tremendous wealth, she's not indulging in luxury. She's just feeding her family traditional good food. Wouldn't you, watching her on your phone, like to do the same? The hair tells us: You could!

You don't need me to point out the deep hypocrisies of Neeleman's down-home corporate enterprise. It's not news. The comment threads on any post—as well as multiple profiles and articles—amply spell out all the status games at play. They'll quickly point out the labor, the time, the resources that must be extracted from all over the world to project this performance of rural simplicity into our social media accounts. It's very toxic, and very beautiful too.

I don't know if Hannah Needleman ever read *Anne of Green Gables* or *Little House on the Prairie* or *Little Women*, but I bet she did. I bet that loving those books is one thing our white American girlhoods had in common. I wonder if Neeleman ever felt Anne's anger, or Laura's, or Jo's. I wonder what happens when her own five little girls rage and riot at each other.

What I know for sure, though, is that the *Anne* books, like the *Little House* books, perfectly explain my own response to tradwives like Ballerina Farm, which is definitely not "always laughing." My response is rage. I feel about Ballerina Farm exactly the same slate-smashing temper that Anne does when Gilbert calls her "carrots." I feel just like Laura in *Little House* when the shopkeeper praises Mary's pretty blond curls and good behavior—like I want to scream and stomp and pull Mary's hair. Like I want to leave the nastiest comment in the world. And then I feel ashamed, as though the bad feelings are something wrong with me. As though bad feelings, like bad hair, are problems that only befall bad little girls.

Those bad feelings are not something wrong with me. The anger that Anne, Laura, and Jo feel comes from a legitimate reason: They are less-beautiful women living in specific nineteenth-century moments when a woman's beauty mattered fundamentally to her marriage options, her options in life. They are angry because they live in a world that pits women against each other and then judges them for their lack of sweetness to each other. They feel a feminist anger. They are right to be mad!

And I'm right to be mad too. Hannah Neeleman's pretty blond ponytail, much like Mary's curled hair in *Little House*, has been put on display on purpose, specifically to create status envy. Bad feelings are the whole business strategy.

What do we do with our bad feelings about unjust worlds? Neeleman has a solution. Buy an apron, buy a hamburger patty. Buy, if you can afford it, an "always laughing" life, with meals made from scratch.

Or you can do something else. You can, as many women have done, put your time into the slow organizational work of changing actual on-the-ground political conditions. You can create environments that, maybe, a little bit, make it easier for women to feel solidarity rather than envy. Building political and social community from scratch is way harder than making a hamburger. Those specific historical political actions are exactly what tradwife "always laughing" history so dangerously elides.

CHAPTER 4

JULIA ROBERTS'S *PRETTY WOMAN* CURLS

There's a moment early in *Pretty Woman*, the 1990 movie that made Julia Roberts Hollywood's most bankable star, when Roberts's costar Richard Gere touches Julia Roberts's hair. Gere reaches for a strand and lifts it—curiously, appraisingly.

This strand of hair: It's not really Julia Roberts's hair. It's a wig. It's a cheap, plastic-y version of an expensive haircut—a blond bob, sleek and aspirationally chic. Platinum strands coil in at the line of Roberts's chin; bangs fall thick on her forehead. The movie's viewers know that Roberts's character worries about this wig. She's concerned that in it she "looks like Carol Channing." She does, in fact, look like Carol Channing! In this early moment, Gere's character has reached out to touch Roberts's hair anxiety. He twists a strand between two fingers.

For viewers, it's a moment delightfully saturated with dramatic irony. Gere's character, even if he recognizes the blond hair as a wig, can't know about the hair hiding underneath Roberts's Carol Channing bob. But we do. We've seen Roberts's real hair—her big, tousled, red curls—flow over her shoulders in the movie's poster, the movie's trailer, in every movie Roberts has made to this point in her career. So we're not wondering how removing the wig will change Roberts's appearance. Our pleasure, we think, comes from waiting to see how the appearance of Roberts's red, curly hair will change him.

Behind this change, though, waits another one—a change that could happen off-screen. When we watch Gere watch Roberts, we're waiting to see if Roberts's curls might offer up some change, some transformation, to the women watching in the audience. To the women learning how to watch each other. To *us*.

~

In the early '90s, no female celebrity was more important than Julia Roberts, and no woman's celebrity felt more tied, more tangled, into her hair. Was this because Julia Roberts's hair, in its most famous moments, itself looked quite tangled? The *Los Angeles Times*' review of *Pretty Woman* called it a "tumbling mane."[1] A 1990 *Rolling Stone* cover story after the movie's release described it as a "striking mane of unruly hair."[2] Tumbling, unruly, a mane: Julia Roberts's wild *Pretty Woman* curls were, in 1990, everything I wanted my hair to be. Because so many people were in love with Julia Roberts, and because loving Julia Roberts seemed inseparable from loving her hair, I never had to think too hard about why I, personally, loved Julia Roberts's hair so much. *Everyone* loved her hair so much. Its lovability seemed obvious, as natural as her unruly red curls.

Consider the key hair moments in *Pretty Woman*. Julia Roberts walking, curly haired, down the streets of Beverly Hills while Patti LaBelle's soundtrack plays: Wild women do, and they don't regret it! Julia Roberts holding hands with Richard Gere outside a Beverly Hills boutique, nervously scratching her hair while Gere says, "Stop touching your hair!" Julia Roberts's long red curls stretched over a pillow. Julia Roberts's dark curls in silhouette as she and Gere eat late night at a dinner, nighthawk style. Julia Roberts's dark curls falling into the Los Angeles night as she leans back over a hotel balcony's edge. Julia Roberts's hair streaming over her shoulders as Richard Gere leans her back over a piano, straining to finally kiss her mouth.

There are other iconic moments in *Pretty Woman*. The "Edward Snaps Vivian's Hand in the Jewelry Box" moment. The "Big Mistake! Huge!" moment. The "She Rescues Him Right Back" moment. In these scenes, Julia's hair is still red and long. But it's not the "untamed" version for which she became famous. In these moments, Julia's curls have been blown out and smoothed; in the case of the jewelry box scene, also re-curled and coiled up.

Romantic comedies tell stories about being changed by love. People who love rom-coms—people like me—love the feeling of trusting that love will change the charming on-screen characters in the most satisfying ways. But the change that feels satisfying shifts from movie to movie. Not every rom-com recommends the same kind of transformation.

This chapter describes rom-coms that have a few things in common, besides their reassuring depictions of love's transformative power. It's a funny list of common elements:

- All the romances take place across a class difference.
- They all involve some kind of sex work.
- They all make curly hair into a metaphor for their characters' love-inspired change.

Pretty Woman has a Pygmalion-style plot, telling a classic story of a poorer, rougher girl being transformed by a wealthier man into an elegant lady (its writers took *My Fair Lady* as a direct model). So, you might guess that Roberts's hair transformations offer an easy analog for her increasing elegance, gained over the course of the movie. You might guess that she starts off curly, crass and low-class; as she becomes sophisticated, her curly hair becomes smooth. At the end, even if she's not rich, she's deeply aware of her own powerful worth.

But that's not really what happens. Unlike women in some other movies we'll discuss, Roberts's hair doesn't undergo a one-way transformation. It doesn't start curly and, by the end, become straight. Her hair mixes it up. It starts curly, gets blown straight, and then curls up again. Even when Roberts's hair shows up in the movie in blown-out, straightened styles, viewers never think that she now has straight hair. She has *straightened* hair. That's different. So here's a better way to describe Roberts's rom-com transformation: by the end of the movie, she's both learned how to act polished *and* how to see the value in her natural curls. It's one reason why it always felt so natural to love Roberts's natural curls: because the movie told us, and her, that her curls are the source of her natural self, her most authentic value.

But here's the thing: Roberts's red curls weren't "natural." No matter how Julia Roberts's hair looks when it grows out of her head, her hair in *Pretty Woman* was definitely styled and curled, if not also dyed.[3] The person who did her hair for the movie was Carol O'Connell, and you can be sure O'Connell spent a lot of time achieving for Roberts a "woke up like this" style that appears curly while, miraculously, never frizzy. Behind the scenes, O'Connell styled Robert's hair to look unstyled, to look natural, to *look like* it told the truth.

Gere's character also changes over the course of *Pretty Woman*. Because he's a man and this movie is kind of sexist, Gere's change doesn't show up in the way his hair, his body, or his manners look. Instead, his change happens in the way he *looks at* Julia Roberts. Learning to see her differently helps him see the world differently. It changes the way he thinks about value, and values, in the biggest sense. He teaches that lesson to the women watching in the audience. The changes in Gere's character that Roberts's curls put in motion roll through us too, and settle into our thoughts about how we, ourselves, appear.

Pretty Woman tells a love story about two people who change. But like all the best rom-coms, *Pretty Woman* ups the stakes on the romance at its heart. It knots that love story to a bigger hope: that love can change the world. The writers of *Pretty Woman*, scripting and rescripting their story at the end of the '80s, had a specific world-altering change in mind. They wanted to make a rom-com about both a change of heart and—wait for it—a change in the economy. I know that may sound surprising. But in very explicit terms, *Pretty Woman* ties its romance to a specific historic event: the rise of a newly financialized economy.

Pretty Woman showed up on our screens when America was facing a crisis about economic value. This crisis mattered to the women in *Pretty Woman*'s audience in all sorts of ways. It was even connected to their own sense of self-worth. So perhaps it's not surprising after all that *Pretty Woman* uses Roberts's natural, wild, untamed red curls to resolve the simultaneous crises of economic and emotional value.

~

"No matter what they say, it's all about the money." These are the very first words of *Pretty Woman*. They're said by a magician. The camera opens on three sets of hands in close-up—hands belonging to the magician and to two (rich, white) women. As the magician speaks, coins appear and disappear in the women's outstretched palms. It's a familiar sight to anyone who has ever been to a magic show. Like *Pretty Woman*'s street walkers, the magician turns a trick—one that's also a financial sleight of hand. But this magician's stage patter quickly gets economically specific. "Let's imagine, ladies," he says, "that you're an S & L officer." The women gasp as the coins disappear. "Where is the money?"

An S & L officer? Really? "S & L" as in the savings and loan crisis that in the years prior to *Pretty Woman*'s release roiled the US economy, leading in 1989 to the biggest stock market collapse since the depression? Yes, that S & L. We're here to see what its trailer describes as a romance, the "funniest movie of the summer." But *Pretty Woman*, in its first words, lays its narrative cards right on the table. Economic anxiety—which may also be an opportunity—provides the backdrop for every romantic moment that follows.

Pretty Woman tells a story, according to its own script, about a man and a woman who both "screw people for money": a sex worker, Vivian (Julia Roberts), is hired for a week to be the kept woman of a financial raider, Edward (Richard Gere). Vivian and Edward meet as she, in her platinum wig, walks Hollywood Boulevard. For reasons even Edward doesn't fully understand, he invites her back to his Beverly Hills hotel. The next morning, the morning after he touches her blond wig, he offers her $3,000 to be his "beck and call girl" for the week. He's spending the week in LA, turning his *own* huge trick. He's buying a company for $1 billion. The movie puts his two deals in parallel: $3,000 for a week of uncomplicated sex with a woman who doesn't understand her own worth; $1 billion for a stretched-thin company with a lot of hidden investment value. Edward thinks he's got it all figured out. He thinks he's made two bargains, that he's got the coins right in his hands. But things don't go to plan. By the end of the week, Vivian and Edward are in love. She's no longer satisfied with their deal of money for access. And for strangely similar reasons, as we'll discuss, he's not satisfied with his. "I want the fairy tale," Vivian finally tells Edward. It turns out, so does he. He changes his financial strategy. He commits to invest in the company he was going to buy, rather than destroy it for his own gain. And he invests himself fully in Vivian, too.

This financial version of *Pretty Woman*'s story may feel cold and mercenary compared to the warm viewing experience rom-coms provide. But *Pretty Woman* is hardly unusual in entwining economic anxiety with emotional desire. Romances have been telling this very same economic story at least since Jane Austen. That's because romances—so often dismissed as trivial, unserious—know exactly what they're doing. They're training their women viewers in Romantic Economy 101.

For all our culture's fantasies about the purity of love—its spiritual, rather than fiscal, value—the romance genre knows that women's romantic experiences are also economic choices. In our world, women—some more than others, obviously—have been systematically excluded from direct economic and political action. So women—again, some more than others—have found a workaround: they take economic action indirectly, through the men they woo, receive gifts from, marry. In such a world, a woman's decisions about which men she desires (or, more accurately, which men she desires to desire her) will always be freighted with economic significance. "It is a truth universally acknowledged," Austen wrote in 1813, "that a single man in possession of a good fortune must be in want of a wife," and the same thing was true in 1990. "No matter what they say," says *Pretty Woman*'s magician, "it's all about the money." *Pretty Woman* doesn't try to say anything else. Edward, *Pretty Woman*'s most eligible bachelor, begins his story as scoped by attentive women as Austen's Darcy at a ball.

When women look for love, they need to learn to look in all the right economic places. Romance teaches them, or tries. Austen's novels, for instance, often compare an upstanding "right man" to some enticingly "wrong man." What usually makes the wrong man wrong is his disreputable, swindler-ish, financial volatility. Right men, on the other hand, men like Darcy, have a steady income. They're landed gentry with endowments in the bank, promising them so many pounds a year. Some other "right" men (like Bingley, to take Darcy's *Pride and Prejudice* counterpart) have come into wealth through what Austen, in the early 1800s, calls "trade"—the emerging manufacturing, market economy based on producing, buying, and selling real things. Austen wants her readers to watch out for wrong men without such assets: men who gamble, men with debts, men looking to scheme.

Austen's novels prefer the steady endowments of the landed gentry but are modern enough to be open-minded about trade. They know that trade, the manufacturing economy, was building real reliable wealth—in fact, as rom-econ since Austen can tell you, trade and manufacturing built much of the wealth that was made between *Pride and Prejudice* and *Pretty Woman*. And here, we need to honestly acknowledge something it can be too tempting for romance lovers to try and ignore: how racialized cruelty nests at the foundation of all modern wealth. Global trade depended on enslaved labor. There's no version of romance that can truly forget this history, because romance, for all its misdirections, always knows that any racialized economy will always put pressure on how women—all women, although again in dramatically different ways—perform race. So in romance, you'll always find racism lurking somewhere, like a madwoman in the attic. In Austen's novels, you see it especially in *Mansfield Park*. We'll see how it appears in *Pretty Woman*.

In *Pretty Woman*, Edward, like Darcy, has inherited wealth. But he's not landed gentry. And he's also not a part of the manufacturing economy. Edward, instead, makes most of his money as a corporate raider. It's a then-new term for someone who opportunistically plays the market against established companies, swinging onto vulnerable corporate boards in much the way a pirate might board a trade ship. This, for Austen, would definitely be wrong man behavior. But in America in 1990, financial volatility had become a new way to be rich. Rather than having land or building things for people to use now, financial wealth came from betting on what might be valuable in the future. Finance isn't magic at all—but like a well-executed card trick, a winning financial bet depends on getting people to look at things the way you want them to, so that in the end the coins are in your hands. Over the course of the '80s, the world of "finance" came to stand in for "the economy" writ large.

Did that also make it the new way to be right? Was finance—despite its slipperiness, despite its greediness—the new way to make a right man?

In a sense, all the corporate "rom-econs" of the '80s—a list that could include not just *Trading Places* and *Working Girl*, which we'll discuss, but also *Secret of My Success*, *Ruthless People*, and *Baby Boom*—pursue research on what scholars call "financial masculinity." Michelle Chihara and Leigh Claire La Berge, for instance, have shown how the media interwove ideas of economics and gender. "Finance was styled," in La Berge's words, as a "form of masculinity and aesthetic comportment."[4] Just like finance represented a shift in the American (and global) economy, financial masculinity meant a shift in romance.

That shift put pressure on American women. To attract the men who were always looking to get maximum return on investment, it seemed you would need to present *yourself* as the most conducive to finance's story. *You* would need to be luxurious, a sign of ever-increasing status. You needed to show that you could, in the financial sense, appreciate. That you could offer, in your body, your tastes, and your potential (all qualities, we will note, that are often evaluated via racialized standards) a more valuable future than all the other women. You needed to be more than beautiful, smart, kind, more than an old-fashioned sentimental heroine. You needed to be a deal. It's an incredible amount of pressure.

Finance had changed the world. *Pretty Woman*, remarkably, wants romance to change the world right back. Its story, taking Richard Gere's character as its example, presents both finance and financial masculinity as problems to be solved. It rejects the world finance makes, including how finance remakes romance. And, using Julia Roberts's curls as a powerful symbol of its position, it vigorously rejects the rules for womanhood that finance provides.

In *Pretty Woman*, Edward aims to buy a ship-building company. The company is owned by a kind, hardworking grandfather named Mr. Morse. In Edward's strategy meetings, he watches video footage of Mr. Morse's property, the vast holdings much like a production-economy version of Darcy's estate. Edward doesn't want the estate. He wants to buy it and divide it up for other investors, for development, for profit. The movie is clear that Mr. Morse—played, by the way, by classic rom-com star Ralph Bellamy—is the better, more honest man.

Pretty Woman takes one of the most controversial types of the new economy, the financial raider, and places him in the starring role. By casting that ruthless figure as its male romantic lead, *Pretty Woman* tackled the question of finance head on, wondering if a happy story could be made of it. Could American women reign in the unbridled ruthlessness of financial masculinity, gaining its resources without succumbing to its cynicism? *Pretty Woman* says yes—especially the right woman, with the right kind of curls.

~

Pretty Woman introduces Vivian to viewers one body part at a time. We start with a close-up of her hip, emerging from black lingerie. She rolls over; we see her slim belly. We stare down at her breasts, in a black bra, as she pulls a tiny white dress over her shoulders. We see her wrists as she decorates them with a wall of bracelets; her inner thighs as she holds a black boot between them, to marker over its scuffs. When a blond head tilts up to show us a face, we only see a close-up of one eye. A hand decorates its lashes with mascara. Significantly, even *we* don't see the moment when she stuffs her hair under the wig. In poetry, this strategy of revealing a woman part by part is called a blazon. If we drew our genres from TikTok, we might call it a Get Ready With Me (GRWM) video. This woman reveals herself, but she also constructs herself. She is becoming a person, incrementally, in front of our eyes.

The blazon form always emphasizes—in, let's be clear, an objectifying way—the beauty of the woman at hand. *Pretty Woman* makes the same point. But it also emphasizes, as GRWM videos do, that the beauty decisions she's making are a performance. *Pretty Woman* does not have exactly the same theory of gender performance as, for instance, Judith Butler, whose book *Gender Trouble* came out the very same month—March 1990—that *Pretty Woman* was released. But *Pretty Woman*, like *Gender Trouble*, knows that femininity is a social role, and also a kind of work.

Pretty Woman, maybe even more explicitly than *Gender Trouble*, also knows that part of performing femininity means playing at race. The movie never hints that Vivian isn't white. But with her big hoops and red lips; her Italian best friend; her mixed-race world of sex workers, pimps, and drug dealers; her affection for Prince; and her Arsenio-hall style "whoop whoop!" fist pump, her feminine performance is defined through racializing gestures. It's implied that her lower-class Southern origins (the character, like the actress, comes from Georgia) mean her tastes and her styles have something in common with women who are Black and brown. Julia Roberts and Vivian are white women, unmistakably. But race, this movie knows, is more than a biological background with an easy Black/white divide. It's a class position and a strategy of performance. Race, like gender, becomes a role that can be played in different ways, depending on what you wear, and what you do, and who you do it with.

Edward pays $3,000 for Vivian's company. He wants to have made a good investment. He wants her to become the most valuable—to him—version of herself. So he sets about changing her performance. He tells her to stop touching her hair, to stop fidgeting, to spit out her gum, to wear clothes that are "conservative" and "elegant." He thinks he wants her to perform like the model women of his elite, white world. These women—like the woman watching the magician in the movie's first scene—are polished, posh, well-mannered, carefully coifed. Most of them have straight or blown-out hair. Most are white.

But the viewer knows: he doesn't really like those women. The movie begins as he ditches his girlfriend; we see him brush past other women who throw themselves in this path. It seems that, despite himself, Edward is on the market for a different kind of femininity.

Their first night together, Edward wakes up to find Vivian's platinum wig hung over a bed post. He gets his first sight of her curls—they're luxuriously spilled over the white of her pillow.

He takes a breath in the dark. The viewers can see it happening: his change of heart has begun.

~

Where did I learn about the power of curls? It's hard to know the answer. Did I learn from reading *Little House on the Prairie*, as Laura stares enviously at her sister Mary's carefully curled golden hair? Did I learn it from reading *Anne of Green Gables*, with Anne's fantasies of dark, curled raven tresses? Did I learn it from watching my mother, who has my same straight hair, wrap her hair around hot rollers in the morning? Somehow, from these sources, I gained the sense that curls were magic. My mother bought me pink foam rollers and taught me how to coil my hair around them before I slept, in the hopes that I too would gain the curls that I longed for, that would earn me praise.

These stories get at the different ways that hair might appear curled. It might look naturally curly, or it might appear temporarily curled, like it does after it's been wrapped on rollers or curl papers. Or it might appear permed, chemically altered. The many times in the '80s I got my hair permed, I was always hoping that the perm would create a different look than it did. I remember asking Allie, the woman who permed my hair, if a perm could give me "big" curls. She promised to try, but it never worked. No perm could make my hair look like I wanted it to—like I woke up with a mess of flowing, romantic curls. When Julia Roberts finally appeared with her big red curls in *Pretty Woman*, it was like she had walked out of my hair fantasies into something like "real life."

"Natural curls," the ones I wanted, and the kind that Julia Roberts's *Pretty Woman* had, seemed to signal something important about a woman's personality, her inner life. Carefully *curled* hair represented an expense—of care, of time, and indirectly, of money. And it also represented a kind of personality. Mary in *Little House* is not only blonder than Laura; she's also better behaved, more feminine. Her carefully *curled* hair shows both that she's better mannered, and, in a more literal sense, better bred. When the shop owner in *Little House* praises her, he's seeing both her beauty and her willingness to sit still long enough to have it cultivated. (Mary's good, in other words, at performing the type of womanhood that finance would later want women to achieve.)

I was after something else. I wanted *curly* hair, not curled hair. I felt about curly hair like I felt about red hair: that both were "wrong" but in an exciting way. Like Anne's red hair (or Vivian's), curly hair would show my wild will, that I wouldn't behave. Good little girls like Mary stressed me out. An ex once praised my straight hair, saying, "Straight-haired women can possess their hair in a way that curly-haired women can't." This seemed to me both correct and a perfect illustration of a difference between us: He admired the calm and self-possession of straight, smooth, hair, whereas I desired the unruliness of naturally curly hair. I wanted hair that I couldn't quite manage; wanted it as a symbol of something uncontainable and willful that was not quite me, but that lived and grew within me. I saw that symbol in *Pretty Woman*; I saw it in women's media in the decades after *Pretty Woman* when similar (if blonder and thus safer) curls appeared on shows such as *Felicity* (which *Slate* described as "a show about a girl with a huge mane of curly hair"[5]) and *Sex and the City*. I still want that wild hair, I admit. And now, after an adult life spent reading nineteenth-century American literature, I have a different understanding of how I absorbed this specific belief about curly hair and personality.

Curls have had meaning throughout hair history, but they came to mean something very specific on the heads of American women, starting in the nineteenth century and continuing into *Pretty Woman*'s era. Curls were often read as a sign—not always, but often—that the woman who had the curls also, to some extent, was not fully white. Racist scientists made up actual charts to "document" the racial meaning of curls. They developed theories about the comparative shape of hair follicles that were literally used in court cases when trying to determine a woman's race.[6] (On TikTok now, controversially, curly-haired women still use categories descended from these nineteenth-century "scientists.") It wasn't just Black and white hair that mattered, although enslavement heightened pressure on that distinction. These scientists built elaborate distinctions between Asian hair, "Indian" hair, "Semitic" hair, and more, and then they put all these categories into a hierarchy, with the typically straight follicles of Anglo-Saxon hair at the top of them all.

Often, racist science interpreted curls as a meeting point between straight Anglo hair and textured Afro hair—as a sign that people from different places on the hierarchy had mixed. That's why, over a surprisingly long history, curls matter to the mixed-race women characters in (racist) fiction. You'll find women with dark, racially marked curls in *Uncle Tom's Cabin* (1852), in the musical *Showboat* (1926), and in the novel and miniseries *North and South* (1982 and 1985)—and these are just a few of the many, many stories I could mention that feature a "passing" plot or, as it was often called, a "tragic mulatta" plot. They are called "tragic mulatta" plots because often the woman's race makes her vulnerable to enslavement or abuse. If known, or if discovered or interpreted, her race disqualified her from proper marriage—from the financial security romance seeks to pursue. The mixed-race character was often threatened with sexual abuse. She often became a prostitute. Dark curls, a full mouth, and an expressive personality were almost always her recognizable features. (Here I will note that the same *Rolling Stone* interview that praised Roberts's "unruly mane" also lingered on her mouth and teeth.)

For women of color, managing their relation to race is an ongoing difficulty. This is true in romance, and it is true in Hollywood, as predominantly white-owned studios make decisions about what kind of woman deserves what kind of story. It would be illustrative, here, to compare the career of two Southern actresses of almost exactly the same age: Julia Roberts and Viola Davis. Davis has had enormous critical acclaim, and she's also spoken eloquently about how difficult it's been for her to be cast in powerful roles or to command a reasonable salary. When *Pretty Woman* came out, Davis was at Julliard. Casting directors, she told the *New York Times*, found her "too dark" and the wrong kind of beautiful to "play a romantic lead."[7] (Davis, in the same profile, mentions how much it meant to her to watch on TV another hair icon we've discussed: Cicely Tyson.)

To avoid the narrow scripts they were allowed to play, some women of color carefully managed information about their race. One famous actress of the mid-twentieth century—one known for her platinum hair—wanted to play romantic leads, and she didn't want to take any shit for it. Why should she? She didn't want to be pressed out of these roles, like Viola Davis would describe happening to her. And this woman did become a Broadway star. She even premiered the stage version of Lorelei Lee, the famous blonde in the early rom-econ musical *Gentlemen Prefer Blondes*, a role played in the movie by Marilyn Monroe. This actress, brilliant and talented, deserved every part she earned. She also made the decision to not talk publicly about her own mixed-race background until the end of her career, 2001, when she published her memoir at the age of eighty-one. In it, she describes the story of her Black grandmother from Georgia. You may, from these details, have guessed the identity of this chic bobbed woman: none other than Julia Roberts's *Pretty Woman* hair doppelgänger, Carol Channing.[8]

As for my own curly-hair fantasies, I can see in retrospect how I absorbed a racializing lesson about beauty and desire, along with a warped sense of how straight hair connected to a privilege I perceived as a pressure. In the '80s I read my grandmother's copy of *North and South* three times. Madeline, its mixed-race character with her exoticized beauty—the character with whom, in the TV version, Patrick Swayze fell in love—was always the woman I found myself wanting to be.

~

Here's a hair theory: Even though modern science has (mostly, we hope) moved away from explicitly endorsing racist nineteenth-century hierarchies, our contemporary hair semiotics still carry those legacies. When many of us look at hair, sometimes we're not only judging whether it's pretty or appealing. We're still interpreting the hair we see as a way to judge where on a social hierarchy people are, where they came from. Whether or not we know what is meant by the phrase *passing plot*, we've still been taught that curly hair might mean someone has passed, or is trying to, from one place on the social hierarchy to another.

Is this theory true? Here's some evidence. Some of the best rom-econs of the '80s tell what are essentially "passing" stories—stories where a character, like Vivian in *Pretty Woman*, learns how to pass into a new social class. It's economic passing, not exactly racial passing (although an economy with roots in racist enslavement will always carry the legacy of racism). And just like in racial passing, economic passing is often marked by a visual trait: the main woman character's noticeably curly hair.

We're going to take a tour through the hair-centric passing plots of three other movies. Watch carefully: I'm going to try to explain their hair tricks. It will take your best slumber-party-gossip skills to follow all these moves. You, woman reading this, gained these skills, even if you didn't realize you were doing it, and you learned them for a reason: because your whole life your hair has been judged in comparison to other women's. That's how we're going to understand these movies' hair too.

Let's start here: It's 1983. Jennifer Beals stars in *Flashdance.* She works in a steel mill; she dances in a burlesque show at night. She longs to become a ballerina. Her hair grows in dark, wild curls.

It's still 1983, just a few months later. Jamie Lee Curtis stars in *Trading Places.* She's a prostitute with uncanny financial sense. She appears on our screens in a tight, red dress. Framing her face are outrageously tight, shoulder-length, red curls.

It's 1987. In *Working Girl*, women are going to work. Melanie Griffith works as a secretary but goes to night school to study business. She doesn't want to stay a secretary. Executives at her company treat secretaries like "working girls" in the slangy, derogatory, sex-worker sense. She wants to make big deals. We see her on the Staten Island ferry, her soft strawberry-blond hair ratted and sprayed into big curling-iron curls.

Can you picture these women? Have you seen these movies, with their perfectly rendered hair plots? I cannot recommend these movies enough. They are corrupt and enchanting, an education in how you've been educated. You should watch them all: Stop now and do it. You should hold in your mind these variously red unruly manes. If you do, you'll see how all of them build over the decade to *Pretty Woman*, with the unruliest red curls of all.

Now: I'm not trying to elide the hair differences here. If you asked me which of these women has the best hair, I would pick Julia Roberts every day of the week, and you would too, or at least, "you" would if you were Hollywood casting directors looking for a lead in your 1990s movie. Roberts's hair is the hair that looks more romantic, because it appears more "natural" and thus more vulnerable and more honest. But the family resemblance remains present and is worth addressing. These are four iconic, successful movies of the financialization era. What is going on with these movies, their sex-work stories, and their curls?

In all these stories, the poorer, curlier-haired woman wins the desire, love, and resources of a Rich White Man—let's call him an RWM. In all these movies, the rich man's ideas of what's valuable change, because of love, over the course of the movie. But the movies have some interestingly textured differences when it comes to what kind of change a man needs. Let's consider some explicit comparisons, get all our hair and narrative evidence on the table.

In *Flashdance* and *Pretty Woman*, the curly-haired heroines, Beals and Roberts, initially astonish, confuse, yet somehow captivate their RWM through their chatty volubility and their seemingly unfeminine knowledge of technology (welding and race cars, respectively). Both movies make a big show of their working-class heroine's charmingly uncultured relationships to the eating of shellfish ("Slippery little devils!" says Roberts/Vivian as her escargot flies through the air). Both movies end as the RWM hands the heroine a bouquet of roses, a symbol of her worth to him, the delicate refined flower he correctly, despite her rough origins, perceives her to be.

This is a good one: Like *Pretty Woman*, *Trading Places* introduces its sex worker character to its RWM while she's wearing a wig. Like Roberts in *Pretty Woman*, Curtis in *Trading Places* (Ophelia) keeps her real hair covered while she's on the job. For both women, there's the real self (and hair), and then there's the fake self (and hair). One reason the audience knows to trust both these sex workers is that both don't really like being sex workers. They protect a real version of themselves, keep it away from their work, and it's this under-the-wig/sex-work woman their RWM falls for. But here's where it gets interesting. When Ophelia in *Trading Places* gets dressed for work, when she wants to look trashier, more fun in bed, she *puts on* a wig of red curls . . . *the same kind of curls that Vivian covers up*. To emphasize the important #hairstudies point here: *Pretty Woman* and *Trading Places* work exactly the opposite wig angles. Underneath her wig, Ophelia has short, light-colored, and "dress for success" '80s hair. You might say that it's similar in cut to Mary Lou Retton's. That's her real self, the person for whom her rich man falls. In *Pretty Woman*, Vivian's highly desirable dark red curls aren't a trashy accessory. It's the opposite. Vivian's curls, with all their complicated associations with race and unruliness and vulnerability, are the real hair self that she keeps protected but lets this RWM see.

You can tell that Griffith, as Tess in *Working Girl*, experiences a different story, because she doesn't wear a wig. Instead, she cuts her hair. It's one of *Working Girl*'s most riveting moments. "If you want to be taken seriously, you have to have serious hair," Tess explains to her best friend, as she chops her permed locks away. Tess doesn't keep a real self hidden under an attractive illusion. She has a working-class identity, and she wants to be rid of it. She wants to move toward wealth, and its hair signifiers, and she does. *Working Girl* tells the story of how

Griffith's real life—her whole life and all of her allegiances, along with her hair—begins to change.

~

In every profile I have ever read of Julia Roberts, someone mentions her hair. I have never found anyone describe her "unruly mane" as anything like "serious." Cutting off her own reddish curls, Griffith's character is heading the opposite direction from Julia Roberts's wild appeal. In order to understand what "serious hair" means in these movies, our hair comparisons have to get more complicated. We can't just compare Julia Roberts's hair to Beals's, Curtis's, and Griffith's hair. We also have to see how Beals's, Curtis's and Griffith's hair compares to that of their RWMs' *other significantly haired* women. You won't be surprised that if *Flashdance*, *Trading Places*, and *Working Girl* all tell stories of RWMs learning how to love the right kind of (variously red curly-haired) (variously sex-worker-y) woman, these stories also include other "wrong" women. All the wrong women are portrayed as villainously dislikable; all of them are rich and polished. All of them have hair that reads as extremely white. For the movies' romances to develop, the RWM must realize that these polished-hair women, despite their wealth, have very little romantic worth. Let's consider them individually:

In *Flashdance*, Jennifer Beals (Alex) spots her rich man (and, uh, boss) Nick with a beautiful woman at the ballet. "What's with the blond, Nick?" she yells at work the next day. The blond is Nick's ex-wife. They sit together on the arts council. This blond, in her one speaking line, rudely asks Alex, "So, you really take your clothes off for money?" (Alex as Jennifer Beals, in this scene, messily yet hotly eats a lobster.) The blond wears a white fur hat over her white-blond hair, in case we didn't get the message that white-blond hair means rich.

In *Trading Places*, Ophelia's RWM begins the movie engaged to a rich white woman named Penelope. Penelope is old money, the niece of the movie's richest men. She has a ponce-y, exaggerated way of speaking that the movie sets up for ridicule. She has incredibly smooth brunette hair, held back by a white headband. We meet her at dinner, where she has no problem eating a lobster. She wears a white dress. She wears white underwear under her white dress. She wears tennis whites. She once sees Ophelia wearing her wig. She gasps in horror.

In *Working Girl*, Tess's rich RWM begins the movie engaged to a rich white woman with a WASPy accent named Katharine Parker. Katharine Parker is Tess's boss. Katharine Parker steals Tess's idea for a "deal," and so Tess steals Katharine Parker's whole life, which in the movie is totally fine, not morally complicated at all, because Katharine Parker is mean and has (as we hear twice in the movie's final scenes) "a bony ass." Katharine Parker, it's worth noting, has curled dark hair—she wears it with a white headband, white plush sweaters, and pearl earrings, in case we didn't get the rich = white message. She's also the character whose judgmental stare and comments—"You might want to rethink the jewelry"—illustrate to Tess that *her* way of having curly hair is wrong.

By the time Julia Roberts appeared with her wild red hair in *Pretty Woman*, American rom-econs had carefully established a pattern of elite white women, with elite hair, being super judgy toward less-elite women, with wilder hair, for whom audiences are meant to cheer.

Viewers had been trained to understand the presentation of hair as a part of romance's economic/class conflict. That conflict builds over the decade of the '80s. *Pretty Woman* presses the plot of all these movies to the extreme. You might say that the hair/class conflict, in *Pretty Woman*, reaches its apotheosis. So it's no surprise that *Pretty Woman* is the movie with the best hair, and (not surprisingly) the most hair judgment. Roberts, in *Pretty Woman*, isn't pitted against a single ex—she's got to handle the rich (white) women in all of Beverly Hills.

Romance means different things to these four movies. But all of them make the romantic tie to economic status abundantly clear, and all of them make hair a symbol of the economic status that the main woman does *not* have, yet will—through romance—achieve.

That's partly why it's interesting that *Pretty Woman* begins with Julia Roberts's hair under a glossy blond wig. It's the moment when *Pretty Woman*, the movie, highlights everything that Julia Roberts's "real" hair is not. Roberts's real hair is *not* blond, or carefully styled, or straight, even though hair that is blond, or carefully styled, or straight has often had—and has, in all these other movies—prestige, cultural power, and the ability to signal status and desirability. When Roberts puts on her blond wig, she's doing so because she believes, or hopes, that the expensive, status-y, straight, white-lady hair will make her more desirable. She's hoping that wearing rich-looking hair will bring rich men to her. She wants to make a deal.

It works. The blond hair looks like money, and it attracts money. It brings Vivian and Edward together, when attraction and money seem like a fair exchange. But, the movie tells us, the red curly hair does something different. It has something to do with, or maybe works as a metaphor for, the transformation in both Vivian and Edward's feelings. In putting untamed red curls under carefully coifed blond, and linking them to change of heart, *Pretty Woman* tells its viewer, explicitly, that Julia Roberts's *Pretty Woman* hair represents a different system of value.

Put differently, in *Pretty Woman*, red curls have value precisely because they're *not* representing the qualities that

America most typically interprets as symbols of wealth. Her hair's power, its value, isn't just noneconomic. In fact, her hair looks valuable because it looks—well, I wouldn't say it looks "poor." But it looks valuable because *it looks like it doesn't care* about looking rich.

~

Pretty Woman, as a movie, cares about being rich. Or rather, it loves almost every sign of wealth—every sign, that is, except for serious hair. The movie loves Roberts's unruly mane; at the same time, it celebrates shopping montages. It's charmed by the idea that a man, with his wealth, could whisk you off to the opera in a chartered jet. It never suggests that being poor and honest could compete with being rich, flattered, and safe. But it does strongly criticize some kinds of wealth, and some preoccupations with wealth. It sees them as signs of damage, and as damaging.

We learn over the course of *Pretty Woman* that Edward pursues his line of work in finance partly because he so badly wanted to destroy the father who had abandoned his mother. We learn that Edward's closest relationships have been with his work and his cruelly money-grubbing lawyer.

As Edward's week with Vivian goes on, Edward starts to see his work differently. He sees it differently because Vivian sees it differently. "So you don't make anything, and you don't build anything?" she says, skeptically, on their first morning together. She sees financial raiding as the equivalent of crime: "It's like stealing a car and selling it for parts."

Vivian, who works selling her body for sex, understands being sold for parts. "Sold by parts," after all, is how the camera introduces her. The movie is careful not to condemn Vivian for her sex work. But it also argues that sex work does damage.

As a prostitute, she turns tricks. Having sex can offer emotional value; it can build a relationship worth having. The movie criticizes sex work for taking sex out of an emotional register and making it extractive, economic. Roberts's character would rather her erotic life be able to create a sustaining world for her. And over the course of the week together, she feels something building with Edward. So when Edward, idiotically (the movie is clear that he is being idiotic) describes her to his gross and finance-loving lawyer as merely "a hooker," one the lawyer himself might hire, she is appalled. "You hurt me," she says, asserting herself as a whole person, with human worth. Her erotic capacity has become integral to her; it's no longer a part she's willing to sell off. Edward recognizes her rightness. He recognizes that her whole way of seeing is better—and that it's better to see her as a whole.

He remembers a childhood spent playing with blocks, fantasizing about all he might someday build. "We don't make anything," Edward says to his lawyer, echoing Vivian's words. "We make *money*, Edward," the lawyer tersely replies. For Edward, after a week with Vivian, this isn't enough. He wants the fairy tale. He wants to build.

In the resolution of its deal-closing plotline, Edward meets alone with Mr. Morse, the man whose company he planned to destroy. "I want to help you," Edward says. They make a deal for Edward's investment. The audience hears Mr. Morse delightedly report its outcome to a room of strategists. They are reversing course from finance, going back to manufacturing. "We're going to make ships!" Mr. Morse crows. "Big, big ships!"

~

The movies I've discussed traverse, historically, the decade in which finance gained hold of the American economy. During that decade, finance, like the magician in *Pretty Woman*, was trying to pull a trick, a sleight of hand. It was trying to tell us where to look, how to find the coins that were moving around. In one hand, we could see the "economy" grow as financiers commandeered huge amounts of wealth. In the other hand, we could see how banking deregulation and predatory economic practices led to a series of economic crises (the S & L crisis as well as the farm crisis, and a catastrophic surge in the global debt crisis) for which everyday people, farmers and taxpayers, paid the bill. Finance (and Reagan's government), as the critic La Berge has argued, wanted us to believe that the money, the future, was in the first hand. It wanted us to believe that finance was the economy at large. It wanted the general public to identify with the sense of growth, rather than with the debt burden underlying that growth. It wanted to tell us a story about how financial growth was *our* future.

All the movies I've mentioned wrestle with this conflict. They are rom-econs helping their watchers learn what economic interpretations they should believe. But none of these movies rejects financial masculinity more directly than *Pretty Woman*. It's a movie that takes up financial masculinity in its darkest terms and makes of it an entirely different story. In fact, the power of *Pretty Woman* might come from how directly, how close to the surface, financial masculinity's corruptions remain. And I don't mean that metaphorically. I mean it literally: they're right there in the movie's own DNA.

Pretty Woman's story went through dramatic transformations between its original script and the version you can watch now. The original script was called *Three Thousand*, and it wasn't a rom-com at all. In fact, according to its author J. F. Lawton, *Three Thousand* was a story about whether "men would rather buy women than respect them." He doesn't use the phrase "financial masculinity," but in crafting a plot about how finance infuses men's treatment of women, he certainly took up the topic. He modeled his movie after the darkly cynical investor drama *Wall Street*, which starred Michael Douglas, Charlie Sheen, and, as their mutual love interest, Daryl Hannah (another hair celebrity, known for her extremely blond hair).

Three Thousand has the same opening conceit as *Pretty Woman*—a financial raider hires a sex worker for a week—but a very different conclusion. In the original script, Edward blithely closes his corporate deal, destroying the legacy of the man whose company he buys. And then, *Three Thousand* ends as Edward drags a raging, weeping "completely broken" Vivian from his limousine and throws her (and her $3,000) literally into the Hollywood Boulevard gutter. The movie makes Vivian the parallel of the destroyed production-economy man. Vivian is not so broken that she doesn't collect the scattered money as Edward's limo drives away. (This Vivian, like *Pretty Woman*'s Vivian, constantly worries about the need to pay rent.)

Between its initial workshopping at the Sundance Institute's Screenwriters Lab and its final production, the script for *Three Thousand* was purchased by Disney.[9] Disney wanted a genre change. And Garry Marshall, who signed on to direct, didn't like how neither character felt like someone you could care about. Disney wasn't initially sure it needed a happy ending, but it didn't want a hardened prostitute. It didn't want a woman who could end up unredeemed, unredeemable, on the street. And it also didn't want a man who couldn't see what real value was.

Three Thousand does not discuss the color of Vivian's hair. But it does discuss hair color. In this version, too, Vivian has a friend and roommate named Kit, another sex worker. We're told she has "dark hair." She likes her hair. But Vivian, who in *Three Thousand* is the "hardened," experienced sex worker, thinks the dark hair is a financial problem. "We should bleach your hair. You'll make more money," *Three Thousand* Vivian tells *Three Thousand* Kit. "If you're going to stick with me, you're going to have to make more money." She wraps her arm around Kit's shoulders, reassuringly. "We'll make it pretty. We'll give it a natural curl or something."[10] It is one (of many) markers of *Three Thousand* Vivian's "hardening" that she has come to see "natural curl" as something she can "give." What's real, what's illusion? This street-hardened Vivian has no idea anymore. There's no natural version of herself hiding under a wig to be rescued or rediscovered. Instead of wigs, this Vivian believes in bleach: a permanent, and economically motivated, hair (and personality) change. This version of Vivian is the one that *Pretty Woman*'s final script revises away.

In its place we find the Vivian that Julia Roberts plays. Maybe we could imagine that Julia Roberts's Vivian retains some of the wisdom that *Three Thousand*'s Vivian has learned. Maybe she's internalized some knowledge about the cruelty that financial logic provokes—the dead end it ultimately leads all women toward. Maybe that's why *Pretty Woman*'s Vivian retains the possibility of returning to a more honest, less financially oriented, self—a self that finds its symbol in her hair. In the early scene when Edward touches Vivian's blond wig, with its wealth aspirations, he wonders what he might find underneath. We wonder what will happen when he finds it. What he finds in her red curly hair is the kind of person, the kind of hair personality, that will change Edward back into the economically responsible version of himself. The audience watches as she changes his heart, a change that redeems both of their economic futures. She turns him away from the fraudulence of finance, and toward love, toward production, toward big, big ships. What does watching this change do for us?

~

The movies *Flashdance*, *Trading Places*, *Working Girl*, and *Pretty Woman* aren't exactly "about" race. They're about romance, and about wealth. But in America, neither wealth nor romance can ever be separated from race. Since the era of enslavement, white Americans have aggressively used race both as a strategy for wealth acquisition and as a justification for maintaining wealth once acquired; romance, meanwhile, has been a strategy for regulating whiteness's "family" boundaries. White America has deliberately deprived people of color of economic access, and it has turned whiteness into the most valuable racial status.

So race, and racial signs, permeate these economically charged movies. *Flashdance* keeps race on our mind through Jennifer Beals's racial indeterminacy. *Trading Places* not only puts Eddie Murphy in a lead role, but it also keeps Jamie Lee Curtis, its working-class sex worker, in close proximity to people of color. (Here I must tell you that Eddie Murphy's character, like Beals's and Roberts's, also has an embarrassing dinner moment with shellfish, which functions in all of these movies as a sign of bad rich-white-person taste.) *Working Girl* aggressively signals Melanie Griffith's Italian/Irish/white-ethnic Staten Island family background. In all these movies, racialized symbols intensify their narratives. They assume that for the American viewer, race makes the "rags" part of rags-to-riches stories more convincingly ragged.

But that makes it sound as though these movies use race as merely a narrative symbol. In fact, all these movies (with the possible exception of *Working Girl*) have something important to say about race.

In *Pretty Woman* specifically, hair brings racial content to the surface and puts it into play. By highlighting gender as a raced performance, by flirting with references to "passing" stories, and by emphasizing Roberts's dark red curls and their long cinematic history, *Pretty Woman* racializes Julia Roberts's curls. I don't mean that her hair makes her appear to be Black, or Latina, or "really" mixed race. My point is more subtle. Her hair, especially as it appears in this movie, with its racializing "Get Ready With Me" opening montage, helps remind the viewer that whiteness itself is a race. Whiteness, too, has a range of identities within it—identities positioned not neutrally, but hierarchically.

In America whiteness works as a luxury commodity, one that even white women will buy (today, as we'll discuss, many of us buy it from Gwyneth Paltrow), because even for women who "are" white—like me, and like Julia Roberts—whiteness is an ideal that we're pressured to pursue and can only ever perform imperfectly. Every advertisement we see tells us that only by reaching toward the impossible ideal of whiteness can we ever become valuable, to ourselves, or to a man. Financial masculinity, with its drives toward the financialization of romance, can only value women who value the race of wealth, which is whiteness. Women in this world are taught that they have to express their desire—in their habits, and in their hair—in whiteness's currency.

Of course, as all these movies also show, even when you embody this deal, you're likely to be rejected as too frosty to be desirable: under America's patriarchal, racial ideology, all women are likely to be screwed.

So maybe the takeaway from *Pretty Woman*, the source of its appeal, is how it explored the darkest attic of the American rom-econ. *Pretty Woman* is a Cinderella story that wonders whether all romance under capitalism is a kind of prostitution. One conclusion you might take from *Pretty Woman*, one rom-econ lesson you could read it as providing, is that what makes a woman the most attractive to an investment-minded man is her ability to be not simply rented but actually owned. Is that why all of us white women wanted Julia Roberts's hair, I wonder? Were white women flocking to the theater all indulging a warped and cruel fantasy about the desirability, to white financial masculinity, of Black and mixed-race women? When Julia Roberts takes off her platinum blond wig to show the darker, curlier, natural version of herself underneath, was she evoking the old idea of passing, of the mulatta who would always be more vulnerable, and thus more possessable, than a white woman could ever be?

Maybe partly. White women are prone to terrible fantasies of how they might gain every kind of white male attention; I wouldn't put it past us. But when I think about what it's like to actually watch *Pretty Woman*, and Vivian and Edward's relationship, and Vivian's hair, and how *Pretty Woman* revises Hollywood's financial fantasies of the decade before, I think something else might be going on with the power of Julia Roberts's red curls.

White women's affection for Julia Roberts's hair—their inclination to see curly hair as a model of wildness, of living without regret—grew from a highly racialized, if not actually racist, set of images and ideas about freedom, constraint, and womanly worth. But despite how problematic these ideas are in their framing and in their origins, the ideas aren't wrong. Highly disciplined white femininity is a problem. It's a problem for everyone, most especially the real women of color living in the world of *Pretty Woman*'s audience and carrying the heaviest burden within whiteness's hierarchies.

So how amazing for women who live in a world where the pressures from whiteness and finance feel increasingly intense to watch a woman, Roberts, inhabit the whitest of milieus without succumbing to those pressures. Who can look around at the absurd displays of white financial aesthetics, and then turn to the richest white financial man of all to call out their absurdities. I won't exaggerate the political efficacy of rom-econs, which so often smother their own most radical insights. Still, I think the real pleasure, the real power, of *Pretty Woman*'s ending is that it offers women viewers the fantasy that American women really *could* give up entirely on serious hair—and that *white* women could lead this charge.

The pleasure of Julia Roberts's curls might come from how they seem to provide real evidence that the best approach to romance, to life, might be to reject the white-femininity rat race all together. Roberts's red curls aren't natural, but they propose—in a dialed-up, fantasy form—that hair expressing a desire for *chilling the fuck out* might be the most desirable hair of all.

BUTCH CUTS

What does a life of the mind look like? How does a lively mind style its hair? These may seem like very foolish questions. Intelligence isn't a matter of appearance, we all know: it's internal, inside you. You can't judge a mind by the hair that covers it.

It's true. There's no actual correlation between hair and brain. But it's also true that, in the mid '90s, when I took my first course on philosophy, aesthetics, and critical theory, we studied several writers—Ferdinand de Saussure, Roland Barthes, Louis Althusser, Jacques Derrida, Jürgen Habermas, and Judith Butler—and all of them had virtually the same hair. On every head, the hair was short and swept back. (The one exception was Michel Foucault, the rebel, who was bald.) These thinkers disagreed about a lot of things, but how to style your hair was apparently not one of them. Their silent hair agreement tells you that hair's important.

Universities are where I learned to think and teach about how things that are hidden, like the unconscious, like ideology, sometimes matter more than what is overtly seen and said. I learned to think about genre, about the normative power that makes some symbols legible and some others not.

Hair was a genre sign, an ideology, that no critical or formal theory class ever addressed. Hair became the hidden curriculum of my theoretical education. Explicitly, in my theory classes, hair was ignored or treated as trivial; implicitly, because all the writers I was taught had virtually the same hair, I was learning that hair was somehow essential to being considered an intellectual. Hair was a system of knowledge-power, a hair styling of things. (It's worth noting that the course's professor, an absolute powerhouse to whom I owe a huge intellectual and personal debt, had fantastic hair, dark and curly and full, much like Julia Roberts's, which, memorably, she wore on the first day of class pulled up in a pink scrunchie.)

You may notice some shared qualities of the authors on my list: They are all white. And only one of them is not a man. Judith Butler, whose *Gender Trouble* I read in that class, was both not a man and queer. When I read *Gender Trouble*, my pink-scrunchied professor and I were two of only four women in the classroom. Butler was the only non-man on the syllabus. Many of the other (male) students had short, swept-back hair that matched the syllabus-assigned hair. I had, at the time, hair down to my butt. *Gender Trouble* describes performances of gender without talking about hair at all. But perhaps, with their short hair, Butler knew they didn't need to talk about hair to know they were making gender hair trouble, at least of some kinds. At least, it felt like a kind of gender trouble to me. In that mid-'90s classroom, I wondered: if I wanted my mind to be taken seriously, did I need to have this life-of-the-mind hair?

I don't know what Butler's hair means to them. One of my favorite phenomena of the pandemic quarantine, many years later, was an Instagram account called Butch Hair Quarantine. Butler's hair isn't included that I have seen, but it would fit right in. The account was a celebration of all the excellent variations of gender-troubling butch hair. The isolation of quarantine meant that many people with butch hair (perhaps Butler among them) weren't able to keep their hair so trimmed, so butch. It was clearly a loss. Looking at that account—pictures of everyday people with butch haircuts, of queer icons with butch haircuts, of non-overtly queer people (Ritchie Valens, Reba McEntire) with butch haircuts—shows how powerful it can be for people the world might inscribe as women to make trouble with the pressure to have conventionally gendered long hair. Indeed, butch hair opens up a whole range of ways for people to be in relation to ideas like *woman*, and also *white*. I have never cut my hair short. In my own mostly gender-non-troubling life, whatever butch hair might have asked or offered me remains theoretical.

As mentioned, *Gender Trouble* was released in March 1990, the same month as *Pretty Woman*. In 1990, Judith Butler already had short hair.

It is probably a coincidence that just a few months later, Julia Roberts, the world's biggest hair celebrity and already ambivalent about it, appeared on the cover of *Rolling Stone* with her hair chopped close to the scalp on the back and sides, a bit longer on the top. It looks very much like Judith Butler's 1990 hair, if Butler had highlighted it and stood in front of a fan. Julia Roberts wanted to make trouble with her celebrity. So she got what you might, if you squint, call a butch cut. Was she also making gender trouble? Not very much. But with her hair shorter, maybe she was hoping that the media would focus less on her body, more on her mind, too.

CHAPTER 5

RACHEL'S RACHEL

"The Rachel" hairstyle is iconic. I don't just mean that it is famous, although it's definitely that. The Rachel has its own Wikipedia Page.[1] It has starred in its own commercial. TikToks, profiles, tutorials, updates, awards. All this; more.

But iconic is something more than famous. When you click on an icon on your laptop, you're transported to another screen, another application. When you pray to an icon in church, you're connected to a higher power. The Rachel is like that—a portal, a conduit, a symbol. The Rachel means more than a character (Rachel Green) on a TV show (*Friends*). Much like the bob in the 1920s symbolized the end of the Victorian era, the Rachel stands in for another dramatic change. The Rachel means the whole decade of 1994 to 2005. It means: The new millennium. The end of the Reagan era, the last leadership of the "greatest generation." The Rachel became an icon of the transition to the global economy, the digital era, the information age.

The Rachel became iconic because America, watching NBC's "Must See TV" lineup one mid-'90s Thursday night, seems to have decided that this haircut, this style, this famously difficult-to-achieve look, was the image of what it was now starting to be. The Rachel was the sign that something had ended, and that something new was slouching toward Thursday nights, between *Mad About You* and *Seinfeld*, to be born.

~

If you google "the Rachel" one image will always appear—you will find it, for instance, on the Rachel's Wikipedia page. In this photo, Jennifer Aniston, the actress who played Rachel Green, stands with her arms crossed, looking directly at the camera. It's an NBC promotional photo, taken in early summer 1995, the end of *Friends*' triumphant first season. It's a photo that, surely on purpose, displays every quality that makes the Rachel haircut so Rachel-y.

First, there's the layers. They're choppy, thick, distinct, extremely in her face. The longest layers curl in; the lower looping ridge brushes along Aniston's clavicle. The Rachel is famed for being "face framing," but here it is also face obscuring. The layers frame so aggressively that they almost completely cover Aniston's slim neck. There's something claustrophobic about them. You can tell they'd be hard to pull back if you wanted them out of your way. A ponytail probably wouldn't work very well. You'd have to use Rachel Green's famous hair accessory, the hair clip.

And then there's the color, her highlights. They're done in thick streaks, clearly unnatural. The layers and the highlights become distinct and visible because of the dramatic teasing of Aniston's hair. At the crown of Aniston's head, highlighted and backcombed layers depart from her dark roots with their own, variously successful escape velocities. The layered streaks of hair, coming forward, give the overall effect of a failed blond firework, or a very weak fountain.

I'm telling you all this like you've never seen the Rachel. But if you're a woman of a certain age, you can picture this hairstyle without me telling you anything about it. You can picture it because it's iconic. Because you saw it on the covers of magazines, on billboards, on buses. At the turn of the millennium, the Rachel was everywhere you looked; it was *the* look. According to *Teen* magazine in 1995, the Rachel was the "biggest 'in' of all."[2]

This photo, the one that keeps illustrating the Rachel, was taken in a photo studio, not the *Friends* soundstage. It's a photo taken in our world, not a televisual one. It's a photo of Aniston wearing a Rachel; Aniston crossing her arms, Aniston looking at us through the choppy layers.

Never mind that Aniston herself did not *like* the Rachel, which she told journalist after journalist was impossible to achieve on your own head. (Aniston's Rachel took so much time to style that she was always both first and last in the *Friends*' stylist's chair.) NBC still used the photo to make Rachel and the Rachel attractive, and to tell its many viewers that a Rachel haircut is how you might cast yourself in the Rachel role. This, it turns out, is something that many (many) women wanted, and indeed still want, to do.

So even if you were too busy or too cool or too head-in-the-sand to watch *Friends*, you may well have seen the Rachel on the not-sandy heads of your actual friends. Or maybe you saw the Rachel when you looked in the mirror. Maybe you, like Aniston, were drawn toward this role. Maybe the one with the Rachel was you.

~

Not me, though. Despite being a woman of exactly the right age, I do not like this hairstyle. I did not like *Friends*. I have never worn a plastic hair clip. If slang had given us the word in 1995, when this picture was taken, I would have called everything about the Rachel—the hair, the character, the show—basic. I didn't want the Rachel haircut in the same way that I didn't want to join a sorority or drink a "cinna-tini" or go on the Atkins diet or do anything else that I thought Rachel or the many women with Rachels might want to do. It wasn't because I didn't want something new. I believed in the something new. But the Rachel looked like the opposite of the change that I hoped the future would bring. As I watched the Rachel spread across the heads of American white women everywhere, it felt to me like watching the spread of a future I didn't want—even though "move to a city with friends" was, in fact, my own life plan.

Unlike the Rachel, which looked to me like bland feminine compliance, I wanted to be countercultural, rebellious, political, brave. The Rachel looked like a sanitized version of these things. I could give you a description of the Rachel—tell you about hair that's been aggressively and unnaturally dyed, chopped, and teased—that might make it sound sort of exciting or extreme. But the Rachel was never any of these things. The color, while unnatural, still stays within friendly white-lady hues. It doesn't really look like rebellion, like the Manic Panic I bought at a thrift store to put long purple streaks in my brown hair. The Rachel doesn't look like going to the thrift store; it looks like spending a lot of money at the salon. And the layers, however choppy, don't look like they could prick or puncture; they're not actually punk.

I was missing something obvious about the Rachel's emerging iconic power. The Rachel looked like compliance, but the haircut was made famous by a character whose story started when she *rejected* the bland predictable white woman's path. When she started out on her own, finding her own way. Rachel got a haircut because, like so many women do—like America was, in its own way also doing—she was going through a breakup. She was, at the very least, "on a break."

I felt superior to Rachel, to *Friends*, and to the women who watched *Friends* and asked for Rachels at the salon. But in retrospect the Rachel shouldn't be so easily dismissed.

The Rachel was powerful because of how it became an aesthetic symbol of an urge I can understand, one that still seems relevant to the Gen Z viewers watching today. Like Rachel, many of us want to break free, and to still be safe. To rebel, yet also to be accepted. To be the future, without giving up the past. To be yourself, and normal too.

~

Friends premiered in the fall of 1994. It's about a group of twenty-something . . . friends, living in New York, trying to launch their adult lives. Monica, a chef, lives, semi-legally, in her grandmother's old rent-controlled apartment; it's painted an off-beat shade of purple, but she keeps it maniacally clean. Her older brother, Ross, works as a paleontologist and has the hangdog manner of someone who's always been a nerd. Joey tries to break into acting; he's sweet but not smart. Chandler does some vague office job and makes anxious sarcastic jokes. Phoebe, the quirky one, is a masseuse.

The pilot episode begins in one of the characters' favorite places: their building's downstairs coffee shop, Central Perk. The friends banter casually about their bad dates. Then, the stakes of the conversation are raised: Ross, the big brother, bombs into the coffee shop with the dramatic news that his pregnant wife has left him. She left him, in fact, for a woman! He's despondent. The friends are comforting. Some new love, they are certain, will surely come his way. And indeed, into that very moment, that very coffee shop, another bomb drops. It's Rachel. She's soaking wet from the rain, wearing a veil and a wedding dress. She has just left her whole life—her fiancé, her father, Long Island—at the altar.

Rachel, viewers learn quite quickly, has always been a privileged daughter, almost a princess. She has always planned to marry a wealthy man. Her father (she calls him, in the episode, "Daddy") has always taken care of her financially; after her wedding, that care will be provided by another man (her to-be husband, an orthodontist unattractively named Barry). But standing at the altar, Rachel realizes she just can't do it. She wants, she thinks, to be her own person; she also thinks that Barry looks like Mr. Potato Head. She's deciding to leave both the father and the potato head. She's bolted into the city in search of her old high school friend Monica. Monica is the only person Rachel could think of who represents another way of life. She hardly knows what this new life might be. But somehow, she is looking for it—a single life, a city life, a new life, with friends.

Importantly, in this first episode, Rachel does not have the Rachel. She just has hair. It's tangled and damp and bedraggled—like your hair might be if it had been elaborately curled and styled, and you then stuffed yourself and your wedding dress into a taxi and rode all the way from Long Island to Greenwich Village, in the rain.

~

In 1994, the same year that *Friends* premiered, I started college, and Newt Gingrich, the conservative congressman from Georgia, led a takeover of the House of Representatives. Republicans hadn't had a majority in the house for more than forty years. When the election results rolled in, I, in my dorm room, was shocked. President Bill Clinton, in the White House, was rebuked. Rachel, meanwhile, was learning how to do laundry. This is literally a plot point in *Friends'* first season: Rachel is so spoiled and unable to take care of herself, she has never learned how to wash her own clothes. (I'm saying this like it's ridiculous, but: I never washed my own clothes before I went to college. So really 1994 was the year when both Rachel and I learned to wash our own clothes.) The laundry episode, "The One with the East German Laundry Detergent," aired on October 20, just two weeks before the election. *Friends* does not specify if any of the characters vote.

But I did: I started doing my laundry and voting the same fall. I had just turned eighteen. I had grown up in the Reagan era, and I was desperately excited for a change in political leadership. I grew up in Iowa, a great state for presidential politics. I had always been politically active and intensely identified with the Democrats and against the evil Republican ogres who declared ketchup a vegetable and wanted to undo the feminist revolution. It's a little hard to remember now, even for me, but when he first ran for president, Bill Clinton seemed bold and cool and new. I was too young to vote for him in 1992, but I volunteered a ton. I knocked on doors, made phone calls. Watching Clinton gain in the polls made it finally feel to me that the world was waking up. I went to college with a sense that the future I wanted was happening. It was a future that would show that the radicals had been right.

And specifically—that the feminists were right. The year Clinton was first elected president, 1992, had been declared "The Year of the Woman." Bill Clinton had seemed proud of his strong, smart wife. Six women were elected to the Senate, partly as a feminist response to the Anita Hill trials. Woman-friendly policies like health care reform were on the agenda, spear-headed by Hillary Clinton herself. Feminism seemed to finally have a place in the mainstream. I felt, as young people often seem to feel, that I had it figured out, and that the world was beginning to see that what I knew was right was also true.

So the Republican takeover in 1994 was devastating to me. Gingrich rolled into power with his "Contract with America," a plan that was based on Reagan's policies. The Heritage Foundation, the conservative think tank that played a significant role in developing the document, described it is as finally accomplishing much of what Ronald Reagan—even with his ketchup and relish vegetables, even with his massive divestment from public welfare—had hoped to accomplish but never fully achieved.[3] I felt like we were in a time warp. There was a hippie Democrat at the helm, and women in the Senate, and yet Reagan's policies on the agenda. Electing a Democrat from a new generation had felt like moving forward. But somehow, we had gone backward too.

~

In the '90s something happened that is often called *postfeminism*.[4] This is not a word I like to use, because it's less a movement than a smug media conception. In the '90s, I did not feel we were postfeminist; I felt extremely feminist. Nevertheless, it seems to be true that other people in the '90s looked around and saw that feminism was no longer something women wanted, nor something we needed to work for, because feminism had either been reached or wasn't actually needed. Couldn't women join the workforce? Didn't women have birth control and abortions and the Victoria's Secret Fashion Show, where they could be proudly sexy on TV? If all these things were normal, what did feminism have left to achieve?

I'm being ungenerous. My point is this: in the late 1990s and early 2000s, feminism, too, felt in a time warp. It was uncertain if feminism was the future, ready to be accomplished, or the past, already accomplished, or the past because it had been tossed over our shoulders, unwanted. The confusion was exacerbated because no powerful movement was working to define what feminist action would look like—like a Victoria's Secret Angel? Like Anita Hill? Like friends living with friends instead of husbands on TV?—so that we could know where we were seeing it, whether in front of us or behind us.

~

Sitcoms are a kind of storytelling built for television, and television is a medium built for the family—in fact, for a particular moment in the American history of the family. Televisions came to be along with the idea of the nuclear family, the 1950s fantasy of the commuting father, the happy suburban housewife, the 2.5 kids. In some of the housing developments constructed for these new suburban families, a space for the television was literally built right into the architecture, where a fireplace or a bookshelf might have been.

So it's no surprise that sitcoms have always had a close relationship with the family. They've always been a mirror to the families watching them—in the '50s through the '70s, *Leave It to Beaver*, *Father Knows Best*, and *All in the Family*; in the '80s, *The Cosby Show*, *Growing Pains*, and *Family Ties*. (These '80s families are all different, but they have some basic similarities; across race and profession, for instance, all the mothers have the same just-at-the-shoulder, lightly hot-rolled, carefully managed hair.) As the TV critic Phil Maciak has explained to me, this means that the sitcom has always had a particular relationship to feminism. Because feminism had long demanded different structures and more resources for domestic life, you could see how America was and wasn't responding to those demands by watching the domestic worlds portrayed on TV. Audience feelings about families and television's representations of families fed into each other in another kind of loop: when shows made particular kinds of families look attractive, those kinds of families seemed normal and appealing in the real world; when real-world ideas of family norms changed, television would reflect those changes. In the era before streaming, sitcoms succeeded financially when they got a lot of advertisers, and this meant advertising dollars were both predicting and shaping what kind of families viewers watched, and what shows could get made.

But also, sitcoms succeed, as their name explains, when they're good at providing viewers a steady stream of enjoyably comedic situations. *The Cosby Show*, to take a now-uncomfortable example, wasn't just Must See TV because it imagined correctly that a successful Black household, with a powerful working mother, was something America could recognize as a family. *The Cosby Show* was also successful because all its actors, whatever else they were, were geniuses at working a bit.

~

In 1994, the president of entertainment at NBC was Warren Littlefield. Littlefield had realized something important about the economics of television: Advertisers had changed how they were willing to spend their money. Advertisers had always wanted lots of viewers, but now what they really wanted was the promise of *specific* viewers: the promise that they could have an audience for directly targeted ads.[5] Advertisers longed to target young people, wanted to lure consumers who might want to spend their money on beer and Diet Coke. These young people, Littlefield was realizing, weren't living in the suburbs with their nuclear families. They were living in cities, with their friends, or they were (like me) *thinking* about living in cities, with their friends. They were the creative class, the workers of the new information age, the dot-com boom. They were, let's say, gentrifiers. They had some money. They still wanted to watch TV.

When Littlefield saw a pitch for a sitcom developed by two young (white) TV writers, Marta Kauffman and David Crane, based on their own postcollege years in New York City, he jumped at the chance.

Some executives felt *Friends* was a risk—that young, unsuccessful, single characters would seem either boring or scandalous.[6] But by focusing on a group of twenty-something friends who live in the same building, played by a cast of actors with remarkable chemistry, *Friends* found a recipe for delivering one excellently hilarious situation after another. You may, personally, find none of the characters on *Friends* very interesting—I myself certainly do not. But watching Joey do his commando lunges or Phoebe give a pep talk to her embryos, you will never doubt their frisson-y affection for each other.

As the pilot episode hints, though, *Friends* had something else to contribute to the sitcom form: a particular kind of seriality. You could watch any episode on its own. But what made *Friends* a hit was the building narrative drama that the character of Rachel introduced to these friends' lives.

Her appearance sets in motion two overarching stories, stories that matter to the show's entire ten-year run, up through the final episode. There's the story of the on-again, off-again romance: Rachel and Ross, and whether they'll get together. And then there's the story of Rachel, and whether she'll get *herself* together as an independent successful woman.

Put differently, for all its normie antics, *Friends* from the get-go sets out to mine for comedy all the situations that emerge when you pit against each other two of America's most familiar stories: the marriage plot and the woman-breaks-free plot.

Can one woman, the show asks—specifically, can *Rachel*—have both? Can you reject heteronormative restrictions and still have the comforting reassurance of a man's desire, of the respect and seriousness that marriage signals? These are Rachel's questions, from the beginning of *Friends*. But they are also feminist questions, and the questions *post*feminism was trying to manage, in the late '90s and still. So it's not surprising that as *Friends* experimented with rewriting the "normal" sitcom rules, Rachel, more than any other *Friends* character, became both the show's style model and the media's object of obsession.

~

"What faith was to the martyrs, what honor was to the slave owners, what glamour is to drag queens," wrote the queer theorist Michael Warner in 1999, "normalcy is to the contemporary American."[7] Yes, of course Americans like individuality—but we want our individuality, as Warner says, "to be the normal kind." I know Warner wrote this because at the turn of the millennium, when *Friends* was becoming America's most famous sitcom, and the Rachel its most famous hairstyle, I was reading a lot of what's called *critical theory*—America's then most famous intellectual style. I was reading a lot of gender and queer scholarship like Warner's, as well as a lot of the French theorist Jacques Derrida. This is maybe why I was more inclined to deconstruct the Rachel than to get one.

What all this reading taught me is that the Rachel signaled a relation to an identity—a person, our runaway bride Rachel Green—who *seemed* like a fixed point of reference, but in fact, was really a shifting signifier. Even though it's an accepted truth that in the late '90s everyone got the Rachel, a better way to describe it is that everyone got a *version* of the Rachel. You got a haircut that signaled to everyone seeing you that you were somewhat like Rachel. You were an individual, like a proper postfeminist woman should be, but in a normal postfeminist type of way. You had a bespoke version of a thing that everyone could recognize. You could feel like you were expressing yourself, while also safely fitting in.

And, to take another term from critical theory, the Rachel became not just a recognizable norm, but what the scholar Lennard Davis would call a "*normal ideal*."[8] We see the normal ideal on screens, where bodies and lives that aren't "normal" in any statistical sense of the term are presented to viewers as the standard towards which we should all aspire. Or a standard to which we could, in our styling, signal both our proximity and our difference.

Critical theory might seem to you very far afield from the concerns of Thursday night Must See TV, or indeed of the chapter that you are now reading. Warner's book doesn't talk about *Friends*, or women's magazines, or women's hairstyles (Warner, famously, is bald.) It's equally as difficult to imagine a character on *Friends* reading *The Trouble with Normal* as it is to picture Michael Warner, in 2001, sitting down to watch *Friends*. Nevertheless, these books are part of the same historical moment. All the characters in *Friends*, in 1999, were living in Greenwich Village, just a few blocks from where the Stonewall protests had broken out, and only a half-hour ride on the C train from where Warner was writing in Brooklyn. When I left college (like the friends) and moved to a city (like the friends), I moved to Chicago, I could have taken the Red Line and a bus to right where Lennard Davis was writing about the "normal ideal," at UIC. We were all of us—me, Warner, Davis, the friends too, and even Derrida, who died near the start of *Friends*' last season—part of the same turn of the millennium moment.

One simple way to describe the intensity of my feeling about the Rachel is that it became *the* haircut of the mid-'90s "normal ideal." Some combination of Rachel, as a character, and the Rachel, as a hairstyle, turned Jennifer Aniston's look into the standard toward which all '90s media coverage pushed us. I could feel her as the standard toward which the media was pushing me. She was the version of breaking up with tradition that tradition could accept.

~

That standard was also one toward which even Jennifer Aniston was pushed. Media coverage of Aniston liked to emphasize that the ability to convincingly play Rachel—this perfectly attractive Normal Ideal woman—was something Aniston had achieved. Primarily, she had achieved it by losing weight.

A famous detail about *Friends*, a quality widely agreed to have not aged well at all, is the show's ongoing bit about how Monica used to be fat. So funny! She was fat! I'd forgotten that weight was a part of the Aniston story too. Her fatness is one of two recurring details in Aniston profiles from the late '90s: She is Greek, and she was fat. The Greekness (the media loved to report that her godfather was the Greek actor Telly Savalas) is one explanation she sometimes offered for the fatness. The other explanation she would provide for her weight is that she really liked mayonnaise sandwiches. Just white bread and mayonnaise, she explained in multiple interviews. She loved them.[9]

Fortunately, as these profiles go, Aniston's agent broke it down for her one day when she had to go to an interview in a leotard. The agent pointed out—by literally pointing at—all the parts that needed to be slimmer. So Aniston gave up the sandwiches and lost weight.

Losing weight works differently than cutting your hair, even though they're physical changes with some important symbolic powers in common. Both changes show a strange interaction of nature, personal expression, and time; what makes the interactions strange is that it's hard to tell where "nature," for instance, stops and "time" or "expression" comes in. Anyone with hair can go get it trimmed right now; you can tell someone exactly how many inches you'd like to lose, and from where, and a good stylist can make it happen. Lowering your body weight, on the other hand (even now, in the Ozempic era) takes time. But how much time depends on a lot of factors, as does growing your hair long. One scholar describes both hair and fat as "active and motile" components of women's bodies—both are always changing.[10] That means that any show of consistency, like keeping the same haircut or staying the same weight, takes labor. Aniston, in interviews, makes the labor of losing weight seem simple. Visiting a nutritionist; healthy eating. Over the course of *Friends*' ten seasons, Rachel's hair changes regularly. But she always stays the same, slim weight.

Slimness, in fact, matters to all the white women hair icons in this book. It's a pattern that's worth mentioning directly, even if we're all familiar with the vast archive of writing on American thinness culture and femininity. Especially in conservative moments (like the one in which I am writing), being "thin," as Tressie McMillan Cottom has argued, "is never negotiable."[11] ("Blonde," she says, "is occasionally negotiable.") The sociologist Sabrina Strings offers one of the best accounts of how American culture has come to associate slimness with another aesthetic ideal: whiteness.[12] But Rachel Green was not living in an overtly conservative moment. What can her aggressively slim body tell us about the conservative pressures underlying her '90s era, or the ideas about whiteness percolating through *Friends* as its characters navigated their new-millennium world?

~

Here's who, in the '90s, I liked better than Rachel Green: Winona Ryder.

Heathers, *Mermaids*, Tim Burton's erstwhile muse: Winona seemed a hero to weirdos like me. She wasn't basic. She was swearing about chainsaws and blowing up the school. She cared about art, she said in a 1991 *Rolling Stone* cover article that I read approximately one million times in my rural Iowa bedroom. "To a true artist, the career stuff shouldn't matter," she opined, smoking a cigarette. Caring about career stuff is one way, according to Ryder, you can detect people who "call themselves actors but are really just posers." It's a two-page article, but Ryder's concern about posers comes up three times. "A lot of young actors and actresses . . . it's so calculated and so posed." It's "a *poseathon*."[13]

Winona Ryder, for the cover of *Rolling Stone,* posed on a bed, dressed in a white negligee. She was nineteen, wide-eyed, beautiful, engaged to Johnny Depp, twenty-eight. (Like Aniston, like everyone, she's very slim.) Her dark hair hits at her chin, tousled and full.

When Ryder railed against "posers" she was preaching a Gen-X gospel that I, too, believed. Although several years older than me, she felt like a peer, partly because like me, and like much of Generation X, she identified her origins in '60s counterculture. Timothy Leary was literally her godfather. She took the name Ryder from her dad's Mitch Ryder album.[14]

In 1993, Winona Ryder starred in a movie, one that would become a Gen X cult classic, about the difference between artists and posers. It was called *Reality Bites*. Like *Singles*, a very similar movie released the previous year, *Reality Bites* tells the story of a group of friends, hanging out in a city, postcollege. They spend a lot of time in coffee shops. Their jobs are jokes. They're broke.

They also have convictions. Winona Ryder's character in *Reality Bites* wants to be a documentary filmmaker. She wants to show what it's like to be a young person with no role models, making a way in the world. She's a little in love with a character played by Ethan Hawke, who angrily and hotly sings Violent Femmes covers at her in dive bars. She's also a little in love with an older character, a TV show executive played by Ben Stiller, who wants to take her documentary footage and turn it into a TV show clearly modeled on MTV's *The Real World*. Winona's character worries: Does adulthood mean selling out, taking the lucrative contract? Does it mean giving up the hot art guy with *clearly bad yet still hot* art guy behavior? Does it mean selling your innovative raw film footage so it can be packaged for the amusement of the mainstream?

In the movie, it does not. Winona never becomes a poser. You don't ever really worry she will. You can tell that Ethan Hawke (and art) will win, because in the movie, Ethan and Winona have almost *the same hair*. This hair is chopped in odd layers; Winona's a little bit longer. It's often unwashed, so a little spikey. It's been dyed before, so it's a little streaked. It hangs in Winona's and Ethan's faces as they peer suspiciously at the mainstream world.

~

In retrospect, Winona and Ethan were probably right to be suspicious of what was happening politically. In 1996, Clinton, much like Reagan before him, swept to a landslide reelection. I was so glad, even though I was also uncertain. I liked Clinton, and I wanted to like what he did. I wanted to think the election was good for women. I wanted to think it was forward motion.

But about his policies, I was becoming unsure. The electoral success of the Republican "Contract with America" had shifted Clinton's presidency and the direction of Democratic Party politics going forward. Clinton responded to Gingrich's success by veering politically to the right. Clinton's strategy was to claim that he offered voters an alternative to both old-timey, stuffy conservative social politics and naive liberal economics. He branded himself as a "third-way Democrat" and styled—literally styled, with a Fleetwood Mac soundtrack—pro-business policies like NAFTA as a mature approach to '60s idealism. It was a turn toward capitalism, but a new capitalism—one that wasn't provincial and driven by Cold War ideology, but rather that courted global finance. Clinton wanted to invest in city infrastructures to support workers in the technology sector, to encourage the dot-com boom.

That sounded okay, but Clinton worried me when he also took up conservative projects like Reagan's old favorite, welfare reform. He put new limits on social services, and, also like Reagan, claimed he was doing so for the good of women and families. And he abandoned Hillary Clinton's pro-feminist policy priority, universal health care. Where was feminism in this third way?

Alongside the policies, of course, was the other part of Clinton's behavior toward women. This was early in Clinton's presidency. It was before Monica. But it was after Gennifer Flowers. It was after Hillary Clinton went on *60 Minutes* and defended her husband against accusations of sexual impropriety. "You know, I'm not sitting here, some little woman standing by my man like Tammy Wynette," Hillary said.[15]

What Hillary meant, I guess, is that she *was* standing by her man, but she was doing it in a new and feminist way. Maybe she meant something like what Winona Ryder meant when she posed in a white negligee to talk about posers; when she became my emblem of radical feminist hotness while also doing the absolutely not-radical thing of getting engaged at eighteen to a much older man. Hillary, like Winona, was doing an absolutely standard thing, but in what felt to her like a not-normal way.

Hillary, it is worth saying, was wearing a headband in that *60 Minutes* interview. Her headband pulled her dark blond hair away from her bangs. The headband was, then, her solution for signifying a new kind of politician's wife—friendly, easy. But it wasn't a good enough solution. After the *60 Minutes* interview, the *New York Times* called the headband "yuppy."[16] *USA Today* quoted a hairdresser who called it "lazy."[17] The headband was gone by the 1992 convention. By 1994, Hillary Clinton was rarely photographed without a carefully styled bob.

~

What did Rachel Green think about Hillary, or Hillary's headband? Rachel never mentions her. 1994 Rachel's busy. She's having a hard time in her new life. In one episode, she bumps into her old friends, her past-life suburban friends—women who are now married, stable, the well-coifed wives Rachel had always planned to be. Rachel knows she wasn't in love with Barry. "But it was a plan," she explains. "It was clear." What will she do, plan-less? What's the way to move forward that doesn't feel like stalling out?

The teleplay writers have a solution: She will bump into the Clinton White House. Literally, in the same bumping-into-her-old-friends episode, she's accidentally delivered a pizza meant for George Stephanopoulos. The episode is called "The One with George Stephanopoulos." Monica has to remind Rachel who George is: "The White House advisor? Clinton's campaign guy? The one with the great hair, sexy smile, and really cute butt?" "The little guy!" Rachel's face finally lights up. "Oh, I love him!" The friends rush to the window with their binoculars. They see George in a towel. They see him without a towel. "Wowwwww."

Is this proof that Rachel Green knew about Hillary Clinton, and her headband, and the headband hate? Who can say. But we do know that *Friends* writers were putting the Clinton presidency into Rachel's social world, and even her erotic world, as Rachel was trying to figure out her post-breakup, post-suburbs, some-version-of-feminism life plan.

~

Rachel doesn't have the Rachel yet in "The One with George Stephanopoulos." Through most of *Friends*' first season, Rachel's hair still grows long and full. Or rather, she has hair that Aniston, in a speech honoring her longtime stylist Chris McMillan, once described as "Greek and frizzy."[18] It is a particular irony that Rachel has this self-described "Greek" hair while the script's writers have a confused Rachel garble Stephanopoulos's Greek name: She calls him "George Snuffleupagus."

But it's just a few episodes after this Clinton/Greekness encounter that the Rachel first appears.

~

Rachel's Rachel hadn't been a plan. "I always had very long hair and would never let anyone cut that much off," *The Mirror* reported Aniston saying. But she let Chris McMillan, who also styled hair for the *Friends* cast, have his way with it. "He just took a razor blade and chopped."[19] (Had he seen *Reality Bites*? I'm sure he had.)

And then, like I said, versions of the Rachel were everywhere. According to the beauty editor of *InStyle* magazine, "People are walking into salons all across the country and asking for the 'Friends' cut."[20] Local newspapers across the country reported on the rush of women coming to salons with Rachel pictures and even, reportedly, VHS tapes of the show.

Friends fan websites typically claim that the Rachel first appears in the episode "The One with the Evil Orthodontist." The evil orthodontist is Barry, Rachel's ex. Rachel and Barry have a fling—they do it in his orthodontist chair—after Rachel discovers that he's planning to marry her ex–best friend Mitzi (played by a very curly-haired and—I promise this will matter in a few pages—pre–nose job Jennifer Grey). Rachel, in Barry's office, buttons up her shirt, looks for her bra. She feels awkward, ambivalent about what she's done. Her new long, chic layers and highlights—her Rachel—frame her worried, friend-betraying, face.

Also in this episode, we see Ross pining for Rachel. He wants her so much! As the season nears its end, and the writers lure viewers with Ross and Rachel's "will they/won't they" serial drama, Rachel's hair becomes central. On the one hand, it's a breakup cut: the sign of Rachel leaving Barry. On the other, it's the sign of her potential future with Ross.

I've never seen anyone claim that the *Friends* production staff had anything to do with the Rachel haircut. But the marketing team—or her marketing team—clearly recognized what was happening. Aniston's hair was intensely Racheled on the cover of an April 1995 *People* magazine. It was Racheled at the 1995 Emmy awards, where Aniston wore a strapless black dress to see if *Friends* would win for outstanding comedy series (that year, it did not). And it was Racheled in all the 1995 NBC promotional shots, like the image I began with.

There are many pictures of the whole cast from that photo shoot, not just of Rachel. But looking at them, you can't help but see how the photos single out Rachel's style, her femininity. In some of the photos from this shot, for instance, all the six friends lie on the same bed and are shot from above, in the style of Annie Liebovitz's famous picture of Fleetwood Mac. (Had the photographer been listening to Clinton's theme song? We don't know.)

Unlike the members of Fleetwood Mac in Liebovitz's photo, however, all the friends but Aniston, despite being in bed, are fully clothed. You can recognize the outfits they're wearing in the other photos. Aniston, however, wears nothing—no clothes (that the viewer can see) but a sheet and her hair, her highlighted layers. The photos show her attractiveness, but they expose her, too. She's there to attract our desire. And also, our scrutiny and judgment.

~

Jennifer Anniston, like Julia Roberts before her, got tired of everyone focusing on her hair. "What am I doing wrong that people are focusing on my hair?" Anniston griped, when being asked about her hair in a November 1995 interview with TV's *Extra.* The question didn't make journalists stop focusing on her hair, nor did it make them stop focusing on their own hair focus. The first time Aniston was featured on *Rolling Stone*'s cover, *Rolling Stone*'s journalist, Rich Cohen, describes watching Aniston be interviewed by NBC's journalist Matt Lauer.[21] Matt Lauer, Cohen smirks in his report, asks Aniston about her hair.

Somehow, McMillan, Aniston's stylist, had created what the *InStyle* editor called "the strongest, newest, style." Rachel's hair became definitive of an era, in the way that—as journalists at the time often noted—Diana's or Farrah's (or Bo's) had before.[22]

Diana had partnered the princess with '80s conservative capitalism. Farrah's loose wave, like Derek's braids, had defanged '60s counterculture. Something McMillan had done with his razors had, in turn, made the Rachel right for her moment too.

When you look at Winona Ryder in *Reality Bites*, you can see the legacy of a style of counterculture: something that Tish and Snooky Bellomo would have recognized, something that came out of punk. The Rachel carries that chopped, razored, aesthetic but only as a distant, ancestral trait.

Maybe we could say: As Clinton's legislation was to '60s idealism politically, the Rachel was to '80s punk rebellion aesthetically. The radical made refined. It was individual and bold and future oriented, but still acceptable, normal, safe.

~

Here is a famous thing about *Friends*: All of the friends are white. But not all of Ross's girlfriends are white. These are two important facts about the show. The first time Ross and Rachel don't get together, it's because he's come back from China with Julie (Lauren Tom), an American girlfriend of Asian descent. Later he tries to date a Black woman, Kristen (Gabrielle Union), and then does date a Black woman, Charlie (Aisha Tyler). Ross's girlfriends are part of how the show tried to compensate for its famous, and much maligned, lack of diversity.

It's true that Ross and Monica were, in an off-screen kind of way, Jewish, and that Joey was Italian. It's also true that Jennifer Aniston, the actress, was Greek. But for all this cultural background, the actual cast members were so white that, as the *Boston Globe* once put it, *Friends* turned the Big Apple into a "homogeneous piece of fruit" that was not just white, but actually "ultra-pale."[23] When the cast of *Friends* went on Oprah in 1995, Oprah suggested herself as a potential "Black friend." "In fact," she went on, "I'm thinking about buying that apartment building next door that y'all are always looking at."[24] It's a joke, sure. But it's also a sign that even Winfrey, for all her wealth, could only imagine herself on the outside of the friends' inner whiteness circle.

Friends' diversity problem was bigger than its cast, as Oprah's hint about real estate makes clear. In New York, between 1990 and 2015, "Gentrifying neighborhoods saw an increase in white population (despite a citywide decrease), and a decrease in black population," according to an NYU Furman Center report. The report also concluded that, starting in 2010, an increasingly significant proportion of those newly urban white people were young adults, exactly the age of the friends.[25] Exactly the age of newly citified me.

The young gentrifiers, like me, were the young white people drawn to cities by Clinton-era investment in urban infrastructure, and also (whether or not we admitted it) in policing. We were lured by the promise of jobs that were glamorous and creative, part of the new economic future. That future, envisioned by young Democrats like me, would be cosmopolitan and diverse, and also safe and familiar. *Friends*, trying to lure viewers, drew upon that fantasy; once it had viewers, that fantasy was intensified.

Given the line *Friends* was trying to straddle, both assuaging white fears about urban safety and indulging their desires for urban diversity, the presence of Ross's women-of-color girlfriends, all of whom are amazing, could be read several ways. You could see these women as a sign of the show's progressive politics, or of its toxic romantic racialism, or as a sign of the impossible pressures on women of color in the postfeminist era.[26]

No matter how you read it, though, the Rachel/Ross plotline mattered to the show's management of race. On the one hand, the fact that Ross kept *not* getting with Rachel gave the casting directors ample space to pad out the show's otherwise homogenous cast. On the other, the fact that everyone wanted Ross to get with Rachel meant that the women of color never felt like they were sticking around. The same thing might be said, too, for Ross's most important girlfriend, Emily, the one he actually marries for a while—Emily is both white and British.

One thing's for sure though: Any woman Ross dates would inevitably be compared, by both viewers and the other friends, to Rachel. That most of Ross's girlfriends aren't American white women throws a spotlight on Rachel and her performance of American white womanhood.

Which means it's worth considering the version of white womanhood that Rachel, with the Rachel, and with the rest of her body, achieves.

~

Guess what? Both Julie's and Charlie's episodes involve dramas of white women's hair.

~

Reader: I know this chapter has a lot going on. This *book* has a lot going on. But here's a moment when some of these goings on come together. Because not only do two of Ross's nonwhite girlfriends have episodes involving hair, but both of these episodes also make jokes about the same hair-famous movie: *10*. I am not even kidding. I don't believe it myself.

These "jokes" aren't actually funny, and they're too intricate to fully explain. Here's a summary. In the Julie hair plotline, Phoebe gives both Julie and Monica bad haircuts. Monica's haircut is bad because Monica wants to look like Demi Moore, but Phoebe mishears and cuts Monica's hair like *Dudley* Moore. "Like in *Arthur* and *10*!"[27] And in the Charlie plotline, all the friends, with Charlie, go to Barbados, where the humidity frizzes out Monica's hair until she looks "like Diana Ross." Monica responds by going to the salon to get, wait for it, cornrows. She feels wildly seductive, tossing her beaded braids like Bo on the beach. To drive home the Bo-seduction comparison, Monica even hums Bo's cornrow sex theme song, "Boléro." The live studio audience laughs and laughs.

What to make of this? I always thought Monica was the pretty one. I like dark curly hair. But the writers seemed willing to mock it. When attractive women of color appeared, it seemed to low-key throw the show into a panic. And I am not surprised that the panic manifested in anxiety about the desirability of white women—anxiety manifested in oh-so-hilarious shenanigans about the racial and gendered boundaries of white women's hair.

~

You can tell why hair matters when Ross and Rachel, finally, get together.

Putting it that way makes the "getting together" seem clear, but it's not. For Ross and Rachel, being together is a perpetual state of confusion. They almost get together a bunch of times, and then they do get together only to break up, and then they get married but without getting together, and then they have a baby and live together but still aren't together, but then in the final episode it seems they are together, although even then Ross makes a joke about being on a break. What's the moment of getting together that counts?

I'm going to say: "The One with the Prom Video." Season 2, episode 14. Feb 1, 1996. In this episode, Ross and Rachel *really for real kiss*. And they decide, at the same time, for the first time, that being together is something they want to do.

But that's not at all that happens in the episode. Like most *Friends* episodes, this one has three plotlines. In "The One with the Prom Video," Rachel and Ross's romance is the A plot. The B plot is about Chandler's friendship with Joey. The C plot is Monica's parents bringing over a box of memorabilia from Monica's old bedroom. It turns out that all these plots, though, are fundamentally about the same thing: race. Specifically, whiteness, and whiteness's hierarchies.

In the B plot, Joey gives Chandler a present: a heavy gold bracelet engraved with the phrase "best buds." The plotline's humor comes from the fact that everyone but Joey knows the bracelet is terrible. That it's ugly and sentimental is not the biggest problem. The big bracelet problem is that this terrible piece of jewelry signifies ethnicity. Joey, the Italian, has gotten his friend a piece of jewelry that looks, as one character says, like "*Goodfellas*." Or, Chandler says, like "Mr. T." Chandler tells us he "pities the fool" who wears this bracelet! What would people think? That he has Italian taste? Or, worse, Black taste? Chandler can hardly stand to put it on.

In the C plotline, on the other hand, the friends, looking through the box from Monica's childhood bedroom, find an old video—a video from prom. It shows Monica and Rachel getting ready together, at Monica's house in their Long Island suburb. Ross, Monica's brother, lurks in the background.

The three actors all wear prosthetics to show their youthful difference. But the prosthetics don't even try to make Ross, Rachel, or Monica look younger—instead, they make them look *worse*. Monica wears an enormous fat suit. Rachel has an enormous nose. Ross has an enormous head of hair and a mustache. The present-day friends, watching the video of the prosthetic high school friends, are delighted. There's so much to ridicule! Monica's clothes could cover the state of Connecticut! Rachel's nose could cover the state of Connecticut! Welcome back, Kotter, they say to Ross!

High school Ross does, indeed, have very much the styling of Mr. Kotter, the famously Jewish teacher at a multiethnic Brooklyn high school in the sitcom *Welcome Back, Kotter*. The characters in Kotter's New York are Italian, Black, Puerto Rican. *Welcome Back, Kotter* aired from 1975 to 1979. It is far, far, more diverse than *Friends*. In it, ethnicity often drives the jokes. But it's never made out to be gross.

But "gross ethnicity" is what's happening in this episode of *Friends*, the one with the prom video. The show makes ethnicity gross by making the thick Jewish hair and the distinct ethnic nose into a triptych with Monica's huge fat suit. Monica isn't just fat. She is aggressively portrayed as *gross* and fat. She's slabbering on a sandwich she never puts down. When Monica gives Rachel a hug, she's still holding the sandwich. "Oh no," Monica literally says to Rachel, "I got mayonnaise on your shoulder." It's like Jennifer Aniston's real-life mayonnaise sandwiches followed her into the show's diegesis, here to disgust us. Or rather, to drive home how disgusting, how comical, how essentially undesirable all these characters were before they (unlike poor dumb Joey with his ugly *Goodfellas* bracelet) left their ethnic pasts, and tastes, and bodies, behind.

~

Or rather: not entirely undesirable, not to Ross. The secret the video shows, that it plays on TV, on the TV within our TV, for all the friends and us to see, is that even then, when her nose was huge, Ross loved Rachel. He stares at her besottedly, literally at her mayonnaise shoulder.

When Rachel, staring at her TV, sees the way Ross looks at her, she kisses him, for real. Rachel kisses Ross because she can see that he desires all the versions of her, even the past versions, the gross ones that others only mine for comedy.

But this true-love-ish moment comes at the apex of an episode that has otherwise emphasized at every turn that to be attractive, to be a person who has an admirable life, means to depart from that ethnic past. The braiding of the episode's plotlines turns the friends' movement into adulthood, and into the city, and into the "normal" world the sitcom *Friends* was creating, into a world where any variation from WASPy tastes and appearances had to be aggressively discarded. In this view, the friends aren't just gentrifiers because they are white, pushing out potential Black friends. They are gentrifiers because they see gentrification as an embodied practice, where only one kind of whiteness can matter or count.

In this episode, Rachel's hair is really, really Racheled.

This is the kiss, the episode's happy ending: Rachel starts it. She walks toward Ross deliberately, in front of all their friends. She reaches toward his face, kisses him full on the mouth.

In screen grabs of the moment, you can see Ross and Rachel framed against the purple paint of Monica's apartment. Ross is taller than Rachel, so to kiss him she must tilt her head backward. She reaches up toward Ross's face, holding it in her fingers, but Ross stands still, arms at his sides. His still pose indicates his surprise. But it has another benefit for us: His arms don't move to obscure Rachel's body, or to crush the shape of her carefully be-Racheled hair. We see in profile how fully present-day Rachel has accomplished a perfected urban whiteness: her delicately slim body, carefully sculpted nose, and expensive, modern, hair. Layered and highlighted, straightened and not too full, Rachel's Rachel falls back from the crown of her head as she steps into love's embrace.

~

You know who else Rachel kisses on *Friends*? Winona Ryder.

Or rather, Rachel kisses Melissa Warburton, her sorority sister from college. Melissa is played by Ryder, cast aggressively against type. The episode, in season 7, makes as much fun of sorority girls as I ever did. Ryder's whole star persona depended on being the antithesis of sorority girls, and Ryder carries all those judgments, all that mockery, onto the *Friends* soundstage. Ryder's Melissa squeals girlishly, in a way we're meant to ridicule, between making entitled demands and oblivious claims. Phoebe mockingly claims to have been in a sorority called "Thigh Mega Tampon," a concatenation of body-judgment terms I could not top myself. When Melissa, Rachel, and Phoebe go to a bar, they all drink a red cocktail in a martini glass that is probably a cosmopolitan but might as well be a cinna-tini.

It's an episode about how far Rachel has come—how far behind she has left her suburban, sorority past. Nothing could more potently show Rachel's distance from her sorority girl roots than making Winona Ryder into a sorority girl, and then having Rachel playing the cooler, non-poser, role.

This episode, "The One with Rachel's Big Kiss," appears midway through season 7, in April 2001. April 2001 was three months after the inauguration of George W. Bush. It was five months before September 11. It was eight months before Ryder would be arrested for shoplifting at Saks Fifth Avenue. I don't know if it was before or after Ryder started regularly taking multiple painkillers. It was definitely after she broke up with Johnny Depp, and after he hatched out the "na" in his "Winona Forever" tattoo.

The joke of the plotline, the ongoing tension, is that in college, Melissa and Rachel had kissed, but Melissa claims not to remember it. So at the episode's end, Rachel kisses her again. And Melissa melts. She effuses. She kisses Rachel back so passionately that Rachel has to push her away by the face. Melissa's only been pretending she didn't remember; pretending because she didn't think Rachel could care. (Melissa's right: Rachel doesn't care.) "You love me!" Melissa gushes. "No one could kiss me like that if you didn't feel what I feel!" The live audience laughs and laughs.

The joke is that the sorority girl has never had any other kiss as good as Rachel's. The joke is that the sorority girl is full of unruly desire she won't let herself admit or express. The joke is that the beautiful sorority girl with her perfect life and perfect boyfriend *hates* her life and her boyfriend, a life Rachel has left behind. The joke, also, is queerness itself.

What if it's not a joke, though? It's true that this episode is full of judginess. But no episode of *Friends* seems so sad or full of longing. These two beautiful, exquisitely slim women, Rachel and Melissa, Aniston and Ryder, with their contrasting media meanings, their different but shared histories with bad men and narrow social horizons, meeting on a fictional street corner, to share the only kind of intimacy prime-time TV knew how to give them: the kind it could easily ridicule.

They have, in this episode, almost exactly the same hair. It's not quite the same as *Reality Bites* Winona hair or early-season

Rachel hair. But it's similar hair, hair with the same extremely distant punk ancestry: straight, razored right at the shoulder.

~

No one has ever stopped talking about Jennifer Aniston's body, Jennifer Aniston's choices. Her plastic surgery, her maybe-second nose job, her hair, her hair, her hair.

Right when *Friends* ended, Aniston's marriage did too. She and Brad Pitt wrote a carefully worded statement about their mutual respect. Then he immediately started showing up everywhere with Angelina Jolie, photographed with all her—and then their—children. Aniston never trash-talked him. As she said in a *Vanity Fair* profile that I quote all the time, "You can only clean up your own side of the street."

Listen: I don't begrudge Pitt and Jolie's relationship. I also think Bill's awful affair with Monica Lewinsky should have been less *media*-significant as a cruelty to Hillary than his throwing her health care project under the bus. It's bullshit that the right-wing media used Bill's many affairs both to attack his legislative agenda *and* to emphasize, over and over, how essentially undesirable Hillary was.

I also think it's significant, and awful, that Aniston became the punching bag in her divorce from Pitt, when it had clearly been his decision, his literal affair. Maybe because Jolie and Pitt were constantly surrounded by children, the media could absorb their relationship into a standard narrative of happy domesticity. Single Aniston, on the other hand, the media wouldn't leave alone. Brad left her, the media said, because Aniston didn't want to have kids. Because she cared too much about her career. She gained a pound. Ten pounds. Look at her belly. She's depressed. She's pregnant. She got dumped again. Look at her boobs. Look at her hair.

Aniston, like Rachel, had done everything right. She had been the normal ideal. It was the source of her power, and she is still living quite comfortably off its resources, so we don't need to spare too many tears, probably, over her suffering. But the ideal she represented, the ideal the Rachel represented, an ideal of carefully managed whiteness and carefully limited freedom, was a punishment for her too. Her hair took her forward and trapped her. No one, not even her, could finally be normal enough, in the long haul.

When Hillary Clinton, a few years later, soft-launched her presidential campaign, she wanted to leave behind her reputation as an unwanted wife, a shrill careerist, a feminist shrew. She wanted to show that she was desirable, modern but appropriate, moving beyond her old life. She wanted to show all that she could balance. So she cut hair. She took the best model she had. The model was, and wasn't, a good one. "Hillary Clinton unveiled a Rachel Green-inflected hairstyle," *Vanity Fair* proclaimed.[28]

~

In 2001, I, like Rachel, was going through a breakup. I was living in a city. For the first time, I was living alone. I was somewhere between Ryder and Rachel—single, sort of alternative, not really. Also for the first time, six seasons in, I started to understand the appeal of *Friends*.

I would work all day, take the train home, and make myself dinner. While I ate, I would watch *Friends* in syndication: It aired at 6 p.m. Then I would go to a coffee shop, also alone, and study for the GRE, work on my grad school applications. I'd be home by 10—just in time to watch *Friends* in syndication again. Twice a night, I'd sink into their friendships as I tried to build myself a future. At 6, they were in one timescape, one season; at 10, they were in another. It didn't really make a difference. No matter which episode I was watching, they always liked each other. Chandler always said something with a weird emphasis. Joey always said something clueless. Phoebe always said something vaguely insane. Rachel always had great hair.

It stopped mattering that I didn't particularly like any of these people as individuals. I liked that they were there. They were there for each other. For better, for worse, they were there for me too.

APPRENTICES

The women keep winning. Whether they're selling lemonade (episode 1), private jets (episode 2), or shots of alcohol (episode 4), they have the same winning strategy: to sell their own sexual availability. Kisses with the lemonade, skimpy stewardess outfits with the jets. Even when they're buying (scavenger hunt items, episode 3), seduction is their art of the deal. The women win so often the producers have to take pity on the men.

Not that I've watched all of this. I don't know how much money Donald Trump would earn from me streaming *The Apprentice*, season 1, but I'm not giving it to him. I've learned about its battle-of-the-sexes, sex-selling details, from reading episode summaries, and from watching clips and trailers on YouTube. Even this long-distance connection feels super gross.

But I felt like I had to talk about *The Apprentice*, and here's why: In winter of 2004, *Friends* was airing its last few episodes. NBC was looking to a new future for Thursday-night Must See TV. Thursday primetime had always been for sitcoms, programming for and about families or chosen families, about friends. But, in 2004, NBC decided to explore a different direction. On Thursday nights, after *Friends* and its queer counterpart *Will & Grace*, but before the drama *ER*, NBC tried out a reality-TV show. It wanted something that would appeal to the same viewers who'd liked *Friends* and *Will & Grace*, viewers who liked watching young, attractive, progressive-ish people move to New York to try to build something new. Maybe these same viewers would think it was fun to watch young people who weren't friends. Maybe these viewers would like *The Apprentice*. Indeed, viewers did.

Jennifer Aniston, like most of the actors on *Friends*, has widely known Democratic leanings. The writers on *Friends* were proud of how they mainstreamed messages about LGBTQ+ acceptance and women's independence. All of that can be true, and yet we still have to mark this sea-change moment: With *Friends* as its lead-in, *The Apprentice* became one of America's top-ten shows. And Donald Trump gained a platform to sell his story about women, and power.

In the opening minutes of *The Apprentice*, season 1, episode 1, Donald Trump introduces himself to Must See TV's viewers. He gives America his message. "I own buildings all over the place. Model agencies. The Miss Universe Pageant." We see clips of huge, looming skyscrapers, and then a model on a runway, thin and lithe in a strappy pink dress. Her blond hair falls to her shoulders. Trump watches from the front row. The message is clear. Her beauty is part of his territory. She's worth attention because she makes herself available to his judgment. She gets attention because her beauty makes her interesting to acquire, to display. (Trump doesn't look like Richard Gere, but you can see their characters' similarity. Unfortunately, no Vivian has yet emerged to turn Trump away from his financial display.)

The show starts with sixteen contestants, divided into teams by sex. All the male contestants clearly put the same amount of time into their short, uniform, hair: not very much. But the women take different strategies. Some, in the opening credits, have suits and tidy high gymnast ponytails. Some have careful blowouts, some have curls. The one Black woman apprentice wears her hair carefully straightened. All of them know that there's power to be had here, if your appearance—your hair—expresses your desire to be something Trump might want.

Look how he likes these women! Look how they succeed! Operating entirely within the narrow frame corporate male desire allows, they can tell American viewers a stirring story about what Trump offers women: the power for a woman—but only a willing one, with the right looks, and alone—to win.

CHAPTER 6

BRITNEY'S BALDNESS

SOMETHING WASN'T RIGHT HERE

"My loneliness," she sings, "is killing me." She's leaning against her locker, lonely. Sitting in a car, lonely. Sitting in the gym, lonely. She may well be lonely, but she projects no sense she's actually alone. The camera shoots her from just a little bit above, as though held by a taller person looking down on her. This gaze is her constant companion. The angle was clearly chosen on purpose. It gives her the chance to look up at the camera through long darkened lashes. She shows off her youth, her small frame, her beautiful eyes. It gives us, watching, a sense of our height. It is uncertain who—us, high up behind the camera, or her, below her lashes—has the most power, or what kind. "When I'm not with you," she tells us, "I lose my mind."

This is 1998. It is Britney Spears's first single, her first video. The success of this beginning would be difficult to overstate. It sold over ten million copies, a number that immediately placed Spears in the company of pop legends like Michael Jackson, Whitney Houston, and Bing Crosby. *Rolling Stone* has called ". . . Baby One More Time" the best debut of *all* time.[1]

In the ". . . Baby One More Time" video, Britney Spears's skin and body are perfect. Every inch ripples, smooth and toned. Her dancing snaps with athletic precision; it makes her pretty hair swing. In the be-uniformed school room scenes, in the street wear cafeteria scenes, in the sporty gym scenes, in the center of an equally youthful and nearly as attractive crowd, Spears manages to convey that, whatever her loneliness, she's both the most popular of these dancers and also, simultaneously, completely nice. ("So sweet, she's so sweet," other women pop stars—Tinashe, Kelly Clarkson—often say about her.) She looks very much as though she hopes and even expects to be admired, desired. But no hint of cruelty lurks behind her extremely knowing performance of her own vulnerable appeal.

Something wasn't right here. Was I supposed to know?

OOPS

"Oops" is a strange kind of confession.

On February 17, 2007, less than ten years after her brilliant beginning, Britney Spears, by then a global pop star, tabloid regular, and divorced mother of two, famously shaved her head in front of a noisy herd of paparazzi. The cameras transmitted the event to all our eyes, framing this hair event as the pinnacle—or, better, nadir—of Spears's intensifying disorder. Whether we had watched Spears with sympathy or schadenfreude, we had all seen her quick marriage to "no-hit wonder" Kevin Federline,[2] her two quick pregnancies, her quick separation; we'd seen up her skirt (this image, too, showed shorn skin). Each new event, warring delightfully with Spears's all-American pop princess persona, seemed perfectly suited to the volatile mediascape of the new millennium.

I remember the frenzy of the moment, the debate about what kind of respect and latitude Spears deserved. A woman's baldness could be punk, ascetic, powerful; it could also be punitive, or even grotesque. What did it mean for Spears? What did it mean to America, in 2007? Was our best response to shame her, or save her?

Both punitive and martyring critical responses to Spears, I would propose, are proxy arguments for a whole crisis of cultural value that took place in the early millennial moment. This crisis took many forms. Millennial America was engaging in new kinds of wars, with new political enemies. It deployed new strategies for surveillance and connection. Arguments raged over whether surveillance could coexist with our freedom, and where the boundary might be between safety and intrusion. Similar debates fulminated about newly prominent kinds of media—tabloid TV news, reality TV.

It's no surprise that as America was sorting out what it stood for, it chose the same moral symbols it always did: young girls and women. Just as 1980s America had taken smiling Mary Lou Retton as an emblem of its austere cold war triumphs, in the early millennium, it chose girlish young women as the ciphers through which America might symbolize its own transformations. It looked towards young women who had been child stars, like Lindsay Lohan, Amanda Bynes, and especially Britney Spears, to represent how America could become something new—less private, more available, less stodgy—while also retaining a sense of its old innocence.

How do you stay innocent while also being exposed? Could you? Should you have to? No matter what we thought about these questions, we all paid attention to how Britney Spears tried to answer them: with the symbolic force of her long, then gone, blond hair.

When you say "oops," what do you admit? I did it; I didn't mean it; I'm not responsible for it. "Oops" is how so many white women ride out moments when we might take responsibility. "Oops" is innocence weaponized. And the story of Britney

Spears shows that the free pass of innocence can always be weaponized reflexively, against you, or me. When your only admission is oops, you can never really be guilty, so you can never really be absolved: You become stuck in a feedback loop, where your every act is more evidence of your lack of control. This is one way to explain what happened to Britney Spears—what was done to her, and also what she did.

Shaving away her blond hair, Spears took clippers to an ideal of American white womanhood—an ideal she had carefully cultivated; an ideal she had exploited over and over to become one of the most famous stars on the planet, and then one of its most debased.

"I was simply out of my mind with grief," Spears offered, by way of explanation, years later in her memoir. And also: "Shaving my head was a way of saying to the world: *Fuck you*."[3]

ONE MORE TIME

In the ". . . Baby One More Time" video, Spears wears three hairstyles. As the video opens, Spears sits, bored, in her school uniform and her school desk. Her blond-ish hair is pulled up into braided pigtails, decorated at the top with glittery white pom-poms and pink bows at the bottom. Then the scene changes, and so does her hair. Dancing now in the cafeteria or a breeze way, she's given up the uniform and the pigtails. Her hair, down, swings over her shoulders. But the hair's not totally down: Behind her bangs, two small sections gather into miniature pigtails. Britney's hair is styled like a real-life Cindy-Lou Who, who wandered out of a Christmas special and into joggers and a sports bra. Later she sits alone (she's lonely, don't forget) on the bleachers of the gym. The Cindy-Lou mini pigtails are pulled further back, now in yellow scrunchies. The scrunchies match yet another belly-revealing bra.

All three styles, with their varying pigtails and brightly colored hair accessories look noticeably little girlish. Grown-ups put such styles into little girls' hair, on purpose, to make them look young, and pretty, and sweet. They also appear girlish because Spears is young: sixteen years old.

But against her youth, her freshness, and her pigtails, Spears gives us other signals. Note how her short skirt brushes above the thigh-high stockings of her school uniform. And her voice, which she has purposefully burned out and lowered so that she will sound, as she puts it later in her memoir, "more R&B." These thigh-highs are sexual; this sound, in America, is eroticized, and racialized; both carry a hint of danger, maturity. Does Spears know what she's doing, when she puts on pigtails with her R&B tone?

A consistently made point in the Spears's think piece archive is that Spears's costuming, in this video and in much of her early career, played into what one sympathetic critic describes as Spears's "Southern Belle-meets-Lolita performance."[4] This critic notes that over and over Spears's trades on her Southern childhood to emphasize her naiveté. Spears grew up in rural Louisiana, a town called Kentwood on the Mississippi border. Despite the fact that at sixteen she'd already had a successful career—appearing on *Star Search*, being cast on *The Mickey Mouse Club*, appearing on Broadway—she played up her rural roots to emphasize her down-home virtues: generosity, hospitality, friendly warmth in the Southern heat. Her golden imagery and her family roots connected her to an old and appealing system of order: an American fantasy about virtuous, celebrated, Southern white femininity. She was too country to be sophisticated or calculating. So, if we thought she looked hot, if she seemed like she was seducing us with the thigh highs and the voice—well, that was probably on us, not her. She helped cultivate our belief that she was ignorant of her own actions. To the extent she was successful in doing so, she was able to wield her erotic power while remaining innocent of its effects on us—or on her.

In this context, the pigtails accomplish something more than simply indicating Spears's youth. They convey a strong message about how someone, maybe Spears herself, wants her to be perceived: as a well-taken-care-of girl. Precisely because Spears's perfectly tied bows make you think of her as a little girl getting her hair done, they also convey the sense of a responsible party looking out for her, taking pride in her, protecting her.

Ironically, it's this conveyed sense of care, I would propose, that creates the conditions for something not right to enter.

I remember singing along to Britney's songs, especially this song, in cars and at parties, in groups and alone. I still believe, we sang with her. Hit me. One more time. Britney's most pleasurable lines were full of bad choices. But the bad choices seemed balanced against a sense of safety, like a house carefully designed to hang over a Los Angeles hillside. Even in earthquake territory, a smart architect with a clear understanding of balance can build a shelter that holds thrill and safety at once.

That's how Britney's lyrics felt: Like every bad choice was cantilevered over specifically cultivated good looks, carefully measured by a proud caregiver. Like her beauty was anchored into a bedrock so solid it could plausibly, would probably, resist the pull of gravity. This person, singing the songs, seemed so fundamentally safe, so secure. Who could actually hit *her* the first time, let alone another time? It seemed safe and enjoyable for her to put on the dangerous fantasy of a woman's masochism because at no point did she actually seem masochistic or endangered.

Her pigtails, seemingly the sign of girlish vulnerability, work just as powerfully as a flex. Someone, the pigtails say, braided this hair; someone tied these perfect bows. Someone knew, wanted us watching to know, as we gazed at her through the downward tilt of the camera, that the whole symbolic order of US Southern fantasies seemed built to protect the person who looked exactly like this searched-for star.

TOO EXCITED, IN TOO DEEP

Within two years, Spears was one of the country's most recognizable stars. She'd had seven top-25 singles and released two albums, both of which went platinum. She was dating Justin Timberlake, the breakout star of the boy band NSYNC. In the videos for her early singles, Spears's hair ranges through styles of white teen love: blondish ratty pigtails at a party ("[You Drive Me] Crazy," 1999); brownish and sad on a football field ("Bottom of My Broken Heart," 1999), blonder and blowing at the beach ("Sometimes," 1999), blondish flippy bob ("Lucky," 2000). In pictures from 1999, Spears had hair that *Cosmopolitan* would later describe as "serving serious Rachel vibes."[5] Like Aniston's, Spears's hair ranged through a spectrum of colors that were not naturally hers but could be considered to *look* natural, on her right, white, body.

Spears's 2000 tour—the Crazy 2K tour, her second—sold out shows across the country. In one glowing review of the tour, a critic for the *Chicago Sun-Times* compared Spears favorably to what it describes as her "blonder competitors" of the pop music moment: "Christina Aguilera, Jessica Simpson, Mandy Moore."[6] Spears might not be as blond, and she might not sing quite as well. But she's "wholesome." She "exudes genuine niceness." "And "Spears has that "It" factor that worked for pinup queens of the past like Farrah Fawcett." It's a telling comparison to a very hot, and very hair-famous, angelic girl next door.

The last nights of the tour, which took place in Honolulu, were recorded and made into a nationally broadcast TV special. Spears wears a perfectly blond bob. The blond isn't natural, but it's more realistic than Julia Roberts's Carol Channing wig. If you'd somehow never seen Spears before, you might believe the color and hair were real. She's a perfect blond emblem of white femininity, entering the stage in a sparkling white crop top and matching white pants. When she turns away from us, we see that a white heart with a distinct iridescent shimmer decorates her white pants on the ass.

Did you notice she was white? She's *so* white. She's white-on-white body, white butt. If you didn't notice her blond hair, her light skin, her shimmery white costumes, the effect drives home when she introduces, midway through the show, her supporting performers: "It's four girls from Houston! Destiny's Child, with 'Say My Name'!"

Note: White-on-white Britney Spears and "Say My Name" Beyoncé Knowles are exactly the same age. On this night in 2000, they are both nineteen years old, glowing with perfect beauty. Beyoncé's hair falls around her face in soft flowing curls.[7] It's a light brown color that hints at blond. Like Britney's, Beyoncé's carefully styled and dyed hair expresses her relation to America's white ideals. But her celebrity can't use that ideal in the same way. Britney, because of her race, can access it in a different version—she can appear closer to its nature. Closer to the kind of protection it's willing to offer some women and not others. Both of these women have dyed hair, but only one of them—Britney—can offer the illusion that her dyed hair is natural. Maybe this difference shapes the songs they sing and explains why Beyoncé's lyrics offer no coquettish fantasy of being hit or hurt. "I am not the one to sit around and be played," she tells us. "What's up with this? Tell the truth!" Even in her lyrics, Beyoncé's performance conveys the strong awareness that she must, and will, take care of herself.

Justin Timberlake, it's worth saying, appears in none of Britney's early videos, but they were often together in performances and on the red carpet. The romance between these two stars undeniably enhanced both of their rising celebrity. But just like Beyoncé and Britney were held to different standards, so were Britney and Justin. "I couldn't help notice," Britney would write later in her memoir, "that the questions [Justin] got asked by talk show hosts were different from the ones they asked me. Everyone kept making strange comments about my breasts."[8]

DON'T LET ME BE THE LAST TO KNOW

In her 2023 memoir, Britney Spears puts forth a theory of hair: that hair works as proof of pleasure. "As performers," she writes, "we girls have our hair. That's the real thing guys want to see. They love to see the long hair move."[9]

It's noticeable that Spears describes her fans as "guys," despite the many young girls who made up her fan base. Even when it's girls in the audience, the male perspective is the one that matters. And "guys" want to know you're not faking it. "If your hair's moving, they can believe you're having a good time," she explains. "They want to see you"—Spears's emphasis—"*thrash* it."

Spears doesn't draw out the sexual parallel she's describing, and she doesn't need to. She's telling us something she believes to be true: For her, performing on stage is like performing in bed. Like the guys you sleep with, audiences are watching to see what's real. They want to know what to believe. An audience, or a guy, will leave satisfied by your performance if your performance—your thrashing hair—successfully communicates that it isn't one.

Spears's theory compels me because it seems true. Or at least, it seems true to me. In the early 2000s, I loved watching Spears's blond hair move. I loved her beauty. I loved the combination of her hair and her beauty, and her choreography that showed off both, while she sang lyrics that seemed simultaneously toxic and trivial. (I didn't *not* love her perfectly toned belly, which, true fact, for a time I tried to somewhat achieve by replicating her ab workout, which I'd read about in a magazine.) I was a (not as young as her) young white woman, and for all my angry punk feelings I was definitely not immune to the idea that being a young white woman really was, or could be, this fun.

Throughout Spears's memoir, her hair stands in for her different parts of herself: her pleasure, her truth, her ambivalent sense of her own identity. Early on, she describes how much she looks like photographs of her grandmother, a woman who had been abused and ultimately killed herself: "same blond hair. Same smile." Later, though, describing how trapped she felt when interviewers cast her as a dumb blonde, she makes sure we know: "My real hair color is black."[10]

But she never describes choosing to go blond, or to keep her hair that way. The only time she mentions dying her hair, it's a black dye that goes wrong, a multiphase disaster. "Trying to get it blond again, I turned it purple," she tells us. "I had to go to a beauty salon to have them completely strip my hair and make it a realistic shade of brown. It took forever to get it right."[11]

Black is her "real" color, but also a bad decision that has to be undone. To become blond, her chosen color, "again," her hair has to be "stripped." She compromises on a shade of brown that's not real but is at least "realistic."

It's interesting to compare Spears's thrashing hair to the carefully tended pigtails of her early career. These styles, and their strategies, may seem like opposites. Definitely, the media saw a transition between her early girlish pigtail videos and the less-girlish thrashing ones (NPR, for instance, described "Toxic" as a sexy "breaking away" from her "90s virginal" image.).[12] It's true that Spears's layered blond haircuts don't impart the carefully tended image of her earliest performances. But Spears's hair theory helps us see the connection. The thrashing hair looks like freedom, like fun, like pleasure. But Spears knows: The pleasure's still mostly there for someone watching over her, someone she's aiming so strategically to please.

I CANNOT CONTROL IT

In the cage is a tiger: a white tiger. The tiger sits, taut under its white fur, with a flickering focus on a trainer who kneels by the tiger's jaw with a handful of treats. The tiger seems to want the treats just a little bit more than it wants to lunge at its cage mate, Britney Spears. Spears, too, ripples with muscular restlessness. From her cage, she talks to us, the people keeping her behind bars. "All you people look at me like I'm a little girl," she purr-speaks into her headset microphone. She bursts open her cage doors with a push. "Did you ever think it'd be okay for me to step into this world?"

It's the VMAs in 2001, one of Britney Spears's most celebrated performances. She is debuting a single that would become a defining hit of the new millennium. The spectacle gives Spears the chance to impose an interpretation of her brand-new, never-before-heard lyrics. At one minute, ten seconds in, the audience hears the song's title: "I'm a Slave 4 U." Its lyrics definitely, literally, fantasize about being a slave. But this carefully choreographed performance keeps our minds off American race and enslavement. This song isn't about the erotics of Black vulnerability: Oh no, no, don't worry. We're seeing our Southern belle, but she's not singing from, say, a plantation. The imagery around her pushes aside real history. Instead, she's in a myth.

Stepping out of her cage, Spears descends into a stage that writhes with fake vines and body-painted dancers. It's a tropical scene with wild beasts and barefoot natives; it's a gauzy scene, with dance moves borrowed from belly dancers. Spears wears green and not much of it: a top that looks like a soft scarf tied tight over her breasts, tiny green shorts, a hip scarf with charms.

The golden shine of her hair and skin make Spears stand out from the rest of her dancers, whose painted bodies have a darkened and only semi-human appearance. One dancer, costumed to look like a zebra, kneels down for Spears to ride. Among these half-beast primitives, Spears glows. Like the white-furred tiger, she looks unusual and rare. Not *quite* a different species. But certainly something more precious. The perfect specimen to cage, to possess.

Her hair falls blond and layered and tousled down her back, trimmed into rough bangs around her face. When she thrashes, her hair ripples and rises and falls. Look at her: There's no hint that she wants to be seen as anything but white, white, white.

Then Spears doubles down on the Edenic imagery. A dancer appears holding—it's so big and terrifying that at first you don't believe it's real—a rippling albino python. Like the white tiger, like Spears's golden skin and hair, the snake's pale color enhances its attractions. In the performance's most famous moment, the dancer hands the snake to Spears, draping it over her shoulders. You have probably seen a picture, or a parody, of this moment. When Spears and the snake turn to face the stage, the crowd roars.

Here's the beautiful ambiguity opened up by a blond, snake-charming Britney Spears: Is she the one being tempted, or the temptress? It's a trick question. Like Eve, her Edenic predecessor, she's both. Seduced, she's in the moment of her fall. Will we fall with her?

"Baby, don't you want to dance up on me?" she croons, ensnaked. The music flows low and bass driven, with a scratchy syncopated loop. Even with the snake on her shoulders Spears's movement hits every strange beat. Her voice in the chorus manages to growl in a babyish way, which is not a thing you would imagine is possible: "I'm a slaaaaave 4 you." Her voice drops several notes on the word *slave*. The falling note strikes a melodic parallel of the lapsarian, Edenic imagery.

She is the snake tempting us, and she is our slave. She'd won't deny it; she's not trying to hide it. It's the simplest and most obvious seduction, yet full of strangeness, of temptations and crimes. She left her cage to step into the slavery of our desire.

Her hair moves the whole performance, except for when the snake rests over her shoulders, pinning her hair down. In these moments, it's the snake—with its yellow scales not quite matching the yellow of her hair—that coils and writhes in its own strange reptilian choreography.

OVERPROTECTED

How would Spears's performances feel different if, in her performances of them, her hair was the dark color she tells us is real? If the hair she thrashed was a darker shade than blond? What different kind of temptation, of plausible safety, of partial apology, could she offer us with her pigtails or her snake or her oops?

More questions: How would Spears's performances be different if we thought her "real" hair was blond rather than carefully highlighted and bleached? She's not naturally blond, her thrashing dark-rooted hair tells us, but she loves being blond. She's expressing how fully she endorses blondness's ambitions. She's happy to make blond hair, white-coded hair, the most valuable, desirable, and stared at. Blondness is a currency that she keeps trading for, and on. How does the fact that she's doing so heighten her appeal?

These are counterfactual questions without easy answers. Spears grew up in Disney's child star incubator, part of a remarkably successful cohort of entertainers. Many of these entertainers, like Justin Timberlake, Christina Aguilera, and Fergie—and Miley Cyrus, slightly later—asserted their artistic maturity by drawing on the signifiers of Black culture. For instance, in Aguilera's video "Dirrty" (2002), she styled her hair in bouncing cornrows. In Cyrus's 2013 VMA performance, she twerked. These are now emblematic performances, structuring how America understands racial appropriation: Aguilera's cornrows shape the title essay in Lauren Michele Jackson's book *White Negros*; Cyrus's twerking spurs a key essay on race and beauty in Tressie McMillan Cottom's *Thick*.

We don't have a great way of describing Spears's appropriation of Blackness, even though it's clearly there. It's not just the voice she purposefully strained to cultivate an R&B sound. Both ". . . Baby One More Time" and "I'm a Slave 4 U" were offered to Black artists—TLC and Janet Jackson, respectively. Spears, in "I'm a Slave 4 U," eroticized Black women's history of vulnerability. But America isn't good at seeing an attraction to Blackness in hair as blond as Spears's increasingly was. Every time you looked at her, you could see the commitment to whiteness her hair expressed. What does it mean to appropriate Blackness when you're always looking as white as possible?

CRY ME A RIVER

It's impossible to explain the cultural power of Britney Spears—at either its heights or its lows—without spending more time than I prefer discussing Justin Timberlake, who is a dick.

Sorry/not sorry. I know he's super talented and funny and clearly smart. Timberlake and Spears broke up in around 2002, and I'm not saying it was his fault. I don't think anyone should be written off forever because they did a shitty job of a significant and public breakup. Spears (she admits this) wasn't a perfect girlfriend: She made out with her choreographer—one of the choreographers of "I'm a Slave 4 U"—Wade Robson. (Robson, like Timberlake and Spears, had been a child star during this dangerous moment for child stars; Robson had been in videos with Michael Jackson.) Timberlake (Spears claims) cheated too. Piecing together different versions of the breakup story leads me to conclude that the relationship was weird and hot and complicated, as one might expect from two very rich and talented world-traveling teenagers who weren't ashamed to wear matching double denim to an award show. Even "Cry Me a River," Timberlake's extremely self-indulgent breakup song, doesn't seem the worst pop music crime in the world. But I still think he's a dick.

It's not Timberlake's fault that the world is misogynistic. But it *is* his fault that his breakup album milked the world's misogyny for his own professional advantage. In "Cry Me a River," Timberlake cast himself as a virtuous and abandoned and cheated-on dude. The world absolutely bought his story, and Spears was punished for it. Diane Sawyer grilled Spears about it in a famous interview, noting that Timberlake was clearly suffering.[13] "What," Sawyer asks Spears, "did you do?" The question implies that Spears owed Timberlake a fidelity no one really thought he'd offered her. Loyalty, sweetness, had been among the bedrock values upon which Spears had built her career. Once Spears's capacity for sexual loyalty was questioned, her career never quite recovered.

It's not just the album. For years, Timberlake dined out on his sexual relationship to Spears. As late as 2009, Timberlake was making jokes about Spears's virginity on *Saturday Night Live*. "Publicly [we] claimed to be virgins," he joked. "But privately," he "hit it."[14]

Also, there's Spears's story in her memoir, which Timberlake has not denied, about how she got pregnant when they were together. In her account, Timberlake pressured her to get a medical abortion so that no one would ever know about the pregnancy. Who knows what part of that story is true. I feel compelled to say that if I were Spears's friend at the time, I would have recommended doing exactly the same thing. But what I find entirely credible, and deeply inexcusable, is Spears's account of how Timberlake managed her pain and grief at the abortion. While she was crying and cramping in the bathroom, he came in and, in the world's most disgustingly dudish attempt at consolation, started strumming on his guitar.[15]

LIKE A VIRGIN

At the 2003 MTV Video Music Awards, Britney Spears played a bride. There were two brides, actually: Spears and her old frenemy from *The Mickey Mouse Club*, Christina Aguilera. They sang "Like a Virgin." They wore white dresses; at the beginning of the performance, veils covered their differently blond hair. Madonna, dressed in a black tux, basically played groom to them both. But only Britney leaned in for a ceremonial full-mouthed kiss.

What's the difference between Eve and a bride? Both figures are on the cusp of innocence lost, of womanly erotics gained. But a bride is a girl in the moment of being chosen. Where Eve falls, a bride is lifted up. A bride has a value that the world knows how to want. Britney seemed to want it too.

The next year, January 2004, Spears was in a professional slump. She got drunk in Vegas. At a chapel, she married a childhood friend; the marriage was annulled the next day. She claims, in her memoir, to have little memory of the event. Even when Spears was (maybe) out of her mind intoxicated, a marriage was what she wanted. She became a bride.

Spears was not lifted up. A bride might be an image of value, but Spears's performance of that value was all wrong. It was white, but not pure. The rural Southernness that had meant one thing in Spears's youth—a kind of plantation elegance—meant something different, and trashier, now. That week on *SNL*, a sketch mocked the event: Spears was played by that week's host, Jennifer Aniston. In it, Aniston speaks in an exaggerated Southern accent, rolls around on a couch wearing a crop top and extremely low-cut jeans. The only laugh line is the cumulative sense of Spears's drunken absurdity. (The bad sketch still works as a positive good for Aniston, who gets to demonstrate simultaneously that she's above Spears's stupid trashy behavior and that she's equal to Spears when it comes to having immaculately flat abs.)

But Spears wasn't done. She was chasing something. She wanted some kind of wanting.

A few months later, she got it, she thought. "It's great that this is happening," a photo caption says, "because it has made me realize that I am growing up, becoming a woman, and things just need to be different." The "this" Spears refers to is her wedding to Kevin Federline, a backup dancer and aspirational rapper. (Federline had, for instance, recently danced in one of Justin Timberlake's videos.) The caption appeared in a September 2004 *People* magazine exclusive cover story about the wedding. In this picture, she's changed out of her gown into a tiny white, lace minidress, decorated with ribbons that loop down over her shoulders, giving the strong impression that Spears's bra straps had slipped out of place. Spears was twenty-four. She was pregnant three months later, and then again. By their second anniversary, Spears had given birth to their second son. She filed for divorce the same month.

From the outside, Spears and Federline's relationship seemed to be, as the reality show about their courtship described it: *Britney and Kevin: Chaotic*. It seemed whirlwind and immature and unregulated. The circumstances are these: Spears met Federline in a Hollywood bar. Two months later, they were married. At the time of their marriage, Federline had a two-year-old daughter and a two-month-old son. He thought it would be fun, after the wedding, to pose in a Juicy Couture tracksuit with the words *Pimp Daddy* embroidered across the back.

The memoir's account of their relationship, though, is surprisingly tender. "Kevin liked me the way I was," she explains. It "felt like such a gift." She talks for three paragraphs about Federline's most important appeal: "We would go swimming, and he'd just wrap his arms around me in the water and not let me go."[16]

Maybe it's a mark of her genuine trust in Federline that in their wedding pictures, Spears's hair is most definitely brown. It's a light brown, which isn't her natural color, but looks like the color she's decided on as being her natural "realistic" shade—about the same color her hair appears on the . . . *Baby One More Time* album cover. In one image, from before the wedding, Britney wears a tracksuit with her hair straight and down at her shoulders, supremely "normal," by which I mean, not glamorous at all. In pictures from later in the evening, she's wearing extensions and her hair now flows down her back. It looks a little ratty, to be honest, in a way that makes me happy (or, at least as close to happy as any of these sad wedding pictures could be). Her hair's not moving in the photograph; it hangs sort of lank and sweaty. Which is how long hair looks if you've actually been dancing and sweating and not worrying about your hair.

TOXIC

Every video, every early performance, seems perfect. As she sings about her bad choices, she conveys the powerful sense of being both well practiced and genuinely pleased with herself. Yet this very pleasure makes her performances and videos now almost unbelievably grim for me to watch. I believe in her pleasure. I think what she was doing felt good to her. She was walking right toward the future we all now know about—the meltdowns, the marriages, the conservatorship—and she was enjoying herself, every step of the way. Was *she* supposed to know that something wasn't right here? Was *she* supposed to know that her watching audience was toxic? ("You're toxic!" she sang, pouring a drink, pulling a man into the mile high club, pulling off the man's mask. "You're dangerous! I'm loving it!") She's full of a joy that I remember sharing, but that I no longer can feel.

Britney Spears is the first fully millennial figure in this book. Her celebrity arched, like a five-act tragedy, over a series of intense cultural changes. A questionable Supreme Court ruling decided the 2000 election for George W. Bush, who, like Spears, built his career by deploying his performance of down-home Southern rural values. The 9/11 attacks shattered an American sense of global safety. Bush rushed into a war, determined to prove that a new set of global enemies were at fault—that they, like the Russians before them, hated our freedoms. That *our* values were pristine. We would purify ourselves of terrorist threats, of any lurking, hidden invader. In the name of righteousness and freedom, Congress passed the Patriot Act. The government said it could keep our freedoms safe by surveilling our every move. We would locate and cast out any possible threat.

Something like surveillance was creeping into media and entertainment, too. Spears's career travelled through a timescape marked by the emergence of two media powerhouses: MTV and TMZ. MTV, like Spears, was born in 1981; they grew up together, creating perfectly programmed spectacles for a mass television audience who could be told exactly when Spears would appear on the VMAs or *Total Request Live*. TMZ, on the other hand, sprung like an unruly god out of Britney Spears's celebrity headaches. The televisual tabloid launched in 2005, the same year as the first widely available camera phones. Building on the gossip-hungry world of bloggers like Perez Hilton (and the MTV-constructed fantasy of *The Real World*), TMZ composed its domain by documenting, for an internet-friendly audience, celebrities caught in moments of surprise, privacy, crisis. The *Media Week* announcement of the channel's launch described how "the site also boasts of an expansive collection of archived star photos and videos" so that watchers could "trace changing hairlines and waistlines."[17]

Media Week had a word for these watchers: *fans*. We might choose Beyoncé's word instead: *haters*. TMZ's reporting is gleefully derogatory. TMZ has now been with us for more than twenty years. On its page "About TMZ" you can read their own account of their "meteoric rise": They had exclusives on Mel Gibson's and Michael Richards's scandals, and they "broke the news of the breakup of Britney Spears and Kevin Federline's marriage."[18] Some of their earliest "stories" consisted of camera-phone footage of Spears and Federline doing not much more than walking around. (The "more" would, obviously, come later.)

TMZ's launch also coincided with the early seasons of Donald Trump's *The Apprentice*. Like Paris Hilton and Kim Kardashian, other celebrities of the moment on whom TMZ kept its many eyes, Trump's appearance on a reality show signaled some new alignment of economic and cultural capital. To see the scions of America's wealthy elite frolicking on reality television, rather than attending the opera or F1 or Cannes, created a pleasurable collision of high culture and low. If these spectacles were trainwrecks, they were taking place within the highly padded safety rails built by generational wealth.

But Spears, on TMZ and in the blogs, didn't have the license of old money to authorize her unruly behavior. Despite her growing wealth and power, the value she'd brought to the table wasn't economic—it was moral. It was about the purity of white feminine virtue, symbolized through blond, cared-for hair. So, when TMZ and the bloggers reported on Spears getting drunk in Vegas, or cheating on Justin Timberlake with her choreographer Wade Robson, they didn't see her creating an entertaining high/low collision like Hilton did. They saw her betraying the very values she'd built her wealth selling.

The documentary *Framing Britney Spears* offers a long catalog of the truly appalling history of media attention Spears received, both before and after TMZ's emergence—question after question about her breasts, her body, her virginity, whether or not she's such a bad example that she should (this is true; Diane Sawyer asks her about it) be shot.

One might be tempted to play heroes and villains here: MTV lifted Spears up; TMZ brought her down. But watching her old videos and performances with the benefit of hindsight, a better account might be that MTV lifted up a version of Spears, one that Spears and her team helped craft, that was always made to be a target. Spears and her management team leaned into her celebrity as a singer meant to be watched, not just listened to. She's obviously not the only one; we all know that video killed the radio star. But Spears didn't just ask us to watch. She asked to be watched over. She built her celebrity into a surveillance state of affairs.

She did so while not understanding (how could any of us have understood?) how media would change once you couldn't control the tilt of the camera. When you couldn't ensure it would focus on your most flattering angle. Spears, not understanding, but not innocent either, gave her image to a country with a profound sense that something had gone wrong, that something wasn't right—a country that needed someone to blame.

CIRCUS

In the most famous photograph from Chartres, 1944, a bald and branded woman carrying a baby struggles through the streets. She's followed by a hounding parade. Next to her are uniformed officers. The uniforms give the event an official kind of air, but what's happening is only partly a judgment by the state. This woman's hair has been shaved because a citizen's tribunal has decided she's a collaborationist. She helped, allegedly, the Germans. She had a daughter with a German soldier. The photo is called *La Tondre de Chartres*. In the photo, the woman seems alone. She was not alone. The Foundation of the Resistance estimates that twenty thousand women across France had their heads shaved as a punishment for alleged collaboration. The shavings were a kind of national purification. The whole country had been invaded. But these women's purity was made to blame. You can see ample, upsetting, video footage of their tribunals. There's no sound, so it's hard to know for sure what the women assent to, or what they say.

Watching the footage, I was strangely reminded of other head-shaving footage I've seen, like documentation of rituals at the Tirumala Venkateswara Temple, in India, where devotees make a religious sacrifice of their hair.[19] These people (not just women) are caught up in a different fervor than the those in liberated France. They're full of hope for a god's favor, or thanks for a god's blessing.

When Spears shaved her head, she evoked an old history of women's heads being shaved. Why are they shaved? As punishment, as penance, as promise. As sacrifice or sanitation. Because they've slept with a Nazi, or because they have lice, or because they want to demonstrate their commitment to a belief, or a God.

Women's hair matters so much, in so many ways, that to remove it completely triggers a profound social response with sometimes incompatible meanings. This woman deserves our scorn, the shaved head says. Our sympathy, or respect. We reject this woman. Or she has rejected something—our standards, our desire, our claim—about us.

ME AGAINST THE MUSIC

Britney Spears shaved her head on a Friday night, at a place in the valley called Esther's Haircutting Studio. Before going to Esther's, she'd gone to her old house—the one she had shared with Federline before she filed for divorce. Federline still lived there. According to her memoir, she wanted to see their sons, but Federline wouldn't let her in. So, in a huge dark SUV, she drove with her bodyguards to a convenience store. She bought a Red Bull while the paparazzi snapped their cameras.

If it's 2007, and dark, and it's after camera phones but before smartphones, and you want to do something shocking to your hair, how do you find where to go? This is a serious question I have, about Spears's drive that night. So many details of what happened are upsettingly well documented, but only from the outside of her moving vehicle. We don't know what was happening in her decision-making mind. The paparazzi followed her from the convenience store to a hair salon. It was closed. Then she found another, Esther's. Esther's had been about to close for the evening when Spears's entourage arrived. Spears's SUV pulled into the parking lot late, in the dark.

But it was an early Sunday morning when I decided to go there myself.

The idea that I could go to Esther's Haircutting Studio came to me as a surprise. The moment of Britney's hair shaving seems so profoundly part of a different world, an entirely different era. I was taken aback to discover that from my Los Angeles apartment, Esther's was only seventeen miles up the 101.

I had the right address on my GPS, and I had seen the pictures and the videos. I had compared the old paparazzi footage to the recent pictures accompanying reviews of Esther's on Yelp (four stars). But still, I could barely recognize it.

Esther's Haircutting Studio sits back from the road, tucked behind a parking lot and wedged between an auto repair shop ("Free Break Check") and what's now a hookah bar. It's a small building with a Spanish style filtered through strip-mall aesthetics and made of dirty peach stucco, although it may have looked cleaner back then. I love Los Angeles, and I know how to recognize its weird burned-out-strip-mall beauty. I could see the care of the potted yuccas under the building's small awning; the palm trees sheltering someone's garden next door. But still I stood in Esther's parking lot full of a bleak question: How lost would America's pop princess need to be to find herself here?

I have watched the footage with the leering paparazzi. In fact, because I watched the paparazzi's footage to write this chapter, I myself am part of its gaze, its still-extending field of sight. In hot dry Sunday morning light, I stood outside the door of Esther's, right where the cameras had been almost twenty years earlier. They clicked and whirred while a clearly very nervous Esther worried around her suddenly famous haircutting studio. Esther sits Britney in a chair; they smile at each other in the mirror, like a hairstylist and a new client are supposed to do. When I looked in the window, my reflection covered both the chair—it looks the same—and the space behind it. I saw myself standing where the cameras show Esther standing as she gently gathered Spears's hair in her hands.

Famously though, Spears shaved her head herself. Esther wouldn't do it. Esther told the media the next day that she tried to talk her out of it. "We all have these hormonal things," Esther claims she said.[20] Esther only cleaned up Spears's messy job, the longer spots left around where her extensions had been glued in.

What would you have done with the hair? What would I have done? Esther and her husband, it seems, sold it. With part of the money, they made a donation to Spears's then-existent foundation, which "helps children in need."

HOLD IT AGAINST ME

Writing this chapter gave me nightmares. I dreamed that Spears was singing, bald and wild and unhinged, in my house. I dreamed that my half-drafted paragraphs were all erased, and no one would tell me why. I dreamed that a man stood at the window beside my bed with a tool I could not understand: Was it something to seal my window shut or pry it open? In my dream, I knew my dog would protect me, if only I could tell her, if only I could move. In my dream I couldn't move. I woke up on sheets drenched in sweat.

In September of 2007, the year Spears shaved her head, she was placed into a now-infamous conservatorship that gave her father and a lawyer control of her person. Britney Spears's conservatorship controlled when she worked, what birth control she was required to use, what and when she ate, what medication she took, how she danced. It's terrifying that legal personhood was stripped so completely from one of the world's most powerful celebrities, and that the watching world registered no objection.

For a long time, in fact, the media consensus repeated her dad's version of the story: The conservatorship was for her own good. Wasn't she a mess? Without his oversight, how would she continue to earn money, to perform? Wouldn't someone take advantage of her, try to gain control of her money? (Of course, he was right that someone would take advantage of her: that someone was him.)

In the last few years, the media outlook has changed. Since #MeToo, particularly, we've come to see Spears's perspective. Feminist cultural critics have become astute observers of the long legacy of Spears's abuse. We've described how the punishment Spears received was archaic in its force.[21] It can feel almost biblical, fantastical. She danced with the snake; she was our fall; she was the temptress we could cast out to purify ourselves. When Spears shaved her head, she withdrew the sign of her agreement to play by the world's misogynistic rules. And so, the world punished her. It punished her rather than admitting that the rules she'd played by and profited from were dangerous, toxic, not innocent at all.

~

Spears's punishment also evokes a particular historical legacy, one tied to the Southern imagery her career had often evoked: nineteenth-century coverture laws. Coverture was a legal system that made wives the legal property of their husbands. Critics now who describe their horror at what happened to Spears are not wrong to see the long and still powerful afterlife of this intensely misogynistic nineteenth-century legal system.

But there's a problem here. Ever since the nineteenth century, white feminists have compared coverture to enslavement. In this account, misogyny and racism are parallel partners—together, they back a system that denies all women personhood, that makes all women slaves.

This account is wrong. White women were, yes, victims of misogyny. But a truer account, one that Black feminists have struggled to make America recognize, is that, under coverture, white women were consistently successful at restoring parts of their legal and social status. They did so by positioning themselves *over Black women*. To do so, they used a horrific medley of social and legal strategies—from playing up their own comparative moral status to purchasing enslaved women themselves. For real white women in the antebellum south, it was a savvy bargain: You would consent to white men looking down on you, as long as they still placed you above the Black women you both enslaved.

This history might give us the best way to describe Spears's particular mode of racial appropriation. Rather than venturing touristically into Blackness, as Aguilera or Cyrus did with their cornrows and hips, Spears always kept Blackness present, but right below her. Even as she sang about her mistakes, her vulnerability, her craziness, her literal enslavement, she was always blonder, sweeter, more "innocent" than the racial other lurking underneath her (sometimes literally) in her performances. With her increasingly blond hair, with her choreographed affirmations of a surveilling patriarchal authority, she could even perform her erotic availability as a kind of white superiority. To inhabit this better-than persona as convincingly as possible, to verify her show of comparative innocence, she offered up her authority as sacrifice. It's not that Spears is the only white woman who gained power this way, but she did it better, more extremely, than any white woman of her era, right up until the point she didn't.

Nothing Spears did merited the shame and punishment that was heaped upon her by the media and the courts and us. But if it is intolerable that the courts stripped her of agency, it seems similarly necessary for critics to acknowledge her accountability. If we want to respect her authority, we have to acknowledge her pleasure in what she was doing, her purposefulness as she put her hair in her pigtails, took the snake on her shoulders. As she thrashed her increasingly blond mane. It's horribly true that Spears consented to something that she could not possibly have understood in advance: that she said yes, in carefully calibrated vocals, to something she did not want. Even so, she consented to our gaze, every dance step of the way.

Spears's legacy is a nightmare for white feminist critics, who still struggle to move beyond failed old frameworks of innocence and guilt, consent and refusal. Until we do, we will never learn to move beyond Spears's triple trap. Like Spears, white women thrash in our cages. We've caged other women with and beneath us. And we're so preoccupied by our own confinement, its pleasures and its miseries, that again and again we fail to recognize our deep non-innocence for the crimes we've asked to be committed against us all.

THE WAY YOU MAKE ME FEEL

There's only one Spears performance that still feels good to me to watch.

Like I said, watching Britney now feels grim. Even her early moments of full-throttle glorious precision feel tainted by the salacious frame of what came later. I know these songs and performances used to feel full of joy. But I can't hear it anymore, and I can't see it. When she thrashes her hair, it doesn't look like a good time. That illusion has, very successfully, been shaved away.

There's one performance, though—one live show that still flips the joy switch in my listening, watching heart. Its joy feels completely real. I can't *not* see it or hear it or feel it. That joy comes with its own dark realizations.

The performance took place at Madison Square Garden on September 7, 2001. In it, Spears triumphs by dancing with a powerful, sinuous, predator, holding her own and unafraid. I'm not talking about the albino snake, although that would be a good guess. In fact, Spears's triumphant, snake-based performance of "I'm a Slave 4 U" had taken place literally the night before. But on the night I'm talking about, there was no elaborate set or costume or animal. She was at the Garden, but only our imagination (and maybe Spears's shimmering green dress) could give it an Edenic feel. Instead, there was just Spears to hold the stage, like a princess with a king, the king of pop: Michael Jackson.

They are performing at a concert to celebrate thirty years of Jackson's solo career. The night is packed with celebrities (Whitney Houston, Usher, Destiny's Child) singing versions of Jackson's songs. But near the end of the night, to perform with Britney Spears, Jackson comes out himself. They sing "The Way You Make Me Feel."

And it is glorious. They are glorious. "I like the feeling you're giving me," they sing to each other, voices strong and full of joy. There's hardly any choreography to fill the empty stage, just the two of them strutting back and forth. The performance rests entirely on their voices and their charisma, their ability to convey to the huge full swell of an arena that they are genuinely, brilliantly, full of attraction for each other. They have to make us believe them when they say: "You're the one for me. You really turn me on." And we do. I do.

Four days later, the towers would fall. New York and the world would change. Less than ten years later, Jackson would be dead, and Spears would be in a conservatorship. A few years after that, Wade Robson, Spears's choreographer for "I'm A Slave 4 U," the man with whom she was maybe, at the time of that performance and this one, cheating on Justin Timberlake, would come forward to admit that he had been abused by Michael Jackson for years. It's almost too easy to say that it really was the last night in the garden, but the metaphor's right there.

You could say, looking at Spears and Jackson singing, that the writing was on the wall of that empty stage. The reason there's so little choreography is because Jackson's taking Demerol; he hasn't been able to rehearse. Rumors about Jackson's abuse of young boys already hang in the air. Jackson's face already shows the effects of his prolonged journey to change the colors and features of his face. Spears, the snake dancer, has already begun to attract the vicious media attention that will surround and smother her.

It's all there, I know it's there, and I still can't see it. When Jackson stares at Spears, her youthful fair skin, her delicate features, her willingness to be wrapped in the coiling muscles of a constrictive force, it looks like he's "never felt so in love before." When Spears looks at Jackson, the face that shows his obsession with whiteness, the legend that devotes all his resources to creating a Neverland of eternal youth, she sees someone who might, if he just held her, "give her ecstasy." For this one moment, together, singing, you believe that they believe it might actually be true—that, finally, their "lonely days are gone."

JOJO WITH THE BOWBOW

Common responses to the name JoJo Siwa include gleeful ridicule (from internet regulars) and confused blank stares (from everyone else). I had never heard of her until I heard students use her name as a joke. Here are some details: In 2013, at eleven years old, Siwa was a contestant on *Abby's Ultimate Dance Competition*, the Lifetime Television predecessor to the slightly more famous *Dance Moms*. But by the 2020s, "reality dance show child star" didn't begin to capture who Siwa had become. She's appeared, as either a judge or herself, on nearly a dozen reality TV shows, each of which has produced numerous social-media-friendly clips of her lispy voice and her famously mediocre dancing. Why could my students casually use her name as a punchline? One student had an explanation. "JoJo Siwa," she said earnestly, "*is* the internet."

For instance, in April 2023, Lifetime television posted a TikTok video made with footage the network had originally aired in 2013, ten years earlier. In this footage, a very blond mom scissors a long, fake blond braid out of her little girl's blond hair. JoJo is the little girl. The braid was a prop—its length adding a special element of challenge—used in one of JoJo's solo dance performances. Someone has carefully banded her fake braid at its bottom, but the hair at the braid's top looks ratty and snarled, like someone stirred it with a fork. In fact, what tangled the hair was the little girl's dance practice, which involved a lot of quick chaîné turns. All the spinning makes a mess of her hair, whirling around her shoulders. After practice, the mom casually tosses the messy braid aside. "Nothing is off limits," the mom gushes, "when it comes to doing what I think will benefit JoJo."[1] JoJo smiles at her mother's reflection as they both gaze into a decorated vanity mirror.

Niche, constantly evolving, less an identity than a meme, JoJo Siwa will be a million different punchlines between when you start reading these paragraphs and when you put this book down. As I write, her latest romantic antics are making *E! News* headlines, more grist for the ridicule meme mill. How long can one person keep embarrassing herself, with bad videos for bad songs, bad makeovers, bad relationships, and bad dancing? By the time these words reach you, she may be entirely forgotten. But then, no one really thought she'd stick around this long. Maybe by the time you read this, she'll be on an upward trajectory—the respected performer she seems to want to be. Or at least an object of sympathy, redeemed.

In all her iterations though, one part of Siwa's celebrity remains constantly noted. I bet you can guess what it is: her hair.

On *Dance Moms*, Siwa had a signature look: a high, blond, side ponytail decorated with a bow. She became "JoJo with the BowBow." At thirteen, she launched her own hair bow product line.[2] You can currently buy eighty-three Siwa-branded bow-related products on Amazon.[3] "Bows," she explained in 2015, to much general hilarity, are "a symbol of power, confidence, believing-ness."[4] The fact that I feel compelled to tell you about this "believing-ness" moment helps me understand how we got to our current JoJo-as-punching-bag state. Every bow, every "believing-ness," is like a pleasurably shootable barrel fish, a joke so available you hardly have to aim. It's hard to lay off the trigger, even though the actual footage of thirteen-year-old Siwa explaining that she knows believing-ness "isn't really a word" is sort of sweet, a little charming, and more than a little sad.[5]

Siwa's bow helped make her recognizable and internet friendly. Put a bow on it, and everyone on the internet knows the joke's about Siwa. Even though she hasn't worn a bow now for years, every new hairstyle earns its own bow comparison. One might say that bows are to Siwa what baldness is to Britney Spears; the bad-decision standard by which all other moves can be internet judged.

Siwa prefers to draw a different connection between herself and Spears. In 2020, when Siwa was a contestant on *Dancing with the Stars*, she and her partner (a woman; Siwa, to more disbelieving internet mockery, has come out as queer) performed an Argentine tango to ". . . Baby One More Time." They wore slinky dresses made of a sequined plaid. (Yes, really.)[6] In the video package accompanying the performance, Siwa talked about how Spears was an inspiration and a model. She claimed that, as two child stars growing up in the public eye, she and Spears had a lot in common.[7] This comparison, too, subjected her to enormous ridicule, at least according to my students. My students love Britney Spears, whom they regard with affection. They perceive Spears as a tragic genius, a real talent who endured real pain. Siwa, on the other hand, constantly overestimates everything—her own talent, her own fame, and even her own suffering. Spears produced constant hits; she was the world's biggest star. Siwa only produced jokes she isn't even in on, and bows.

But I think Spears and Siwa have more in common than some of my students can see. There's the blondness, for one thing, the constant hair performance. In the 2023 TikTok clip of the 2013 TV show, JoJo's mom gets out her bleach. She wants to make absolutely sure that JoJo's hair matches the long, fake blond braid. "I've been dying my hair since I was two, one and a half," eleven-year-old JoJo explains cheerfully to the camera. "I'm a natural brown, so I have to dye it so it looks like I'm a natural blonde." She's got to cover up what she lispingly describes as her "brown ruts."

And then: There's the baldness. Siwa has a bald patch on the side of her head. My students told me she'd lost her hair because of years of wearing her ponytail too tight; that it was a case of traction alopecia brought on by her own commitment to her bad hairstyle taste. That's not what Siwa says. According to her own TikTok on the topic, she got a bad stress rash while on *Dance Moms* as a kid. She picked at her scalp so much she damaged "every single follicle." She brings the camera close to her scalp. "You can see I have a little bit of one right now."[8]

Siwa's partial baldness typically brings only more unfavorable comparisons to Britney. Spears really lost it, the logic goes; Siwa only endured a rashy imitation of Spears's disorder. Why's she complaining? She's only getting what anyone who grew up watching Britney Spears, as Siwa grew up watching Britney Spears, should have known to expect.

Siwa's actually not complaining. She just still has a rash. It's 2023, it's 2013, it's now. What's changed? Things might be different around women, celebrity, and hair—certainly the media likes to perform its own redemptive distance from the circus that punished Spears. But in the circuits of the reality internet that Spears's celebrity helped cement, time gets lost, recycled, renewed. We've moved past the moment when Spears was a *Saturday Night Live* spoof whom everyone could mock; we're now in an era when we lift up Spears by mocking Siwa. It's hard not to think that there's damage at some deep cultural follicle, some rut at the root, that's altered what kind of female celebrity can grow.

CHAPTER 7

GWYNETH PALTROW'S BODY HAIR

Think about the thick weight of Gwyneth Paltrow's hair, her *head* hair—its rich color. Imagine pulling it back over a brush, the actual resistance that all those thick strands would offer. Imagine that if you placed your palm on the back of your own neck, the hair that met the skin at the edge of your little finger was, like Paltrow's, heavy and mobile and golden.

Paltrow's blond makes me remember two girls in my small hometown, sisters whose similarly blond hair swished through my childhood. The older sister was too old for me to know well, but the younger one was about my age and sometimes we would find ourselves in the same amoeba of little girls, smooshed up together in my friend Nikki's low-ceilinged attic bedroom. I remember braiding this younger sister's hair, and how she seemed to have about three times as much hair as I did, how it always looked lush, never stringy. We were just kids, unevolved, but we were learning to organize ourselves. Hair was a kind of order. Her hair felt in my hands like popular girl hair.

When I look at Paltrow, whose hair I have never touched, I think about the girls I knew in childhood, and I wonder what Paltrow was like at slumber parties. Was she generous? Was she mean? When you're that beautiful, you don't have to be mean to be powerful. The girl whose blond hair I would sometimes braid had a big house and a hot tub, and I wasn't jealous of her exactly, but I absolutely felt the difference between us. Her hair was the sign of this difference, and it was also the difference itself. This girl wasn't mean, either, but then she didn't need to be, or not often. She had a hot tub and her hair, and precisely because neither was something she had earned, both felt like signs that she was a different order of creature, one to whom the world and others should inevitably defer. I loved to braid her hair because it was such beautiful hair. My pleasure in the experience was another confirmation of her superiority, a recognition she took as her due.

When you are little girls, hair is a matter of what grows from your head. When we were slightly older, my friends and I spent slumber parties considering the hair beginning to thicken on our legs. Sometimes we practiced shaving them. Foamy soap, combs for razors. We discussed who needed to shave, whose mother wouldn't let them. Who looked "like a gorilla" or "a peasant." Questions about armpits, inner thighs. Parts of these matters we would discuss overtly. Other parts we—I at least—kept hidden. As we grew older, our judgments of each other's hair and its management did not decrease. But we grew away from slumber parties, and our bodies became less intimately known to each other. What correlation there was between enviably thick head hair and problematically visible body hair was not always made clear. We based our judgments less on what we had touched, and more on what we were allowed to see.

It is quite possible that when Paltrow was a very little girl at slumber parties, her own thick blond hair was not yet what it is now. So maybe she did not, as a girl, have the superior-girl feeling that my friend did. Maybe Paltrow knew another little girl with superior hair and wished it was hers. Maybe she had hair in other places of which she was less proud, hair that she hid. Either way, I am certain that Paltrow knows the deep slumber-party memories her own hair stirs in the particular kind of white woman, like me, who is her target demographic. Even if Paltrow wasn't that girl at the slumber party then, she's that girl now.

~

I have spoken to Gwyneth Paltrow three times. Our first interview took place on a February afternoon in 2016. We talked for an hour that was truly so transformative for me that I had to process it later with my therapist. I was there to interview her but, by the time we were done with our iced coffee–laced conversation (me: whole milk latte; her: almond milk matcha), I felt I had come to understand something important about myself and my own ambivalences about femininity. These felt relevant to the political moment, as 2016's presidential campaign was kicking into election-year gear. We both had the sense, that February day, that the world was on the cusp of a great change. Paltrow's company goop had just moved to its first California offices. She hoped goop would be a part of the world's transformation. It was, but not in the way either of us knew to expect.

In that conversation, I learned that Paltrow has thought a lot about being a woman—a woman like Hillary Clinton, or herself—whom other women ridicule. She has thought about judgment, and competition, and how it hurts us. One reason Paltrow so carefully tends to her image is because she wants to put better ways of looking at each other on display. She wants to see, literally, women more generously; she wants us to see ourselves more generously. She helped me see myself more generously.

But still, I'm here writing this. I'm going to write about the social media appearances of Gwyneth Paltrow's body, Gwyneth Paltrow's hair, and specifically the non-appearance of Gwyneth Paltrow's body hair. I am going to be critical. My criticisms create more ambivalent feminine feelings. Paltrow offered kindness to me, and opportunity, at a moment when I deeply needed those things. I accepted both. Doing so makes me feel like I entered into a kind of contract with her, one I am now betraying. Am I doing something wrong, or something right? In this world, sometimes all we can reliably count on is the kindness we personally extend. But at the same time, interpersonal kindness often becomes the contract white women use to account themselves square for systemic wrongs. I have often relied on the shelter of this false contract myself.

Paltrow comes at the end of this book for a reason. In it, I've been interested in how white women, with their hair, shaped whiteness between the elections of Reagan and of Trump. Gwyneth Paltrow, I am sure, hates Trump with a burning passion. But 2016, it turns out, was a year of victory for them both. And so, in this chapter, I'm asking a question that feels both painful and necessary: What can Paltrow's strategically crafted and highly lucrative image teach us about how white women's desires—Paltrow's desires, and mine—tangled together with the desires of all the many white women who desired to elect Donald Trump?

~

Gwyneth Paltrow, starting goop, meant well. She still means well. She aims to empower women to care for themselves, to ask questions about things that matter. She tries to keep it real. In 2008, at home with two young children and facing the kind of career impasse and ambivalence many women with caregiving duties encounter, she began an email newsletter that was a way for her to reach out into the world. Paltrow called her newsletter *goop*. In it, she gave recommendations, talked about how she was choosing to build and live her life, and shared her favorite recipes (banana muffins; turkey ragu). Since then, goop has expanded from a simple email into a multi-pronged and social-media-driven business venture: goop makes clothes, food, vitamins, vibrators. It sells, currently, 129 "clean hair products."[1] Paltrow has built this wellness empire in what she conceives as a feminist fashion: with women, and for women. She purposefully hires mothers, whom she regularly praises: "That bitch will get it *done*."[2]

The women in this book have used their hair to perform white womanhood in many ways. Some women, like Bo Derek, have positioned themselves as the preferred erotic other to Black women; some, like Mary Lou Retton, or Britney Spears, have positioned themselves as the innocent alternative to Black girls. Gwyneth Paltrow does none of that. She is the only central figure in this book who didn't overtly build her fame around her sexual, narrative, or symbolic value to white men. She is the only woman who, in the moment of her rising fame, articulated a feminist, pro-women, pro-equity politics at all. She started goop as a mother, and she's never hidden her experiences of middle age. She gained her greatest fame during the era of Barack Obama. She's hosted a fundraiser for Obama in her own backyard (Julia Roberts was there). She called him handsome, thanked him for supporting equal-pay legislation, and called herself his biggest fan.[3]

2008 was also the year that Hillary lost her first major campaign, and the year that a judge committed Britney Spears, another blond mother of young children, to a conservatorship. (Paltrow's children, Apple and Moses, were born in the same three-year stretch as Spears's sons, Sean Preston and Jayden James.) Clinton, Spears, and Paltrow were some of the favorite media punching bags of the Y2K era. All three women faced protracted ridicule for their domestic, maternal choices. It is a telling comparison, one that shows how many ways there are for women to do womanhood *wrong*, how few ways there are to do it right. It's also telling because Paltrow designed goop to celebrate the same activities—having and acting on preferences—which Spears had just been legally denied.

With Clinton's defeat and Spears's legal case as the background, the rhetorical case Paltrow makes for goop's feminism might feel stronger. In our world, even the most powerful women—even the blondest, the most beautiful—can, like Spears, be categorically denied the rights and pleasures of personhood. If that's true, isn't it urgent, even necessary, to create spaces where women's intimate experiences are talked about and taken seriously? Where women's questions are assumed to be valid, rather than signs of ignorance or incompetence? Where women's ability to determine what they eat, imbibe, enjoy, or optimize is celebrated and valued? Goop has been very good at valuing these abilities. Indeed, shortly after our 2016 interview, goop would be valued at over $250 million.[4]

Girls grow up judging each other's appearances. Paltrow and goop gained power in a cultural moment when technology changed our access to those appearances. She understood how social media shifted and intensified women's opportunities for insight, for concealment—for judgment. She did so right as Trump was rising to power.

We know something about Trump's elitism and racism. It's very different than goop's stated politics. Paltrow, and goop, promote a language of inclusion, feminism, and self-respect that's meant to feel empowering to women of all races. But partnered with goop's words, we always see goop's image. Goop's web design is white, and I don't mean a little bit.[5] Its media presence cultivates an atmosphere that's simultaneously "natural," hyper-disciplined, and extremely expensive. And to sell goop's products, to build its brand, Paltrow leans into qualities of her personal appearance that have long been coded white.

Among these remain two of goop's most unchanging and potent symbols: Paltrow's long, thick blond hair, and her perfectly smooth, pale skin.

~

Gwyneth Paltrow joined Instagram in 2013, the same year that Britney Spears joined Instagram—and also the year that I joined Instagram. (Was 2013 a particularly good year for white women joining Instagram? Apparently.) We all joined Instagram three years before the bright 2016 February day when I found myself hiding in the bathroom of goop's Santa Monica offices. I had closed myself into the gray tiled space to try and compose myself before interviewing Paltrow for *Self* magazine. I stared intently at the perplexing array of grooming products that goop's bathroom counter displayed: soaps, lotions, foams. I think they were supposed to offer me something like "self-care," which seemed like the kind of thing a reader of *Self* magazine might find interesting. But they mostly just stressed me out. I'm not good at products. What would I even talk to Paltrow about? I had just turned forty. I took a selfie, and I took a picture of the products. I didn't post either picture to Instagram.

Instagram launched in 2010. It was started by two dudes, Stanford graduates, who initially developed the application for people who, like themselves, wanted to drink fancy bourbon and brag about it. "Burbn," as the app was initially called, allowed users to check in at a location and post an image of whatever whiskey or bourbon they were, at that specific time and place, consuming. When they received venture funding to launch the app, they changed its name and broadened its focus. But it's useful to remember Instagram's origins if you're trying to understand what it's come to mean in the American media landscape. Ever since its conception, Instagram has catered to our competitive, socializing desires for luxury intoxicants—intoxicants that are simultaneously delicious and harsh; that are dangerous to indulgently consume.

Within three months, Instagram had a million users. In eighteen months, it was worth a billion dollars to Mark Zuckerberg, who bought it to enhance Facebook's value a month before Facebook's initial public offering.[6] Instagram had been built specifically to exploit a gap in the moment's social-media ecology: Where platforms like Blogger, Facebook and Twitter prioritized words, Instagram was made for images, and specifically for images taken on the go. It was released only on the iPhone, to take advantage of iPhone 4's new, exciting camera. It was made for people who wanted to look, closely and consistently. It turns out that was a lot of us.

We are now so firmly enmeshed in the smartphone era that it can be difficult to remember how radical a change smartphones made. Phone-based social media made so many interstices of our lives—the small moments that had passed unseen, alone, observable only by ourselves—into scenes of contact and revelation. That these points of connection were intensely politicized, we now well know. Perhaps most famously, Trump's brilliantly deceptive and all-capsy deployment of Twitter fed lies to his followers in every cranny their smartphones pried open: while they waited for breakfast, walked into the gym, sat in the bleachers at their kids' baseball games.

Instagram has not been a campaign tool in the same way; its images don't exactly deliver talking points or policy changes that could be reported easily on the news. It encouraged a different kind of politics. What started as posting pictures of your "burbn" became posting pictures of your pretty breakfast, your workout, your victorious kid. The status-driven consumerism of Burbn's initial idea expanded. We could compare everything we had to what someone else had: their coffee, workout, or kid. It turns out we didn't need alcohol. The competition itself was intoxicating. It became especially so when performed in a wholesome-seeming "cute kid!" guise that rarely had to acknowledge itself as such. You could pose with your cute kid and your beautiful hair. You could make other mothers think about their hair and whether it was beautiful enough. You could sell products to make that hair more beautiful. Instagram's pictures might or might not tell you how to vote. But they pose steady questions about resource allocation—the stuff of which politics is made.

Resource competition over products that create thick hair or glowing skin may seem frivolous in comparison to other resources—money that might be spent, for instance, to build a border wall in Mexico. But the realms of the aesthetic, the embodied, and the domestic are those within which women are intensely judged, and within which they judge, generously or not, each other. We should consider it a serious political event, in my opinion, that Instagram gave every woman all the judgment of a slumber party to carry around in her purse or pocket, while removing from that slumber party all intimacy, accountability, and physical acts of care. These political consequences start in the heart, in desire, and move up the chain of command, shaping economies and infrastructures in ways that are dangerous to ignore.[7]

Such resource competition, in fact, drives a huge economic market with intensely political undertones: the market for "wellness." Wellness's territory is our interiority. It wants to get at every possible interstice that social media can touch. It stakes a claim in our most intimate lives, and we pay to follow it there. According to the extremely gross consulting firm McKinsey (to whom I gave my email to research this chapter), in 2016 companies like goop were growing wellness into what would become, the end of Trump's first term, a $1.5 trillion market.[8]

Instagram can seem like a place of benevolently shared wisdom, where anyone with an iPhone can gain a following, and where anyone, no matter their appearance, can be pictured, be seen. In these ways, becoming a wellness influencer can be presented as sort of radical, or even feminist. Paltrow herself told me that "one of the upsides of social media is that people can really connect to different paradigms of beauty," different "ideas of how women look."[9]

But as one media scholar, Mariah L. Wellman, proposes, an influencer's "positionality" can trump other qualities as she works to build her following. By positionality, Wellman means that when we look at an influencer, we automatically position her on a spectrum of social identities our world teaches us to care about. To put it in the words of one influencer Wellman interviewed, wellness influencers do the best when they're "thin and toned, curvy in the 'right' places, white, [and have] long hair."[10]

Paltrow's Instagram famously challenges many mainstream norms of body care. I believe her that she's glad body ideals are changing. But when thin, white, long-haired wellness influencers like Paltrow praise the diversity of social media, it's often to costume themselves in an ethical status they have extracted from the self-presentation of influencers with less-privileged positionalities. You will notice, in Paltrow's images, that her own visible commitment to whiteness's beauty ideals never wavers for a minute.

In the wellness market, Instagram has been the most significant social media. Recently, tradwife influencers like @BallerinaFarm have gained an increasing share of the lifestyle and wellness Instagram market. But in 2016, Gwyneth Paltrow's company goop was one of the most successful. At the center of goop, always, was Paltrow herself. You could say that in 2016, not only did Gwyneth Paltrow mean well, but, at least on Instagram, wellness also meant Gwyneth Paltrow.

~

Here's a great hair moment from Amy O'Dell's recent biography of Gwyneth Paltrow. O'Dell tells us that, for the early-career movie *Flesh and Bone*, Paltrow's stylist thinned out the ends of Paltrow's hair, apparently so she would "look poor."[11]

This isn't the only moment offering a general sense that Paltrow's thick hair makes her seem rich. I read an essay once that described hair like Paltrow's as "patrician hair." I can no longer find this essay, so it's possible I invented this concept and injected it into the observations of some actual stylist, who, in the essay I remember, was not only talking about Paltrow. The stylist was making a comparison between Paltrow and the similarly luxurious blond hair of Blake Lively. Lively is an actress who solidified her career playing a character who is not quite based on Gwyneth Paltrow. On *Gossip Girl*, a show for teen girls that aired between 2007 (when Britney Spears shaved her head) and 2012 (when I started wondering if I should join Instagram), Lively plays Serena van der Woodsen, a powerful and beautiful blonde attending a fictional girls' school based on Paltrow's actual girls' school, Spence. Serena/Lively is not identical to

Gwyneth and neither is her hair: Although blond, Lively's hair conveys a different impression of silk and hot rollers.

These subtle differences, while important, mostly serve to underscore their common nobility. Both women seem made of a different kind of stuff than the rest of us, or at least than me—the kind of stuff that leads you to grow up and date (but only for a judiciously brief time) Brad Pitt. And then to take up a career selling the ideal of yourself to other, envious girls, who long to share the slumber party "that girl" feeling. This stylist's use of the word *patrician* pulls slumber party hierarchies into a broader scope. Paltrow and Lively, like my childhood friend, seemed connected at the root to something deeper, richer, and more powerful. Whatever that nobility was, their blond hair was its visible sign. They were noble by nature.

Lively, around the same time that Gwyneth and I started our Instagrams, began her own social-media intensive image project, the short-lived but amazingly named Preserve. Preserve: to keep, to hold back, to break down and boil and protect for a later season. Just like Lively's image is an iteration of Paltrow's, preserves are a kind of goop. Lively, like Paltrow, has politics that tilt toward the progressive, and aesthetics that shine like bright jelly in a jar: feminine, flavorful, and elegantly contained. Are preserves natural? They are nature that has been rearranged through human labor and knowledge into a condensed and enduring presentational form of itself. Preserves are natural, I think in the way that Paltrow and Lively's hair is natural, which is to say, nature that is highly processed and procured at great effort.

Paltrow with goop, like Lively with Preserve (or other celebrity beauty lines, like Jennifer Aniston's LolaVie) sells an act of shared effort. She shares, on Instagram, about products she really uses, so that we can consider using them too. This reality effect isn't unique to Paltrow and isn't her invention. As long as there's been an American mass market for femininity, self-revelation is a common product that's been sold: "Here's how I do it," women's guides have said since the nineteenth century. When a woman you like, or are like, or would like to be more like, shows herself in process before you, that act of sharing creates a kind of credibility—a sense of trust.

Sharing feels feminist to Paltrow because sharing seems to push back against femininity as fantasy, and particularly against femininity as a fantasy that women must try to uphold in solitude, anxious and insecure. I don't totally disagree. Given the choice between goop-style transparency and many other kinds of feminine fantasy, transparency is what I'd choose.

But there are different kinds of sharing, and different strategies for feminism too. The girl with the beautiful hair at my slumber parties was sharing and, to an extent, trusting me. She was showing me the hair privilege she had so that I could see how I did not share it. She was letting me draw close because she liked my admiration and envy, and I liked drawing close because it was a pleasure to touch the hair I admired. The moment of sharing forged an intimacy between us, one where all my feelings about her, even the negative ones, helped intensify a social order. Her hair was thick and lush; mine was thinner, but also silkier. (This might raise slumber party questions: Did my silkier hair, like Lively's silky hair compared to Paltrow's coarser hair, signal a difference between our body hair?) We could weigh the comparative power between us, noting subtle differences that only intensified our shared set of values.

It's like we were making a shared hair country, right there in that slumber party bedroom. We didn't need anyone to build a wall. Inside our borders was white femininity, shared if unequal. Outside those borders was Other Hair.

In every image, every Instagram post, Paltrow invites her viewers—invites me—into that same intimate slumber party evaluative feeling. All of us watching know whether or not, and to exactly what degree, we have what Paltrow has. No one can ever perfectly obtain white femininity, but some of us have more access to it than others. And for a time, no one was more successful than Paltrow at selling as self-care—and even self-pleasure—the costly, onanistic, asymptotic journey toward white America's feminine ideal.

~

Several years after I interviewed her, Paltrow posted a reel on Instagram that helped me understand the world that goop had made. It helped me understand something about how Paltrow's hair mattered to the post-Trump world that I was living in.

Here's what happens during this reel's extraordinary nineteen seconds: Paltrow stands alone with her brush in a bathroom, her hair loose around her face. She looks at her camera—we are like her mirror—with her expression blank. In her left hand, Paltrow holds a goop-branded brush, made of a pale unfinished wood. The brush, you can't help noticing, is basically the same color as Paltrow's golden hair.

But Paltrow doesn't brush her hair. Instead, with great care, Paltrow brushes her *skin*. Or as she puts it, she "dry brushes" her skin.

What is dry brushing? It is a "detoxing" technique, an "ancient modality," according to goop's website, that the video exists to model for you. Starting with the back of her right hand, Paltrow drags the brush's bristles over her bare skin. She works her way up—forearm, upper arm. She makes sure to get her inner elbow, the back of her arm. As her brush reaches her shoulder, she lifts the sleeve of her faded red T-shirt, so as to *really brush* her shoulder. The moment of extra exposure, combined with the fact that her T-shirt says CLAM BAR, drives home the sense that we're seeing something intimate and exclusive. Paltrow's fresh flesh lines up with the Hamptons' seafood restaurant we're learning that she loves. One arm now fully brushed, Paltrow switches to her second arm, working her way up. Then, the video loops so that the arm brushing starts again. I said the video lasts nineteen seconds, but really it lasts forever. Like white femininity itself, it never gets to the end.

You may rightly note that this is not, technically, a video "about" Paltrow's long hair. Paltrow's hair—blond and flowing, as always—merely accessorizes the central brushing event this video displays. (In another dry-brushing video, Paltrow sits in a sauna, carefully dry brushing each of her thighs, as her hair floats over her shoulders.) The purpose of the reel, instead, is to recommend dry brushing, and also to sell you a brush.[12] Goop's web page describes how dry brushing "wakes your senses up like no other practice, feels absolutely incredible, and leaves you with silky-smooth skin and an allover [*sic*] body glow." It's the glow, the feeling, that apparently we are meant to see when we look at this carefully brushed, and perfectly smooth, skin.

But here is the thought experiment I want to propose, an experiment that makes hair's meaning visible.

Imagine how different, how truly radical, either of these dry-brushing videos would become if there was the slightest, remotest sense that it was Paltrow's arm *hair*, rather than her arm—or, even more shocking, her *leg hair*, rather than her legs—that Paltrow's brush was gently untangling. Imagine Paltrow with downy arm hair, or with stubbly-haired legs. With coiled hair growing between her thighs.

Such a video would be an astonishing piece of performance art, and I would like to see it. But it would spoil the advertisement for the dry brush. If Paltrow had body hair—I think this is fair to say—we would notice her body hair. Whatever "glow" she was feeling or radiating seems unlikely to shine through the surprise her body hair would cause. So, although this brushing video nominally is about a feeling, a sensory state, rather than about hair, in fact, its capacity to advertise this "ancient modality" depends on hair: on how Paltrow has no *body* hair at all.

~

Does body hair correlate to race? Good question. In the nineteenth century, racist pseudoscientists answered yes definitely. Such science used both head hair and body hair to categorize racial differences. From hair texture and distribution, the racist scientist could distinguish between Black, white, Indian, and Asian. But just as importantly, hair was used to carefully measure difference between these categories. You might not be surprised that for nineteenth-century racist scientists, there were hierarchies within whiteness, and that the Anglo-Saxon race was considered the pinnacle of human existence. Hair could distinguish between white and Black, but also, for instance, between "Anglo-Saxon" and "semitic."

Today, scientists offer conflicting accounts of what, if anything, body hair means as a "racial" marker. But strangely, or maybe not, nineteenth-century strategies for measuring hair texture—categorizing curls from one to four, for instance—will now show up on social media. TikTok and Instagram are full of posts about how visible body hair matters to experiences of belonging—as a #greekgirlproblem, for instance, or a #easterneuropeangirlproblem.

I've had students write about the shame they've experienced around their arm hair and their mustaches, and they've all perceived this shame to be a part of an ethnic othering. These women's experiences reveal the legacy of nineteenth-century racism, and the lingering belief that body hair signals fine gradations in racial hierarchies.

When I was in college I read a famous book about visual culture, John Berger's *Ways of Seeing*. In it, he explained why so few images in the history of Western art include women's body hair. "Hair is associated with sexual power, with passion," he wrote, and it's the convention of Western art to minimize women's power, erotically and otherwise, so that men can hold power's monopoly.[13] Across centuries, in almost every iteration, art's ideal white woman's body has remained hair-free.

This long visual history helps explain why removing body hair can feel like a natural practice, even though it's a relatively new historical phenomenon. Safe razors and effective depilation cream only became available in the early twentieth century. But once it became possible for women to consistently remove their body hair, doing so quickly became a cultural mandate, one that women comply with at rates that are almost shocking.[14] Body-hair removal is so normalized that women's bodies with all visible body hair depilated feel and look like the "natural ones."

You can tell that body-hair removal has become "natural" because body hair itself can feel weird—whether difficult, intimate, or just gross—to discuss. Even books focusing on the intimate world of beauty products sometimes leave body hair by the wayside. One prettily designed book of celebrity beauty interviews conducted by a *New York Times* beauty editor, called *Skin Deep*, includes an interview with Gwyneth Paltrow. Throughout, the book describes serums and stylists; it tells you one of Paltrow's choices for shampoo (Shu Uemura, $23 for 75 milliliters).[15] But it doesn't tell us about anyone's leg hair. We don't know which razor Paltrow uses, or if she still shaves—we don't know if she waxes, or how often, or if she's had enough laser treatments that the hair on her armpits, calves, or inner thighs no longer grows. We only know that it's never there for us to see.

Maybe that's because removing your hair isn't really a marker of "beauty." Hairless bodies have become the baseline from which beauty can begin. Or even more—the baseline from which "womanliness" can begin, at least if you mean the kind of womanliness that Western visual culture can be willing to accept as such.

Western culture has a million tests for femininity, as anyone reading this book surely knows. Body hair isn't the same as ovaries, or breasts, or hormones. But like breasts, body hair remains a way to visually measure the hormone levels that medicine decides are womanly. These measures, much like the test used to measure "normal" quantities of body hair (it's called the Ferriman-Gallwey hirsutism test) are highly subjective—which sadly has not diminished their power to aggressively regulate bodies and their genders.

And even more so than breasts, body hair has become a way to visually measure what we might call the attitudes that our culture has decided are womanly. Because the ideal woman—unlike almost every real woman—is hairless, our culture has made the *desire to remove* unwomanly hair into a womanly trait. We're supposed to be disgusted by our own body hair, to worry if we look like a gorilla or a peasant. And if we're not disgusted, ashamed, worried, we're seen as a problem. To simply grow the body hair that your body grows becomes insubordination that merits aggression in response.[16] (It's a structure that runs parallel, although with different stakes, to the discipline that can be directed toward Black women who don't straighten their hair.)

Breanne Fahs, the author of the book *Unshaved*, a feminist discussion of women's body hair, tells a story about giving her students an extra-credit assignment: go unshaved and write about it. A right-wing media outlet reported on the assignment. Fahs got death threats.[17] Body hair is both an everyday reality and hot to touch.

~

Instagram has many, uh, virtues, but it isn't very searchable. You can find goop posts telling you "How to get a smooth bikini line" but can't locate them all at once. So, I searched goop's main page. On the day I started doing this research, goop had more articles on shaved ice (six) than on shaving itself (three). It's an interesting ratio, giving that no matter shaved ice's popularity, this refreshing desert seems less central to goop's image than smooth skin.[18]

Goop, at least so far, also doesn't produce its own line of shaving products. Instead, it vends a select group of products from a company with the vaguely hot name of Fur. Fur makes products like "shave cream," "fur oil," and "ingrown eliminator serum." The shaving cream is unisex and meant for anywhere on the body. But most of the Fur products available on goop focus on pubic hair, or, as goop's articles put it, "the bikini line." "Where exactly the bikini line might be has wavered considerably from decade to decade," one article tells us, "and we've arrived at a place where anything—from minimal trimming to maximal waxing—goes." The article quotes Fur's founder, who wants specifically to "validate the bush."[19] Both Fur and goop handle the topic of pubic hair with goop's characteristically practical and non-shamey tone. You might want to laser; you might want to wax; you might not. It's all good.

But as against that open-minded rhetoric is the visual messaging of goop's media empire. For instance, accompanying both of goop's bikini-line articles are images that zoom our eyes in on a woman's bikini-clad pelvis. We can't see her face or her feet, but we can see her toned belly and thighs, the string of her tiny bikini being pulled suggestively away from her hip to show a glimmer of untanned, carefully groomed, hair-free skin.[20]

Neither picture would give any definitive sign of the woman's race, except for how both pictures, despite the way they're cropped to focus our gaze on the bikini line, show the lower edges of the model's long, flowing, smoothly textured wet hair floating into the picture. Like Paltrow's dry-brushing reel, this picture partners the ideal depilated body with the ideal long-haired head. The image captures, and sells, a kind of racially coded hair perfection. I have spent a lot of time looking at goop's Instagram. It shows variety, at least when it comes to skin tone. But there's never any body hair, ever, anywhere, that I have seen.

~

You might receive the same message about fur's (lack of) desirability, although admittedly in a very different (and differently upsetting) form, from looking at a much older advertisement than the one on goop. This advertisement was from 1893; it promoted a "Curio Hall," or what's more casually known, then and now, as a freak show. On the advertisement is a drawing of a "freak," who is "living proof of Darwinian theory: A MISSING LINK!" The drawing shows a young girl sitting cross-legged between two gorilla-like creatures. The announcement tells us she was "rescued" from "Siam." She is covered in darkly drawn body hair.

The name given to this girl by her "rescuers" was Krao. She performed as a freak (a word I will now stop using) for decades. This drawn advertisement is not the only image of her. The manager of the show, "Signor Farini," posed for a photograph with Krao to prove that she was real. It became so famous, as the hair historian Sarah McBride Gold has carefully demonstrated, that political cartoons could use it as an easy cultural reference—the kind of image everyone knew about whether or not they'd been to this particular curio show, just like everyone knows about Spears's baldness and Paltrow's vagina egg, even if they've never looked at goop or TMZ.

The famous portrait of Krao is shocking; when I first saw it, I audibly gasped in dismay (a stranger sitting next to me looked at me in alarm; when I showed her the portrait, we were both alarmed). In it, the white showman sits with the young girl in his lap. Their cheeks press intimately together. The girl's arms cling around his neck. In these ways, she's posed as a daughter might be.

But the rest of the image highlights their differences: Krao's not a daughter but rather something like a pet. Farini clutches one of the girl's calves awkwardly in a fisted grip; her other leg stretches (it's thin; she's only seven years old, and tiny) across his chest. He wears a carefully tailored suit; the little girl he clutches is naked. All her skin is exposed to the camera, to us. And so is all her body hair.

Krao made money because viewers believed she was only half evolved, "the half-way point in the evolution of Man from the Ape" as an advertisement promoting her show proclaimed.[21] Her captor has posed her closely to himself to highlight the difference between them: his civilization and whiteness, her barbaric animality. Her body hair is the main visible evidence of her half-evolved status.

Krao has dark hair covering her abdomen, arms, throat, and legs. The photographer carefully posed Krao's nude body to show that her leg hair grows fully over her thigh and hip. Her legs are carefully crossed to just barely conceal her genitals, while strongly implying that hair grows there too. The photograph has been processed to emphasize her dark hair, which is the main selling point of its advertised "scientific" claim about human evolution and difference. In 1892, the advertisement tells us, you could go to see Krao at a theater for ten cents.

~

What lesson can we take from comparing these two advertisements, goop's "Bikini Line Confidential" and Farini's ad for a befurred little girl whom he claims is a missing evolutionary link? I have not done the inflationary math to compare the value of ten cents in 1892 to the $55 (or four interest-free payments of $13.75) it costs to buy Fur "Fur Oil" on goop today. I'm not sure which is more expensive. But paying either amount seems to me a demonstration that you have some interest, place some value, in the same thing: proper body hair as a standard and measure of human, specifically womanly, status. You're showing that you believe body hair matters to status. And in a deep, hard-to-see way, you're literally buying into a pattern that links status, and hair, to race.

This may seem like a reach. After all, the goop advertisement for the Fur product line doesn't mention race explicitly at all. The advertisement of Krao's body hair (which is made to look like animal fur) promotes an evolutionary, rather than racial difference. But put together, these images show body hair as a key marker of what we might call, following Wellman, the "positionality" of humanness. On this spectrum of humanness, the very hairy are foreign, half evolved, hardly more than animal. The most human are the ones with the most ideal hair arrangement: smooth, abundant head hair; smooth, hairless bodies; and light skin.

In the nineteenth century, claims about race and hair—McBride traces several of them—were made explicitly. Such overtly racist claims might now seem out of date, except for how goop, and other wellness influencers and product lines, still sell the link between body hair and status today. Wellness culture, like nineteenth-century freak shows, sells and patrols—the patrolling is part of the selling—the belief that womanliness is a ladder, and that a bespoke whiteness boosts you toward a higher rung. One sign of whiteness that both goop and the freak show sell is hair that grows abundantly, healthily, but only in one place: the head.

That is the power lurking behind Gwyneth Paltrow's dry-brush ad, too, and the "incredible feeling" that dry brushing promotes. That incredible feeling, the one that's so hard to see, might best be called whiteness.

We usually think about whiteness, a racial term, as a physical reality or a social position rather than a feeling, or—to use a word that seems to suit the goop aesthetic—a "vibe." But we have to consider whiteness as a feeling to understand the considerable power of Gwyneth Paltrow, or her hair. Because part of whiteness *is* a feeling—indeed, it is the right feelings, the right desires, and the right desires about desirability. It is an abstraction rather than a reality. It can feel good to approach it, I know from experience. But you can never actually get there. You can only approach it on infinite loop. Which is good news for Paltrow, because as long as whiteness remains beyond our grasp, she can sell the hope of achieving it.

Here's what I would propose: Whiteness sometimes feels like a woman's perfectly smooth, hairless skin.

~

According to the profile I wrote about Paltrow in 2016, Paltrow's hair that day was "pulled back into a loose bun." She wore jeans and sandals and an off-the-shoulder top and looked so good in her gold necklaces that I bought two knock-offs myself.

In 2016 I was (although I didn't know it yet) beginning to get divorced, and Gwyneth Paltrow was finishing getting divorced. My still-unconscious uncoupling feelings were one of the reasons I was taking a lot of selfies and posting many of them to Instagram. I was trying to recognize myself, and I was trying to be recognized, and I was using pictures to help me aestheticize, or maybe anesthetize, the rupture my unruly desires would cause. Pre-divorce selfies are a thing I can now spot in other people's Instagram feeds. But I cannot spot them in Paltrow's, even though the first years of Paltrow's Instagram are also the years of her divorce. How could you spot them? What would distinguish them? Selfie recognition isn't just an event for Paltrow; it's her major product. This is partly why her Instagram feels to me both so desirable and so dangerous. Recognition is romantic, but in the real world there's no way around it: Rupture hurts.

And yet: Where do we see that hurt? Where are those Instagram shots? What's the context that makes wellness urgent? In the years since Paltrow and I started our Instagrams, the world has become more threatening to women, and goop's marketing empire has grown. The salves she sells have found an audience among progressive, high-end consumers in our disaster-ridden world. I am entirely sure that progressive middle-aged women are suffering from the fears our world intensifies: climate, class stratification, police and government brutality; the retraction of social support systems, health care, basic safety. As I write, all women in America—some much more quickly than others—feel ourselves slipping down a slope toward a world where our most intimate experiences are surveilled and controlled (perhaps this is why so many of us are fascinated with the fate of Britney Spears).

I know that progressive and privileged white women feel these dangers, because I am one of those women. But the dangers I perceive remain beyond the edges of what goop is willing to picture. The world of goop, like Paltrow's carefully maintained body hair, remains blissfully smoothed. This is not the only indication that her empire might not be the tool for sisterhood and solidarity she believes it to be. Rather, it is one sign among many that white wellness culture is a zone where politics, and collective struggle, get rerouted back into an essential solipsism.

"Self-care isn't selfish!" Paltrow has said in promotional ads on Instagram. Well. When white women spend hundreds on shaving cream and hair serum it isn't the same as when they divest from public schools, but it too is a kind of resource privatization. It's money spent to soothe and polish the self in a world getting rougher.

Self-care as a concept comes, famously, from the Black feminist intellectual tradition. Audre Lorde understood "care of the self" to be an act of "political warfare" because she was fighting against—and vividly describing and naming—South African apartheid, the effects of Reaganomics, and a cancer diagnosis all at the same time. In the context of lived pain, both systemic and cellular, Lorde praised the radical potential that could come from Black women teaching each other self-nurturing in a world that cared about them only as resources for extraction. "It requires an enormous amount of mutual, consistent support," Lorde wrote, "for us to be emotionally able to look straight into the face of the powers aligned against us and still do our work with joy."[22]

Gwyneth Paltrow, too, turned to self-care because of cancer. Her father, whom she loved deeply, died miserably from stomach cancer while she was helping to care for him. "While he was having radiation and the surgery and everything, and eating through a feeding tube," she told me in an interview, "I'm pushing this can of processed protein directly into his stomach, and I remember thinking, "Is this really healing? This seems weird. There's a bunch of chemicals in this shit.'"[23] Wellness was an answer for Paltrow, a way to understand a world that seemed full of hurt, and a medical system that seemed not to take her seriously. She, like Lorde, wanted her questions to be listened to. This was her path to founding goop.

"It's not a luxury," she insisted, about goop, in the same interview where she told me about her father's death. "It's aspirational." Lorde too was aspirational. But placed next to each other, you can see how Lorde and goop aspire toward materially different worlds.

~

How does a project that understands itself to be inclusive come to perpetuate the exclusions it claims to hate? Another way to ask this question might be: How is it that even as more and more prominent white women in America—Paltrow, Taylor Swift—have openly claimed feminist identities, many of the basic changes for which feminist politics have advocated become increasingly out of reach for most women?

I want to propose that goop, like much of white feminism, has relied on a kind of optical illusion, a trick, one that allowed it to see itself as advocating for "women," when in fact it was only advocating for *some* women. I don't think white feminists did it on purpose. They were falling for the trick too. But nevertheless, they relied on an understanding of womanhood that made many women's struggles, many women's questions and experiences, harder to see. Like body hair, those experiences were shaved away before goop's picturing began.

Goop's happy to include, in its feminist mission, anyone who considers herself a woman. For goop, womanliness isn't a matter of genetics. Instead, it's emotional, behavioral. Considering yourself a woman, in goop's Instagram visual logic, means admiring the discipline it takes to pursue a thin, elegant, "well" body. It means wanting to be seen as orderly, desiring to be desired. These qualities, not coincidentally, are the same as those coded white. Goop advocates on your behalf as long as you indicate, with your money and desire, that you see all the emotional and physical qualities associated with white womanhood—indeed, with *Anglo* white womanhood—as the peak of what women can achieve.

Once you concede to that set of expectations, it doesn't matter what racialized traits you've inherited, or if you're XX or XY. You have declared yourself willing to join the race that white femininity always is—a competition, a rat race. On this expansive track, anyone is welcome to take their mark. But on this seemingly open field, the legacies of race are preserved in the starting points we're assigned. White women aren't exactly closer to the finish line of white womanliness, because there is no finish line; no one ever really wins. But it still matters that white women can place themselves ahead of everyone else, in the lead.

Because body hair is such an intense symbol of a person's desire for womanliness, it becomes the perfect metaphor for the sleight of hand that goop has learned so perfectly to execute. To say that you mean well for women, that you want wellness for women, to say that women's selves are worth caring for, and then to take only a perfectly depilated women's body as the emblem of that cared-for woman, is to lift up a woman who has already agreed to have only the right desires about how her body should be. You are only taking care of the women who our racist, misogynistic, class-based culture defines as worthy.

And so, you are cutting off (placing beyond the bounds) your capacity to look at or question the historical power structures through which those definitions have been imposed.

Doing so, for goop, has both positive (or, "positive") and negative consequences. On the one hand, and on the upside for your profit margin, you will never have to give up or even acknowledge the inherently unjust privileges you have. Instead, you can enjoy how those values create the conditions for your luxurious celebration. But on the other hand, if, for all your questions, you're never questioning misogyny's basic values, you will never actually eradicate its harms. You can talk about inclusiveness all you want, but you will never become free.

~

The same month that I interviewed Paltrow, two significant cultural events took place.

First, Donald Trump shocked the nation by coming in a shared second at the Iowa caucuses, while Hillary Clinton nearly lost to Bernie Sanders. These results both felt like anomalies. The prevailing sense I had was that Clinton was bound to win the coming presidential election, and that no matter these early victories, Trump was bound to lose. It felt, culturally, like we had turned a corner toward a kind of racial equality, where many of the culturally powerful appeared to want a more equal world. When I interviewed Paltrow, I had not yet come to understand that the progressive, generous ways she was describing the world were completely compatible with the world for which Trump was building his campaign. Paltrow hated Trump. But like him, she was banking on luxury whiteness. Trump's body has little of Paltrow's perfect discipline. But what Trump offered the white women who voted for him was the promise that he could provide exactly the kind of luxury femininity that goop sells.

The second cultural event may seem minor in comparison. It's a picture on Paltrow's Instagram. For all her hair pictures, this one may be, surely inadvertently, her most astonishing picture of hair and race.

The photo features two children, two girls, walking and holding hands. Because this photo pictures these girls from behind, what we see of them is their hair. One girl's hair grows straight and blond down her back, just like her mother's—Gwyneth Paltrow's. The other girl's hair is dark and textured, forming a soft circle around her head. Or, as this girl's mother, Beyoncé, will describe such hair just a few hours later in her Superbowl halftime performance: "I like my baby heir with baby hair and afros." In her performance of *Formation*, Beyoncé did not wear an afro, but all of her in-formation dancers did. It was a celebration of black political aesthetics, marked by a lyrical and visual embrace of black hair. Beyoncé's dancers were not joining the whiteness rat race.

For this gorgeous celebration, for her display of the wrong hair desires, Beyoncé faced a heated backlash from a MAGA-fomenting country. The American electorate choose to see Beyoncé's celebration of Black femininity—of her daughter, her daughter's hair—as something that needed to be punished, squashed, put down.

Both girls in Paltrow's photo are adorable. Clearly this photo was posted with sincere love and pride. Here's what I wonder about it: When Paltrow posted this picture, did she see how the sweetness of the image sits alongside the risk it also shows, the unequal American playing field that these two beloved girls walk toward? If she didn't, what blindness kept her from it? And if she did, how does she square that knowledge with the actions she has taken since 2016: building an empire that enhances the cultural value of white, privileged femininity—an empire that is therefore dangerous to the sweet young girl whose hand her own daughter holds?

ICE QUEENS

Elsa's hair comes down at the end of the bridge. The song's bridge, that is—the melodic shift before the final soaring chorus. While singing the first two verses, Elsa has climbed a mountain. She's conjured a castle from her own cold hands. Now, standing in the shelter of her icy craft, she sings the lyrics she's been building toward: "One thought crystalizes like an icy blast / I'm never going back, the past is in the past."

As she reaches this key phrase, Elsa reaches toward her head and pulls away a jeweled comb that's been holding in place her carefully coiled hair. She flings away the comb. She reaches for her hair, pulling it loose from its tight, anxious, bun. A long, luxurious silver braid unravels over her shoulder. Radiant, released, she sings: "Let it go!"

You have heard this song. You probably have also seen it. The scene from the hit 2013 movie *Frozen* when the ice queen, Elsa, sings "Let It Go" has been viewed on YouTube more than nine hundred million times.[1] Even if you are not one of those viewers, you may have seen a little girl out in public—school, Halloween, the grocery story, the mall—dressed in one of the many million *Frozen* costumes Disney sold.[2] The song, and the imagery that accompanies the song, captured the imagination of American girls at the end of the Obama era. I have seen rooms full of girls standing in costume, singing along with Elsa: "It's time to see what I can do / To test the limits and break through. . . . no rules for me, I'm free." In this 2013 blockbuster, Disney chose the same symbol of freedom that Phillis Wheatley Peters had chosen two hundred years earlier—blond hair. Lo, as Wheatley Peters wrote, it moves divinely fair.

I too have sung along with Elsa. I've sung "Let It Go" when I felt myself raging and wanted its magical release. The song let me imagine an elemental power latent within me—a power I could let loose to destroy all the rule-making world. I could let down my hair. I could, especially, let go of my obligatory performance of a warmth I didn't feel.

Women are supposed to be warm. That's one of the most important rules. Smile, make people comfortable. Take children and other soft creatures into your lap, wrap those who are hurt in your arms. Offer them the heat of your body. Let your love flow like warm milk your body might one day make. Even women with no children and women who still are children are tasked with delivering a consistent maternal warmth. Few behaviors draw the world's judgment more quickly or completely than a woman being frigid, being cold.

What if we could just let that expectation go?

Elsa appeared in the middle of the Obama era. When I first heard little elementary school girls singing along, I felt we were headed into a better future, one shaped by the feminism I heard in its lyrics. Watching Elsa, I thought we could imagine an era when warmth and niceness weren't the standards by which powerful women were judged. It was such a beautiful fantasy. What if the world of warmth judged us, and we could, like Elsa, just turn away and slam the door? Wouldn't it be such a wonderful release to say, "I really don't care, do U?"

~

"I really don't care, do U?" These words appeared on the back of Melania Trump's jacket in 2018. Many watchers expressed their shock and disapproval. Trump (and here Trump will refer to Melania) was on her way to visit a Texas center for children, several of whom had been separated from their families due to her husband's immigration policies. Donald Trump for years had been aggressively callous, unconcerned with the actual people his policies and words harmed. But many Americans still held Trump to a higher standard. Was she really saying she didn't care about children? How appalling: especially appalling because she was a woman. Whatever else she did, she should care.

The First Lady was unapologetic, about both the jacket and the policies. "It was for the people and for the left-wing media who are criticizing me. I want to show them I don't care. You could criticize whatever you want to say. But it will not stop me to do what I feel is right."[3] The storm never bothered her anyway.

Picture after picture was snapped of Melania getting into and out of huge black SUVs. The pictures were supposed to be of the jacket, and the words. But they also included Melania's long hair, which flowed loose down her back, swung back and forth over her shoulders, blew in the breeze. Melania Trump was the first consistently long-haired First Lady in at least seventy-five years. She is the first First Lady to regularly appear in public with her long hair down—let go.

~

It's not just Trump. By now, Donald Trump's MAGA world has given prominent positions to many women, most of them white. And it has made long and straight white women's hair into one of the recognizable symbols of the MAGA movement. A short list of prominent Republican politicians and staffers whose hair echoes Trump's flowing style might include Kimberly Guilfoyle (ambassador to Greece and Donald Trump Jr.'s ex), Nancy Mace (representative from South Carolina), Kristi Noem (secretary of the Department of Homeland Security), and Lauren Boebert (representative from Colorado).

All these women in Donald Trump's close orbit chose, for their Instagram profiles, hair that falls in soft, carefully blown-out, gently highlighted waves. It's long hair that speaks to a nostalgia for the past, the era when America was great. But it's also distinctly modern and technological, dependent on curling irons and probably extensions. It's a look that shows what happens to the past when it moves into the "again." It's a style that's sometimes called "Utah curls," after the Mormon influencers who made them famous: long hair with a wave added with an iron halfway between the root and the ends, which are left alone. These curls are basically the opposite of Julia Roberts's *Pretty Woman* curls: They always emphasize that the wearer's hair has been curled but naturally grows straight. Like Fawcett's angelic feathers, Utah curls are a performance of the natural that requires time and commitment. In the time it takes the long hair to grow, the time to get the not-curly-curls just right, they express the wearer's long-term loyalty to Trump's look, to MAGA's cause.

And on MAGA women, they are everywhere, with only subtle variations. Pam Bondi (attorney general) and Karoline Leavitt (press secretary) have similar hair in slightly shorter versions, hitting at the shoulders rather than flowing over them. The younger women tend toward a middle part, while Trump's comes more on the side. Boebert wears glasses, Noem wears a cowboy hat. Trump's stepdaughter Ivanka sometimes shows similar soft curls; often, though, her cool blond has been straightened, much like Gwyneth Paltrow's.

It's not just the famous MAGA women—the women whose hair appears in the news: Long hair matters to the whole MAGA empire. Every woman who has appeared on the cover of *Evie* magazine—the Peter Thiel–funded publication that its founder Brittany Hugoboom refers to as "conservative Cosmo"—has the same MAGA flow. (So, predictably, does Hugoboom.) MAGA mothers train up their girls in the same styles. Take, for instance, one so-called "popular item" on Etsy: MAGA hair elastics. Made of stretchy fabric in shades of red, white, and blue, the hair elastics come in various prints. You can get GOP elephants, stars, and hearts, and the words "TRUMP 2024." "Makes a great stocking stuffer!" says one review. Presumably you'd gift them to someone who wanted to indicate—or whose mother wanted them to indicate—that they could pull back women's rights and their ponytail at the same time.

Or there are the official photos of Donald Trump signing his anti-trans discriminatory executive order 14201, "Keeping Men Out of Women's Sports." In these pictures, Donald Trump sits in the oval office with his own comb-over the punctum at the photo's center. Around him cluster women and girls, rows deep. They are, presumably, athletes—they want to excel, to win. Some wear sports jerseys. Some wear Siwa-style bows, some have curls, some have braids or ponytails. Almost all of them are white. And all of the white girls, all of them, have long, ready-to-flow hair.[4]

I love long, flowing hair. The real, physical object of long women's hair seems to me a symbol of womanly power, womanly appreciation. But I look at Trump and all these long-haired MAGA women and executive order witness girls, all the way to the littlest one, and I find myself asking: How could you possibly be so cold?

~

I'm not against Elsa, or her beautiful rejection of the past. I love her braid. But one of the lessons I take from the horror I feel when I watch a Kristi Noem press conference is how much she, like me, felt drawn to a long-hair fantasy of womanly power. Both of us probably sang along with Elsa. Both of us wanted to feel free.

I don't think Trump or Noem or Hugoboom drew their long hairstyles directly from Elsa, obviously. Noem's glossy "Utah curls" aren't the same as Elsa's icy braid. But I do think Elsa's anthem, its hair rhetoric, helps us understand something about the flowing feminine locks that style MAGA's regressive policies. Elsa helps us see how impoverished white women's fantasies of freedom sometimes are.

Collectively, if not individually, white women have seemingly come to conflate the emotional burdens imposed by the patriarchy with the compassion demanded by a feminism based on collective caregiving. It's true that the patriarchy has unjustly tasked white women with posing as the benevolent heart of white American policies. This emotional demand is very different from the feminist mandate to act in solidarity with other women. But solidarity, for many white women, *does* require sacrifice—it means giving up a privileged position, a moral status. It turns out that's something many white women don't want to do. We want to free ourselves of the burdens of compassion while still luxuriating in care ourselves. Like MAGA hair, we want to be let loose and kept up all at once.

And at the most extreme versions, white women enact and endorse Trump's brutal policies—they withdraw resources, care, warmth, justice, from the world's most vulnerable. They misinterpret this brutality as a justifiable rejection of the unfair affective demands women have long faced. According to this MAGA logic, letting go of the caregiving and the solidarity work of feminism can feel—and, with long hair, can look—like the most feminist action of all.

Trump's world seduces white women with many promises, but maybe the most pernicious is the fantasy that we'd be able to keep thinking about ourselves without apologizing for or even recognizing our privileges. That white women's hair has become one of MAGA's most recognizable symbols shows us how complicit with privilege white women's hair remains.

CODA

CRITICAL HAIR STUDIES

As I reach the end of this book, I'm confronting a question that many people have asked me: What's the right thing for white women's hair to do?

Here's one of my favorite things I do with my hair. At holidays, I sit on the floor in front of one of my nieces. I hold my head still against the gentle resistance of her brush, the tug of her hands looping and smoothing as she spirals a braid around the crown of my head, twists it in a bun. If she says "pin," I hold a single bobby pin up for her easy reach. I feel its metal slide as she tightens the coils against my scalp. I used to be better at braiding than either of my nieces; now I am not. Both nieces have gentle firmness as they pull and separate. It's a skill I have not managed to teach either of my sons, despite their own long hair. They might, but don't, want their own hair brushed and braided. They might, but don't, worry about torn hair. My sons can braid; I made sure to teach them. I taught them how, every time the hair overlaps, you have to run your hand all the way down the section so that the mass of *hairs* keep working like *hair*. But there are other braiding lessons I didn't quite know how to teach them, because no one had needed to put those lessons into words for me. I don't articulate them to my nieces.

They know how to find a balance of gentle and firm because they've felt pleasure and pain on their own heads.

My hair, unlike that of either of my nieces, always presents itself as a tangle. Their hair grows blond and thick, like my grandmother's, their great grandmother's (also like their mother's, my sister-in-law). I have spent the last twenty years of my life chemically treating my hair so it looks blonder and—if not thicker—at least fuller. "Volumized." My hair's bleached ends split and knot. It grows thin in its last several inches. When my nieces do my hair, they are learning old crafts, how to braid and brush. They are also learning bigger lessons: how we take care of each other. And they are learning, with their hands, the damage I do to my own hair in my efforts to make it blonder—like theirs.

~

So often, women go to hairstylists hoping for transformation. We hope that with some magical move of scissors, a bit of bleach or some dye, problems far beyond our hair might be solved. Our confidence boosted, our reputations improved. Good hair days, and good life days, all the rest of our days! I feel this hope, and maybe you do too, every time I sit down in my stylist's (her name is Ashley Garcia) chair.

It's not surprising, in this context, to feel the hope that a hairstyle could also solve the problems raised by our hair itself. I, too, would like a hairstyle that could sever my hair from the complexity of my white privilege. So often over the last many years, I've wondered if there was an easy hair fix. There doesn't seem to be. Mary Lou Retton's hair was cut short; Gwyneth Paltrow's grows long. Neither are free of danger. Even these beautiful hours spent with my nieces are full of mixed messages.

The problem is this: Hair is full of power. Power is always political. It's a resource. So the question of what to do with your hair, or mine, can't be separated from a larger ethical dilemma: What should anyone do with the power they have? So many options. Listen, lead, protect, proclaim. Reign. Here I sit cross-legged among my most beloved girls: a crown of bleached-gold hair braided around my head. This crown is real. I have to reckon with it the authority it gives me, with my nieces, and in the world.

This book has aimed to untangle the different kinds of power white women have used their hair to seize. I've tried to show how women's personal hair decisions are not just political; they're also historical. A resource like long, flowing, smooth hair might gain or lack an exchange value in one political context (for instance, the end of '70s counterculture) that might change in another (for instance, Trump's cabinet). That means that white women have gained power with short hair and long, with bleach and with braids. The historical specificity determining the power at play in every hair decision means that no one haircut, no particular approach, will consistently wash the drama of white femininity out of my hair, or yours. The power a woman's hair has is too context specific. And whiteness itself is a powerful collective fantasy backed by very real infrastructures. No one person's hair decisions will knock those structures down.

But the limits on our personal power don't absolve us of responsibility. If America's institutions of "serious" knowledge making, like the white men who founded and still often sustain them, regularly fail to offer methodologies that consider the daily practices of women's power, women's lives offer their own skilled training in understanding hair's power. We should recognize this training as such.

So rather than proscribing a specific hairstyle, what I can recommend is a particular kind of hair *study*—what I often call critical hair studies. Critical hair studies means looking at the media representations of women around us—as I have modeled in this book—and remembering, always, that if a woman's hair grabs our attention, that grab is a function of power reaching out to you. The same ideas I've used to help us understand what hair is *doing* can help us see how to do hair better. So, to return to my opening schema: Hair conjures the *natural*, it *expresses* desires and values, and it is *temporal*. These terms give us a set of questions:

- What ideas of "nature" does your hair reinforce? Who benefits from those ideas? Who's excluded? How does creating a sense of something "natural" conceal economic privilege, or cultural/social capital?
- What desires does your hair express? What vision of beauty and style? In what currency, what social standards, does your hair invest?
- What kind of time does your hair take or represent? What does the temporality of your hair say about its relation to your own resources, time, and place?

These questions can apply to your hair; they can also help us understand the hair in the media around us, the hair we're being taught to desire. Look at, for instance, long MAGA hair through this framework. Thick and lustrous, always down, this hair performs a robust sense of thickness, of internal correctness—a unified vision of what "natural" hair should be. The consistent hair shows a fully desired embrace of that particular standard. No roots ever show, and no limpness. Any variation in thickness is remedied, clearly, with extensions, even though we never hear these women talk about their extensions. This hair visibly requires a huge commitment of time. This hair, in other words, is a hoard of resources in perfect replication of their resource-hoarding policies enacted in our world. You can never look at these women without seeing how willingly they endorse Trump's narrow vision—expensive, compliant—of what a woman should be. Only within this narrow image can they be angry or powerful. Trump can claim all day long to be "protecting women," but MAGA hair shows us a different story. The only women he will protect are women who sacrifice their individuality, and an honest accounting of how they use their resources, in order to protect him.

Or take my own hair, my long braid twisted by my nieces up on my head, dark and gray roots clearly showing against my bleached highlights. I offer no image of MAGA polish. No one looking at me would think I'm naturally blond.

But everyone looking can see that I think, if ambivalently, that blond is beautiful. Looking at me, you might guess that I take great pleasure in my long, bleached hair and its close proximity to a powerful social currency, and also that I'm wary of those pleasures. Your guess would be right.

~

The ethics of power remain difficult to parse for everyone, but they pose specific problems for American white women, who have historically found themselves in an aslant relationship to power's most overt operations. We have so much power. But when we measure our experiences against those of white men, our powers can sometimes look paltry, insignificant, only ("only") second class. Looking at our power from this blinkered perspective, it's easy to think of our social position as one of weakness. It can make heightening the forcefulness of our hair—which we might do in many different ways, depending on context—feel "empowering." I've taught young women in college classrooms for twenty years, and almost all of them, regardless of geography or social class or political outlook, have been taught that their empowerment is inevitably a good thing. You go girl, morning network television tells us! We see women in power with beautiful hair, with expensive extensions, cuts, and dye jobs. "You're worth it," the hair ads tell us. Won't your hair feel good? If it feels good, isn't it?

But not all "empowerment" grants the same powers, or to the same people. Something we might call "empowerment washing" happens throughout the worlds of art, media, and politics, whereby art or media touts its capacity to empower women, while mostly reproducing familiar old hierarchies. Just because women—white women or otherwise—have historically been denied some kinds of power doesn't mean that all their deployments of power are ethical. A woman having power might be good for women . . . but it might not. A television show or a social media account might claim to be "empowering," but if it hides the time, care, or money a woman's "natural-looking" hair really takes, it's erasing its ability to show what her embodied life is really like. It's basing the power it offers on a fantasy, or a lie. Especially when the power a white woman gains comes in the form of white male approval and attention, as the MAGA ice queens' power does from Trump, women collectively are most likely to lose. Our decisions about power should be guided not only by the pleasures we hope to experience, but also by the world we want to create.

White women are widely and rightfully considered unreliable narrators of our own experience, and it's true that we are skilled at redeploying to our advantage the lies of which our white femininity is made. But if some meaningful reconfiguration is to come in what white femininity can mean and do, white women need to practice better understanding what our hair has taught us. Just as we have practiced ponytails and buns and braids and twists, we need to practice reading how our hair has created harmful fantasies and how it has constrained our lived realities, perpetuating the hierarchies of our world. We need to practice using our hair's social power, as we should practice using all our powers, for collective rather than private good.

I hope that when my nieces touch my hair, they're learning something from my ambivalence and damage about all the ways that power isn't pure. It's a negotiation, and it always will be. I also hope that they are learning, through this careful time I spend braiding and brushing *their* hair, that *they* are a resource. I am sinking my time into caring for them, in the hopes that they are learning strategies for caring for all the women they will encounter. I am expressing how much I love them, and their natures, however those natures grow. I am teaching them about the tools they have, and that their hair is one of those tools. I hope I am teaching them to use those tools with care.

ACKNOWLEDGMENTS

One Christmas when I was very little, my Uncle Jeff gave my Grammy a framed print of a painting by Edgar Degas. In the painting, one woman brushes another woman's long red hair. As soon as she unwrapped the painting, Grammy—who was not inclined to warm displays of sentimental appreciation—gasped. I remember it *perfectly*. Her eyes flooded, full of gratitude. Jeff had gotten her the painting because he knew it would remind her of some of her most precious childhood memories: having her own thick hair washed and brushed by *her* mother, who had died suddenly and too young, and whom she still urgently missed. Grammy hung the painting over her sofa, where it stayed the rest of my childhood.

The painting confused me. I knew Grammy loved it and that it reminded her of love. I had a hard time squaring Grammy's tender feelings with what I felt I could clearly see in that painting—which was one woman brushing another's hair *way too hard*. What was I learning about my much beloved grandmother, her hard-working mother, how love worked between them? The painting, this work of art, helped me understand something about the lessons in power and pleasure that Grammy, when she brushed *my* hair (gently, most of the time), was trying to teach me.

This is just one of many stories from my own life, and from many other women's lives, that are the foundation of what this book knows. Storytelling and hair brushing and holiday memories and art/media sharing are the kinds of research it's hard to acknowledge in footnotes or a bibliography. So I am acknowledging all the skull-based knowledge and painting/movie/magazine-passing wisdom of the women around me here: Thank you to everyone who told me stories about their hair, to everyone who brushed my hair and who let me brush their hair, and who texted me pictures of hair. This list, my friends, is *deep*. But I'd especially like to thank Carolyn Bassett Madison, Lindsley Armstrong Smith, Sherry Mesle Morrain, Nancy Hiles Johnson, Ann Mesle, Ashley Garcia, Mel Micir, Zelda Roland, Nicole Neal, Virginia Jackson, Koritha Mitchell and all the participants in the C19 femininities seminar, Barbara Hiles Mesle and her coven, Abbey Studer, Norma Derry Hiles, Kay Mesle, Nora Parker Mesle, Charley Mesle, and Braid Academy.

Huge thanks to my agent Tanya Mckinnon, who believed me when I told her, "This is the book!" even though it definitely *wouldn't* have been a book without her. Our many conversations as I was drafting *Tangled*'s proposal are woven through so much of the final story it tells, particularly the chapter about Gwyneth Paltrow.

One of Tanya's gifts was connecting me to Amy Caldwell, my editor, who was the perfect editor for this book. Our conversations about writing and women and hair and microgenerations offered pleasures and insights way beyond what the final manuscript could contain. Thanks to everyone at Beacon: Caitlyn Meyer, Thea Smith, Marcy Barnes, Louis Roe, Susan Lumenello, Molly Woodward, Brittany Wallace, and the designers who worked on the cover.

Phil Maciak read some of the very first paragraphs that would become this book and was its stalwart companion all the way to the end. Thank you so much for my hat, and for everything.

No conversation about hair is ever purely scholarly in the conventional sense, but scholarship can make hair conversations better. I'd like to thank Elizabeth L. Block, Glenn Amandson, Sarah Anne Carter, the artists Shani Crowe and Melanie Bilenker, and the many people who I don't know personally but whose scholarship I cite in this book. One of these I must cite by name: Paulette M. Caldwell, whose fiercely powerful work I have returned to time and time again.

Ashley Garcia styled my hair through a pregnancy, a divorce, a remarriage ("Sarah, wear it *down*"), and all the life in between. I am grateful to her for taking care of my literal roots. Thanks to Vanessa Arce-Mendez and Lydia Guido, owners of the Beauty Box.

Thanks to the library staff at the Edendale and Echo Park branches of the Los Angeles Public Library. I'm so grateful to them and to this beautiful institution for supplying me with endless gymnast and celebrity memoirs, encouraging smiles, and amused questions.

Thanks to Amor Ayala Luna, Sophia Hammerle, and Ruby Telles, for your support and feedback in the writing and researching of this book. Thanks to USC's Gender Studies Department for making space for these powerhouse students and thinkers, specifically Hye Min for bringing them my way.

Thanks to Phil Maciak, Sarah Ahrens, Morgan Fahey, Marie Rutkoski, Arielle Zibrak, Sophia Hamerle, Josh Kamensky, and Caleb Smith, for careful eyes, ongoing conversations, and for last-minute readerly assists. Lauren Teukolsky sent hair products and clear instructions to my house at one moment when they were desperately needed.

Thanks to all the women who remind me every day—in texts, jokes, cocktails, long walks, late nights, hard questions, easy questions, fashion recommendations, tears, hair holding of various kinds—that love is a material practice. Kati, this especially means you.

Thanks to my amazing family, in all its iterations and generations. This is a book about women, but I am lucky to come from a family with excellent men: my wonderful father, brother, uncles, chosen uncles, and grandfathers. Caleb, Elliot, Asher, Van, and Luna: You are the best possible pack. I love you, and I love that all of you have strong opinions about your own hair. Caleb, thank you for all the ways you lift me up. I love every day I spend writing and thinking and star watching with you. More of this good life!

This book is dedicated to my mother, Dr. Barbara Hiles Mesle. It's so hard to imagine a different world, a better one, while also doing the daily work of caring for people who live in *this* world. But that is indeed the work of feminism, and it is work at which my mother excels, more than almost anyone I know. I am so grateful to my whole family, my mother especially, for always modeling for me that the only way forward is to keep your eyes on the stars and your feet here on earth, getting muddy.

NOTES

INTRODUCTION: **DISCIPLINE AND PONYTAIL**

1. Ruth Wilson Gilmore, *Golden Gulag: Prisons, Surplus, Crisis, and Opposition in Globalizing California* (Berkeley: University of California Press, 2007), 50.
2. Jasmine Nichole Cobb, *New Growth: The Art and Texture of Black Hair* (London: Duke 1.
3. Michelle Obama and Meredith Koop, *The Look* (New York: Crown, an imprint of Penguin Random House, 2025).
4. Priya Elan, "Swimming Caps for Natural Black Hair Ruled Out of Olympic Games," *The Guardian*, July 2, 2021, https://www.theguardian.com/sport/2021/jul/02/swimming-caps-for-natural-black-hair-ruled-out-of-olympic-games-alice-dearing.
5. Paulette M. Caldwell, "A Hair Piece: Perspectives on the Intersection of Race and Gender,"
6. *Duke Law Journal* 1991, no. 2 (1991): 383, https://doi.org/10.2307/1372731.
7. Phillis Wheatley Peters, "Liberty and Peace, a poem. / By Phillis Peters," Evans Early American Imprint Collection, University of Michigan Library Digital Collections, https://name.umdl.umich.edu/N14772.0001.001, accessed September 13, 2025.
8. Alice Walker, "In Search of Our Mother's Gardens: The Creativity of Black Women in the South," *Ms.*, May 1974, https://msmagazine.com/2023/04/13/in-search-of-our-mothers-gardens-creativity-black-women-south/, accessed September 13, 2025.

CHAPTER 1: **BO DEREK'S CORNROWS**

1. Steve Lohr, "Stars Rise Quickly in Poster Boom," *New York Times*, February 2, 1980, https://timesmachine.nytimes.com/timesmachine/1980/02/02/112062428.html?pageNumber=27, accessed September 13, 2025.
2. Lauren Michele Jackson, *White Negroes: When Cornrows Were in Vogue . . . and Other Thoughts on Cultural Appropriation* (Boston: Beacon Press, 2019), 21–23.

3. Kim Kardashian (@kimkardashian), "BO WEST," Instagram, January 29, 2018, https://www.instagram.com/p/BejDGW4FRRS/?hl=en, accessed September 13, 2025.
4. Chimamanda Ngozi Adichie, *Americanah* (New York: Knopf, 2013).
5. *In My Own Words*, season 1, episode 2, "Bo Derek: In Her Own Words," Reelz TV, 2020, https://ondemand.spectrum.net/tv/reelz/18510632/bo-derek-in-my-own-words/.
6. Bo Derek (@boderek), "Hey! It's just a hairstyle I wore in the movie '10,'" X, January 31, 2018, https://x.com/boderek/status/958801333355556864.
7. Max Boot, *Reagan: His Life and Legend* (New York: Liveright, 2024).
8. Ronald Reagan Presidential Library and Museum, "Ronald Reagan's Filmography," https://www.reaganlibrary.gov/reagans/ronald-reagan/ronald-reagans-filmography, accessed September 29, 2025.
9. Cay Brown, "Why Did Ronald Reagan's Hair Stay So Dark and Full, Even into His Nineties?" Quora, https://www.quora.com/Why-did-Ronald-Reagans-hair-stay-so-dark-and-full-even-into-his-nineties, accessed September 29, 2025.
10. Ronald Reagan Presidential Library and Museum, "Military Service of Ronald Reagan," https://www.reaganlibrary.gov/reagans/ronald-reagan/military-service-ronald-reagan, accessed November 23, 2025.
11. *The Last Outpost*, directed by Lewis R. Foster (1951, Paramount Pictures), https://www.imdb.com/title/tt0043725/.
12. These thoughts are indebted to Cheryl Harris. Cheryl I. Harris, "Whiteness as Property," *Harvard Law Review* 106, no. 8 (1993): 1707–91, https://doi.org/10.2307/1341787.
13. Paulette M. Caldwell, "A Hair Piece: Perspectives on the Intersection of Race and Gender," *Duke Law Journal* 1991, no. 2 (1991): 383, https://doi.org/10.2307/1372731.
14. Patricia Hill Collins, *Black Feminist Thought: Knowledge, Consciousness, and the Politics of Empowerment*, 10th-anniversary rev. ed. (New York: Routledge, 2000), 130.
15. In Collins's words, "[T]he visibility of Black bodies themselves reinscribes the hypervisibility of Black men and women's alleged sexual deviancy." Collins, *Black Feminist Thought*, 130.
16. Shirley Anne Tate, "Race and Ethnicity," in *A Cultural History of Hair in the Modern Age*, ed. Geraldine Biddle-Perry (London: Bloomsbury Academic, 2018), 116.
17. Caldwell, "A Hair Piece," 384.
18. Cicely Tyson, *Just as I Am: A Memoir* (New York: HarperCollins, 2021), 190.
19. *In My Own Words*, season 1, episode 2, "Bo Derek: In Her Own Words," Reelz TV, 2020, https://ondemand.spectrum.net/tv/reelz/18510632/bo-derek-in-my-own-words/.

20. Mark Malkin, "Bo Derek Looks Back on Her Career, Past Relationships and Acting with Trump," *Variety*, August 14, 2020, https://variety.com/2020/film/news/bo-derek-linda-evans-10-donald-trump-1234734836/.
21. Mik Awake, "What Cornrows Mean," *GQ*, June 28, 2019, https://www.gq.com/story/what-cornrows-mean. Previous versions of this article provided a dead link to an article of *People* magazine. As I have revised this chapter, I have noticed that Google's AI assisted search provides inconsistent results, reflecting perhaps an inconsistent digital record. Eunice Ann Collins's inactive Twitter account can be found at https://x.com/eunicecollins?lang=en.
22. Akatidanse, "Bo Derek had time today," Lipstick Alley, January 31, 2018, https://www.lipstickalley.com/threads/bo-derek-had-time-today.1416907/page-2.
23. Jackson, *White Negroes*, 1–6.
24. *Sneak Previews with Roger Ebert and Gene Siskel*, "10 (1979) movie review," YouTube, https://youtu.be/k-aBS5twrTc?si=vh6smTKZMQWWKkTJ, posted June 6, 2019.
25. Chadwick Roberts, "The Politics of Farrah's Body: The Female Icon as Cultural Embodiment," *Journal of Popular Culture* 37, no. 1 (2003): 87, https://doi.org/10.1111/1540-5931.00055.
26. "The '10' Bo Derek Braided Hairstyle in High Demand in 1979," CBS 8 San Diego, YouTube, https://youtu.be/8YYM-18txQ4?si=i15j8yINrvtLPcVA, posted October 14, 2020.
27. Tressie McMillan Cottom, *Thick: And Other Essays* (New York: The New Press, 2019), 58.
28. Steve Lohr, "Stars Rise Quickly in Poster Boom," *New York Times*, February 2, 1980, https://timesmachine.nytimes.com/timesmachine/1980/02/02/112062428.html?pageNumber=27, accessed September 13, 2025.
29. Rogers v. American Airlines, Inc., 527 F. Supp. 229 (S.D.N.Y. 1981) https://law.justia.com/cases/federal/district-courts/FSupp/527/229/2369655/.
30. Hoover Institution, "Abraham D. Sofaer," https://www.hoover.org/profiles/abraham-d-sofaer, accessed September 29, 2025.

MANIC PANIC

1. Sarah Laskow, "Manic Panic Isn't Just a Hair Dye Brand: It Was the First Punk Store in America," *Atlas Obscura*, November 4, 2016, https://www.atlasobscura.com/articles/manic-panic-isnt-just-a-hair-dye-brand-it-was-the-first-punk-store-in-america.
2. The Bellomos' site, Tish & Snooky, https://www.tishandsnooky.com/queensofcolor. Among places where Lauper praises Manic Panic: Mackenzie Wagoner, "Cyndi Lauper's 5 Rules for Girls Who Just

Wanna Have Fun with Beauty," *Vogue*, June 24, 2016, https://www.vogue.com/article/cyndi-lauper-beauty-rules-hair-color-makeup; Shammara Lawrence, "Cyndi Lauper Reveals Why She Still Loves Having Pink Hair," *Allure*, December 12, 2017, https://www.allure.com/story/cyndi-lauper-pink-hair-hsn-touch-of-cyn.

3. *Billboard*, "The 100 Best Album Covers of All Time: 2. The Beatles, 'Abbey Road' (1969)," August 7, 2023, https://www.billboard.com/photos/best-album-covers-of-all-time-6715351/99-2-the-beatles-abbey-road-1969-album-art-billboard-1240/.

CHAPTER 2: **MARY LOU RETTON'S BOB**

1. Mary Lou Retton and Bela Karolyi with John Powers, *Mary Lou: Creating an Olympic Champion* (New York: McGraw-Hill, 1986), 16.
2. Retton and Karolyi, *Mary Lou*, 1.
3. Rachael Denhollander, *What Is a Girl Worth? My Story of Breaking the Silence and Exposing the Truth About Larry Nassar and USA Gymnastics* (Carol Stream, IL: Tyndale Momentum, 2019).
4. Erin Blakemore, "How Gymnastics Became a Deeply Beloved Olympic Sport," *National Geographic*, July 15, 2021, https://www.nationalgeographic.com/history/article/how-gymnastics-became-a-deeply-beloved-olympic-sport.
5. Retton and Karolyi, *Mary Lou*, 79.
6. Retton and Karolyi, *Mary Lou*, xiv.
7. Irvin Molotsky, "Five Receive Kennedy Center Honors for 1984," *New York Times*, December 3, 1984, https://www.nytimes.com/1984/12/03/arts/five-receive-kennedy-center-honors-for-1984.html.
8. Here are the hair instructions given on the 2018 DCC tryout FAQ: "Hair should be worn down and in a current hairstyle that compliments your features. Make sure your hair does not hide your face. You may call Tangerine Salon, our official hair care partner, at 972-393-9200 to schedule an appointment to get the look and style that best suits you for your audition. Click here for a list of services and pricing." Dallas Cowboys, "Cheerleaders: FAQ," June 1, 2018, https://www.dallascowboys.com/news/cheerleaders-faq, accessed September 8, 2025.
9. Denhollander, *What Is a Girl Worth?*, 18.
10. Lesley Visser, "US Gymnasts Hailed; Coach Sees Silver' for New Men's Olympic Team," *Boston Globe*, June 4, 1984.
11. Renee V. Lucas, "Fashion—The Crowning Glory," *Philadelphia Daily News*, April 11, 1984.
12. Robbie Andrew, "Busy-ness Retton: Athlete and 'Businesswoman,'" *Sun Sentinel*, May 1, 1985.
13. Bela Karolyi and Nancy Ann Richardson. *Feel No Fear: The Power, Passion, and Politics of a Life in Gymnastics* (New York: Hyperion, 1996), 147.

14. Ronald Reagan Presidential Library, Trip to California: Breakfast with U.S. Olympic Team Medalist at the Century Plaza Hotel in Los Angeles (cut camera), August 13, 1984, Master Tape #128, https://catalog.archives.gov/id/137880490.
15. Ronald Reagan President Library, Trip to Texas, Victory '84 Fundraising Dinner, October 2, 1984, https://www.reaganlibrary.gov/archives/photo/c24764-01; Elizabeth Kastor/*Washington Post*, "Cashing In on That Winning Smile Those Who Assumed, Once the Olympics Were Over, That It Would Be Goodbye, Mary Lou, Can Guess Again," *Newsday*, October 23, 1985.
16. Max Boot, *Reagan: His Life and Legend* (New York: Liveright, 2024), 466, 514.
17. Boot, *Reagan*, 514.
18. Rick Perlstein, *Nixonland: The Rise of a President and the Fracturing of America*. (New York: Scribner, 2008), 114.
19. Boot, *Reagan*, 399.
20. Retton and Karolyi, *Mary Lou*, 21–22.
21. Retton and Karolyi, *Mary Lou*, 82.
22. *Simone Biles Rising*, directed by Katie Walsh, Netflix, 2024, https://www.netflix.com/title/81700902.
23. Boot, *Reagan*, 477.
24. Vidal Sassoon, *Vidal: The Autobiography* (London: Macmillan, 2010).
25. Paddy Calistro, "The Man Behind Wash 'n' Wear Hair," *Los Angeles Times*, February 26, 1993.
26. Caroline Cox and Lee Widdows, *Hair and Fashion* (London: V&A, 2005), 49.
27. Kerri Strug and John P. Lopez, *Landing on My Feet: A Diary of Dreams* (Kansas City: Andrews McMeel, 1997), 173.
28. Strug and Lopez, *Landing on My Feet*, 176.

CHAPTER 3: **ANNE SHIRLEY'S CARROTS**

1. Margaret Atwood, "Nobody Ever Did Want Me," *The Guardian*, March 28, 2008, https://www.theguardian.com/books/2008/mar/29/fiction.margaretatwood.
2. Toni Morrison, "Foreword," *The Bluest Eye* (New York: Vintage, 2007), xi. Morrison here speaks specifically about the racializing project of culture as I will explore in what follows; she seeks to take a girl child to understand the "demonization of a whole race."
3. Robin Levinson-King, "Anne of Green Gables: The most popular redhead in Japan," *BBC News*, May 8, 2017, https://www.bbc.com/news/world-us-canada-39809999.
4. American Girl Dolls, "Our Story," https://www.americangirl.com/pages/our-story, accessed December 13, 2024.

5. Denise Martin, "Megan Follows on *Anne of Green Gables* and Her Racy New CW Series, *Reign*," *Vulture*, October 17, 2013, https://www.vulture.com/2013/10/megan-follows-on-reign-anne-green-gables.html.
6. "Americans Love CBC's Anne: [FINAL Edition]," February 21, 1986, *The Gazette*, D1; Clifford Terry, "PBS Takes In the 'Green Gables' Tale," *Chicago Tribune*, February 21, 1986.
7. Harriet, Van Horne, "An Orphan's Idyll on PBS," *Newsday*, February 15, 16, 1986.
8. *Out* magazine in 2015 on the legacy of the sexual rebellion Madonna enabled: Nathan Smith, "Still Virginal," *Out*, March 10, 2015, https://www.out.com/music/2015/3/10/virgin-madonna-30th-anniversary.
9. Melanie Rawn, *Dragon Prince: Book I* (New York: DAW Books, 1988), 398.
10. Laura Ingalls Wilder, *Little House in the Big Woods* (New York: Harper & Row, 1973), 161.
11. Wilder, *Little House in the Big Woods*, 167.
12. The most significantly red-headed biblical figure is Esau, son of Isaac and Rebecca, and twin of Jacob. According to the King James translation, Esau "came out red, all over like an hairy garment" (Genesis 25:25), and his thick red hair matters in several episodes of his life.
13. Ruth Mellinkoff, "Judas's Red Hair and the Jews," *Journal of Jewish Art* 9 (1982). Also quoted in B. Ayres and S. E. Maier, *A Vindication of the Redhead* (Springer International, 2021), 202; and J. C. Harvey, *Red: A History of the Redhead* (Black Dog & Leventhal, 2015), 72.
14. Tressie McMillan Cottom (@tressiemcpd), "My Gen-X Molly Ringwald Theory of Pop Culture," Instagram, https://www.instagram.com/reel/DE7_jbWJqUU/?utm_source=ig_web_copy_link&igsh=MzRlODBiNWFlZA==.
15. John J. O'Connor, "'Anne of Green Gables' on Public TV," *New York Times*, February 14, 1986, https://www.nytimes.com/1986/02/14/arts/anne-of-green-gables-on-public-tv.html.
16. Nick Coleman and Staff Writer, "Critic's Choice," *Minneapolis Star Tribune*, February 17, 1986; Harriet Van Horne, "An Orphan's Idyll on PBS," *Newsday*, Feb 15, 1986, 16.
17. Noel Holston, "A Movie Steeped in Old-Time Romance," *Orlando Sentinel*, March 26, 1986.
18. Angela Y. Davis, *Women, Race, and Class* (New York: Knopf Doubleday Publishing Group, 2011), 12.
19. On bonnet shame, see Arielle Zibrak, *Avidly Reads Guilty Pleasures* (New York: NYU Press, 2021).
20. Robin Bernstein, *Racial Innocence: Performing American Childhood from Slavery to Civil Rights* (New York: New York University Press, 2011), 7.

21. Filmmaker Dream Studios, *Carrots! A Compilation*, YouTube, posted June 13, 2017, https://www.youtube.com/watch?v=mguQ-gkEfBo.
22. bell hooks, "The Oppositional Gaze: Black Female Spectators," in *Film Theory: Critical Concepts in Media and Cultural Studies*, ed. K. J. Shepherdson, Philip Simpson, Andrew Utterson (Oxfordshire, UK: Routledge, 2004), 233–48.

FARM BALLERINAS

1. Hannah Neeleman (@ballerinafarm), https://www.instagram.com/ballerinafarm/, accessed September 11, 2025.

CHAPTER 4: **JULIA ROBERTS'S PRETTY WOMAN CURLS**

1. Sheila Benson, "Pretty Woman: Roberts' Legs, a Cold Heart," *Los Angeles Times*, March 23, 1990.
2. Steve Pond, "Pretty Woman, Indeed," *Rolling Stone*, August 9, 1990, pp. 46–47, 49–50.
3. If you're interested in the question of Roberts's natural hair—which, yes, I am interested in the question—you can look at several pictures of a young Julia Roberts made available to you by the wonders of the internet, and in some of them she looks more or less red, more or less curly.
4. Leigh Claire La Berge, *Scandals and Abstractions: Financial Fiction of the Long 1980s* (New York: Oxford University Press, 2014); 5. Michelle Chihara, "What We Talk About When We Talk About Finance," *Los Angeles Review of Books*, September 18, 2015, https://lareviewofbooks.org/article/what-we-talk-about-when-we-talk-about-finance/.
5. Heather Schwedel, "The Great Felicity Reckoning," *Slate*, April 30, 2024, https://slate.com/culture/2024/04/felicity-tv-show-keri-russell-dear-ringer-suits.html.
6. For a history of hair and trials regarding racial identity, see Walter Johnson, "The Slave Trader, the White Slave, and the Politics of Racial Determination in the 1850s," *The Journal of American History* 87, no. 1 (2000): 13–38, https://doi.org/10.2307/2567914.
7. Jazmine Hughes, "Viola Davis, Inside Out," *New York Times*, April 12, 2022, https://www.nytimes.com/2022/04/12/magazine/viola-davis.html.
8. Carol Channing, *Just Lucky I Guess: A Memoir of Sorts* (New York: Simon & Schuster, 2002), 8.
9. Scott Meslow, *From Hollywood with Love: The Rise and Fall (and Rise Again) of the Romantic Comedy* (New York: HarperCollins, 2022), 31.
10. J. F. Lawton, *Three Thousand*, screenplay draft, 1987, SellingYourScreenplay.com, https://www.sellingyourscreenplay.com/wp-content/uploads/screenplay/scripts/Three-Thousand-filmed-as-Pretty-Woman.pdf.

CHAPTER 5: RACHEL'S RACHEL

1. "The Rachel," *Wikipedia*, https://en.wikipedia.org/wiki/The_Rachel, accessed September 29, 2025; Hedy Phillips, "Watch as Jennifer Aniston Forgets All About Her Iconic 'Rachel' Haircut in New Uber Eats Spot," *People*, February 20, 2024, https://people.com/jennifer-aniston-forgets-rachel-haircut-uber-eats-commercial-8597700.
2. "Your Look," *Teen* 39, no. 11 (November 1995): 24, 26.
3. Jeffrey Gayner, "The Contract with America: Implementing New Ideas in the U.S.," Heritage Foundation, October 12, 1995, https://www.heritage.org/political-process/report/the-contract-america-implementing-new-ideas-the-us.
4. On the problems with post feminism, see Elaine J. Hall and Marnie Salupo Rodriguez, "The Myth of Postfeminism," *Gender and Society* 17, no. 6 (December 2003): 878–902.
5. Saul Austerlitz, *Generation Friends: An Inside Look at the Show That Defined a Television Era* (New York: Dutton, 2019), 8–11.
6. Austerlitz, *Generation Friends*, 62–63.
7. Michael Warner, *The Trouble with Normal: Sex, Politics, and the Ethics of Queer Life* (New York: Free Press, 1999), 53, http://catdir.loc.gov/catdir/enhancements/fy0645/99044356s.html.
8. Lennard J. Davis, *Enforcing Normalcy: Disability, Deafness, and the Body* (London: Verso, 2014), 154.
9. Heidi Parker, "Jennifer Aniston Needed to Lose 30 Pounds Before Landing *Friends* in the '90s," *Daily Mail*, September 18, 2019, https://www.dailymail.co.uk/tvshowbiz/article-7477609/Jennifer-Aniston-needed-lose-30lbs-landing-Friends-like-What.html.
10. Helana Darwin, "The Pariah Femininity Hierarchy: Comparing White Women's Body Hair and Fat Stigmas in the United States," *Gender, Place and Culture: A Journal of Feminist Geography* 24, no. 1 (2017): 138, https://doi.org/10.1080/0966369X.2016.1276889.
11. Maureen Dowd, Patrick Healy, Tressie McMillan Cottom, and Lydia Polgreen, "Four Opinion Writers on 'Wicked': 'Women Deserve Rage. We Have a Lot to Be Angry About,'" *New York Times*, November 29, 2024, https://www.nytimes.com/2024/11/29/opinion/wicked-cynthia-erivo-ariana-grande.html.
12. Sabrina Strings, *Fearing the Black Body: The Racial Origins of Fat Phobia* (New York: NYU Press, 2019), https://doi.org/10.18574/9781479891788.
13. Anita Karl and David Wild, "Winona Ryder Beats the Heat," *Rolling Stone*, May 16, 1991, 45, 46, https://www.rollingstone.com/tv-movies/tv-movie-news/winona-ryder-beats-the-heat-237419/.
14. Karl and Wild, "Winona Ryder Beats the Heat," 45.

15. *60 Minutes Overtime* Staff, "Hillary's First Joint Interview—Next to Bill in '92," CBS News, February 1, 2013, https://www.cbsnews.com/news/hillarys-first-joint-interview-next-to-bill-in-92/.
16. Karen Lehrman, "Opinion: Beware the Cookie Monster," *New York Times*, July 18, 1992, https://www.nytimes.com/1992/07/18/opinion/beware-the-cookie-monster.html.
17. Elizabeth Snead, "Hillary's Hair Bands: Zippy or Just Dippy?" *USA Today*, February 7, 1992.
18. *InStyle*, "Even Jennifer Aniston Had Trouble Styling the Rachel Cut," October 24, 2018, YouTube, https://www.youtube.com/watch?v=PoJi86aJGbI.
19. Brigit Grant, "Talking Crop; I'd Shave Off All My Million Dollar Hair for the Right Part," *The Mirror*, February 14, 1997, 12.
20. Laurie Lucas, "'Rachel Cut' Finding Its Way into Manestream: Its Flexibility Has Made the Modified '60s Shag a Popular Style in Salons Nationwide," *The Press-Enterprise*, November 26, 1995.
21. Rich Cohen, "Jennifer Aniston: The Girl Friend," *Rolling Stone*, March 7, 1996, pp. 34–38.
22. Lucas, "'Rachel Cut' Finding Its Way into Manestream."
23. Contemporary discussions of *Friends*' whiteness include Mike Duffky, "Sitcoms' Lack of Diversity Obvious as Black and White," *Chicago Tribune*, March 6, 1996, and Traci Grant, "Newton's Matt LeBlanc Finds Sitcom Success at 27," *Boston Globe*, April 28, 1995.
24. Quoted in Shelley Cobb, "'I'd Like Y'all to Get a Black Friend': The Politics of Race in *Friends*," *Television & New Media* 19, no. 8 (2018): 708–23, https://doi.org/10.1177/1527476418778420. Cobb also notes: "In 2016, the Oprah Winfrey Network uploaded three portions of the episode to YouTube. [. . .] The segment in which Oprah tells them to get a black friend is not included."
25. NYU Furman Center, "Report Analyzes New York City's Gentrifying Neighborhoods and Finds Dramatic Demographic Shifts," *The Stoop*, May 9, 2016, https://furmancenter.org/thestoop/entry/new-report-analyzes-new-york-citys-gentrifying-neighborhoods-and-finds-dram.
26. Amanda Mitchell, "Julie, Charlie, and the Women of Color *Friends* Failed," *Marie Claire*, May 16, 2021, https://www.marieclaire.com/culture/a36522146/friends-women-of-color-romantic-racism/.
27. Julie's haircut is bad because Rachel sabotages it, so that Julie's hair will be cut like Roddy McDowell "in *Planet of the Apes*," not Andie McDowell "in *Four Weddings and a Funeral*." It's worth noticing that Rachel pushes Julie, via hair reference, not only out of the romance genre but also fully out of the human species.

28. Mattie Kahn, "Hillary Clinton Debuts Wind-Tousled, Bouncy Hair as Anna Wintour Endorses Her," *Vanity Fair*, July 9, 2013, https://www.vanityfair.com/style/2013/07/hillary-clinton-haircut?srsltid=AfmBOopn5EhYEXjJN3ZmiNxrbq4YRjkIqiUrWcdjz8XU4rgAtayD2ZCU.
29. Siwa, Jojo (@itsjojosiwa) "Replying to @Megan Decker" TikTok 2022-7-26, https://www.tiktok.com/@itsjojosiwa/video/7124784523396631854?lang=en.

CHAPTER 6: BRITNEY'S BALDNESS

1. Rob Sheffield et al., "The Hundred Greatest Debut Singles of All Time," *Rolling Stone*, May 19, 2020, https://www.rollingstone.com/music/music-lists/greatest-debut-songs-singles-990470/britney-spears-baby-one-more-time-2-990475.
2. Jimmy Kimmel called Federline "the world's first ever no-hit wonder" in a sketch during the 2006 American Music Awards. TMZ reported that Spears was "pissed." TMZ Staff, "Britney—The Plot Thickens," TMZ, November 22, 2006, https://www.tmz.com/2006/11/22/britney-the-plot-thickens/.
3. Britney Spears, *The Woman in Me* (New York: Gallery Books, 2023), 8, 25.
4. Jennifer Musial, "We're Country: Britney Spears, Southern White Femininity, and the American Dream" Feminist Formations 31, no. 3 (2019): 72–94, https://doi.org/10.1353/ff.2019.0031, 74.
5. Charlotte Chilton, "50 Amazing Photos of Britney Spears's Hair Evolution Through the Years," *Cosmopolitan*, March 30, 2021, https://www.cosmopolitan.com/style-beauty/beauty/g34817732/britney-spears-hairstyles/.
6. Jae-Ha Kim, "Britney Spears Proved the Pop Singer's "It" Factor," *Chicago Sun-Times*, March 23, 2000, https://www.jaehakim.com/2000/03/britney-spears-it-factor/.
7. Destiny's Child Brasil Fãs, "Destiny's Child—Say My Name (Live in Hawaii 2000) Britney Spears," February 27, 2016, YouTube, https://www.youtube.com/watch?v=pxgxa4DuaSU.
8. Spears, *The Woman in Me*, 89.
9. Adrian G. Uribarri, "Salon has a Close Shave with Britney: A Harried Stylist is Recovering from the Media Frenzy After the Tabloid Celebrity Lops Off Her Locks at a Tarzana Shop," Febuary 18, 2007. *Los Angeles Times* (1996–), 1.
10. Spears, *The Woman in Me*, 209.
11. Spears, *The Woman in Me*, 10.
12. Spears, *The Woman in Me*, 21.
13. "The Decade In Music: Britney Spears' 'Toxic' (2004)," NPR, November 13, 2009, https://www.npr.org/2009/11/13/120385043/the-decade-in-music-britney-spears-toxic-2004#.

14. *Primetime*, "Britney Spears," aired on November 12, 2003, on ABC, posted by Britney Online, YouTube, https://www.youtube.com/watch?v=FyI6PTuLYgw&lc=UgyLjtuabZvtVx69HX54AaABAg.
15. *Saturday Night Live*, season 34, episode 21, "Immigrant Tale," featuring Justin Timberlake, aired May 9, 2009, on NBC, YouTube, https://youtu.be/k9N9kMD7qCk?si=xoicKbqgCZxt-jxs.
16. Spears, *The Woman in Me*, 77.
17. Tauber, Michelle, Todd Gold, Julie Jordan, and Ulrica Wihlborg, et al., "Britney's BIG DAY." *People*, October 4, 2004, 64–74, 77.
18. Spears, *The Woman in Me*, 110.
19. Mike Shields, "AOL Launches TMZ.com," *Mediaweek*, December 8, 2005, https://web.archive.org/web/20060219061419/http://www.mediaweek.com/mw/news/recent_display.jsp?vnu_content_id=1001656883.
20. TMZ, "About TMZ.com," https://www.tmz.com/pages/about/, accessed September 29, 2025.
21. Chris Rock features this temple in his documentary *Good Hair*, Roadside Attractions, HBO Films, Zahrlo Productions, Urban Romances, Lions Gate Entertainment, Chris Rock, Kevin O'Donnell, et al., Lions Gate Entertainment, 2009.
22. The Britney Spears Foundation, https://web.archive.org/web/20041102011049/http://www.britneyspears.com/foundation-bsf.php, accessed September 29, 2025.
23. Among these, one of the best is Philippa Snow's "Breaking the Waves: Britney Spears and Lars von Trier in Lockdown," *Los Angeles Review of Books*, May 8, 2021, https://lareviewofbooks.org/article/breaking-the-waves-britney-spears-and-lars-von-trier-in-lockdown/.

JOJO WITH THE BOWBOW

1. LifeTime Television (@officiallifetimetelevision) "She's the Repunzel of 2013," TikTok, April 5, 2023, https://www.tiktok.com/@officiallifetimetv/video/7218590739725405486?lang=en.
2. Nickelodeon (@nickelodeon), JoJo Siwa, Instagram, https://www.instagram.com/p/BQ6nHLAlG3d/?taken-by=nickelodeon, accessed September 29, 2025.
3. Amazon.com results for "jojo siwa brand," https://www.amazon.com/s?k=jojo+siwa+brand&i=beauty&crid=1G9ONCRZV443C&sprefix=jojo+siwa+brand%2Cbeauty%2C79&ref=nb_sb_noss, accessed September 29, 2025.
4. "JoJo Bows: Why Are Schools Banning 'A Symbol of Believing-ness'?" *The Guardian*, March 7, 2017, https://www.theguardian.com/society/shortcuts/2017/mar/07/jojo-bows-siwa-schools-ban.
5. CBBC, "JoJo Siwa and the Giant Bow Craze," YouTube, February 28, 2017, https://www.youtube.com/watch?v=K_snn76M4ds.

6. Witsay Fan, "Jojo Siwa and Jenna Johnson Argentine Tango (Week 3): *Dancing with the Stars*," January 14, 2022, YouTube, https://www.youtube.com/watch?v=TbSBpPz93_U.
7. Ryan Gajewski, "Jojo Siwa Shares How She Relates to Britney Spears After 'Hard' Experience with Child Stardom," *ENews*, October 4, 2021, https://www.eonline.com/news/1304815/jojo-siwa-shares-how-she-relates-to-britney-spears-after-hard-experience-with-child-stardom.
8. Siwa, Jojo (@itsjojosiwa) "Replying to @Megan Decker," TikTok, July 26, 2022, https://www.tiktok.com/@itsjojosiwa/video/7124784523396631854?lang=en.

CHAPTER 7: GWYNETH PALTROW'S BODY HAIR

1. "Clean Hair Products," Goop.com, https://goop.com/clean-hair-care/c/, accessed May 28, 2025.
2. Taffy Brodesser-Akner, "How Goop's Haters Made Gwyneth Paltrow's Company Worth $250 Million," *New York Times Magazine*, July 5, 2018, https://www.nytimes.com/2018/07/25/magazine/big-business-gwyneth-paltrow-wellness.html.
3. Michael S. Schmidt, "Obama Sticks to His Script for Star-Struck Celebrities at Hollywood Fund-Raiser," *New York Times*, October 9, 2014, https://www.nytimes.com/2014/10/10/us/obama-sticks-to-his-script-for-star-struck-celebrities-at-hollywood-fund-raiser.html.
4. Brodesser-Akner, "How Goop's Haters Made Gwyneth Paltrow's Company Worth $250 Million."
5. Here I quote the media studies scholar Bridget Conor: "Cosmic wellness and Goop are saturated in white and I mean this at all levels—the landing pages of the Goop website and Instagram feeds, the majority skin colour of the employees and spokesbodies of Goop led by GP, the celebrity guests at the #inGoophealth conferences. The overall palette is one that is bleached out, minimal and 'pure.'" Bridget Conor, "'How Goopy Are You?' Women, Goop and Cosmic Wellness." *European Journal of Cultural Studies* 24, no. 6 (2021): 1261–81, https://doi.org/10.1177/13675494211055735.
6. Evelyn M. Rusli, "Facebook Buys Instagram for $1 Billion," *New York Times*. April 9, 2012, https://archive.nytimes.com/dealbook.nytimes.com/2012/04/09/facebook-buys-instagram-for-1-billion/.
7. Elizabeth L. Block's book *Beyond Vanity: The History and Power of Hairdressing*, for instance, carefully traces the archives of women's hairdressing to show how seemingly intimate practices shape infrastructural systems from international trade to urban architecture.
8. Shaun Callaghan, Martin Lösch, Anna Pione, and Warren Teichner, "Feeling Good: The Future of the $1.5 Trillion Wellness Market," McKinsey & Company, April 8, 2021, https://www.mckinsey.com

/industries/consumer-packaged-goods/our-insights/feeling-good-the-future-of-the-1-5-trillion-wellness-market.

9. Sarah Mesle, "The goop Magazine Cover Story: The Full Q&A with Gwyneth," goop, September 19, 2017, https://web.archive.org/web/20170919053956/https://goop.com/goop-magazine-cover-story-full-qa-gwyneth/.
10. Mariah L. Wellman, "'A Friend Who Knows What They're Talking About': Extending Source Credibility Theory to Analyze the Wellness Influencer Industry on Instagram," *New Media & Society* 26, no. 12 (April 17, 2023): 7030, https://journals.sagepub.com/doi/10.1177/14614448231162064.
11. Amy Odell, *Gwyneth: The Biography* (New York: Simon & Schuster, 2025), 69.
12. As of 2025, it costs $25. It is the only goop product I've bought: the "Ultimate Dry Brush."
13. John Berger, *Ways of Seeing* (London: British Broadcasting Corporation and Penguin Books, 1972), 55.
14. According to studies quoted by Breanne Fahs in her book *Unshaved*, 91 percent of American women regularly remove their leg hair; 93 percent regularly remove armpit hair. Breanne Fahs, *Unshaved: Resistance and Revolution in Women's Body Hair Politics* (Seattle: University of Washington Press, 2024), 10. A 2016 *JAMA* article reported that 84 percent of women removed their pubic hair in some way. (Britney's bare pudendum was a scandal, but imagine what drama the sight of untrimmed pubic hair might have caused.) Tami S. Rowen et al., "Pubic Hair Grooming Prevalence and Motivation Among Women in the United States," *JAMA Dermatology* 152, no. 10 (2016): 1106–13, https://jamanetwork.com/journals/jamadermatology/fullarticle/2529574.
15. Since the 2017 publication of *Skin Deep*, goop has become more regular about selling hair products so this information may not accurately reflect what Paltrow currently uses on her head. In the *Skin Deep* interview, she expresses some hesitation about it: "I have dry, damaged, bleached hair, and they work for me. That's the one area I can't find a nontoxic product that works well." Bee Shapiro, *Skin Deep: Women on Skin Care, Makeup, and Looking Their Best* (New York: Abrams, 2017), 178.
16. See, for instance, Helana Darwin, "The Pariah Femininity Hierarchy: Comparing White Women's Body Hair and Fat Stigmas in the United States," *Gender, Place and Culture: A Journal of Feminist Geography* 24, no. 1 (2017): 138, https://doi.org/10.1080/0966369X.2016.1276889. Darwin proposes that "body hair and body fat are active and motile, components of women's bodies that never truly go away; rather, these unruly bodily matters continually lurk just beneath the surface, rendering all women discreditable."

17. Fahs, *Unshaved.*
18. Significantly, one article that appears on goop, "Lingerie Drawer Update," sells lingerie and a dry brush to help "prepare your skin to be seen." The model for this article is toned, blond, and perfectly depilated, https://goop.com/style/trends/the-lingerie-drawer-update/, accessed June 4, 2025.
19. Editors of goop, "How to Get a Bump-Free Bikini Line at Home," goop, updated August 1, 2025, https://goop.com/beauty/skin/tips-for-smooth-bikini-line/.
20. In addition to the above, see a second article here: "Bikini-Line Confidential," goop, https://goop.com/beauty/bath-body/bikini-line-confidential/, accessed June 4, 2025.
21. Quoted in Sarah Gold McBride, *Whiskerology: The Culture of Hair in Nineteenth-Century America* (Cambridge, MA: Harvard University Press, 2025), 118.
22. Audre Lorde, *A Burst of Light: Essays* (Ithaca, NY: Firebrand Books, 1988), 123.
23. Mesle, "The goop Magazine Cover Story."

ICE QUEENS

1. That number comes from just this one post and doesn't include other versions like the "sing-a-long" posts. Walt Disney Animation Studios, "Disney's Frozen 'Let It Go' Sequence Performed by Idina Menzel," YouTube, December 6, 2013, https://youtu.be/moSFlvxnbgk?si=-Oiu-TYECRnjhtIQ.
2. In the first year of *Frozen*'s release, Disney reported three million *Frozen* dresses sold in North America (which, as this *New York Times* article points out, is "roughly the number of 4-year-old girls in North America." Binjamin Appelbaum, "How Disney Turned *Frozen* into a Cash Cow," *New York Times*, November 18, 2014, https://www.nytimes.com/2014/11/23/magazine/how-disney-turned-frozen-into-a-cash-cow.html.
3. Brittany Raymer, "The Media's Mistreatment of Melania Trump," *Daily Citizen*, July 27, 2020, https://dailycitizen.focusonthefamily.com/the-medias-mistreatment-of-melania-trump/.
4. Danielle Kurtzleben, "Trump Signs Order That Seeks to Ban Transgender Athletes from Women's Sports," *All Things Considered*, NPR, February 5, 2025, https://www.npr.org/2025/02/05/nx-s1-5282137/trump-transgender-sports-executive-order.